FOLK
SONGS
out of Wisconsin

Street band, Black River Falls, ca. 1900.
Photo by Charles Van Schaick.

Musicians on the *Dell Queen,* a Wisconsin Dells tour boat.
Photo by H. H. Bennett, courtesy H. H. Bennett Studio, Inc.

FOLK SONGS
out of Wisconsin

Edited by H A R R Y   B.   P E T E R S

Published by
THE STATE HISTORICAL SOCIETY OF WISCONSIN

Madison, Wisconsin
1977

FOLK SONGS OUT OF WISCONSIN
is a contribution of
The State Historical Society of Wisconsin
to the American Revolution Bicentennial celebration,
and was made possible in part by a grant from
The Wisconsin American Revolution Bicentennial Commission.

Library of Congress Cataloging in Publication Data:

Main entry under title:
Folk songs out of Wisconsin.
1. Folk-songs, American—Wisconsin.
I. Peters, Harry B.   II. Wisconsin. State Historical Society.
M1629.F687   784.4'9775   77-1793   ISBN O-87020-165-4
Printed and bound in the United States of America

INTRODUCTION

In January 1973, shortly after the death of Professor Helene Stratman-Thomas of the University of Wisconsin, A. J. Blotz asked me if I might be willing to undertake the completion of a project to which his late wife had been extremely dedicated. This was a book of Wisconsin folk songs which she had collected and recorded throughout the state during the 1940's, under the auspices of the University of Wisconsin and the Library of Congress. Although I had had little previous experience with this musical genre, I agreed to look at her unfinished manuscript materials. What follows in this present volume owes largely, and directly, to the intelligence and imagination of Professor Stratman-Thomas, whose notes contained a wealth of imagery and insights into the popular culture of Wisconsin. To a large selection of melodies from her compilation I have added some folk songs collected by Franz Rickaby in the 1920's and by Asher Treat and Sidney Robertson in the 1930's.

When these collectors crisscrossed Wisconsin to record the folk songs which appear in this book, they were in search of songs that had entertained the early inhabitants of the state—songs which transmitted familiar legends and stories, songs which expressed moods, life styles, and varied aspects of culture. Usually these were songs that had already enjoyed long life spans, many enduring for generations, having been handed down from singer to singer, often enriched by individual variations. To say for certain which songs were invented in Wisconsin is difficult if not impossible, for even songs which mention Wisconsin personalities and locales are sometimes merely adaptations of songs that were composed and sung elsewhere. (After all, one of the charms of folk music is that it grants the balladeer freedom to insert names and places to suit a particular situation.) In any event, all of the songs in this collection were—and in some instances still are—sung by ordinary people within the boundaries of Wisconsin. Broadly speaking, these were the "popular music" of their time.

Such a definition of folk music does not, of course, satisfy present-day musicologists and social scientists, who have created precise and highly refined categories for analyzing and codifying "folk music." There are a number of good reasons for this. After 1790, when American copyright law formally protected musical as well as literary creations, singers and writers of songs were largely forced to register their own works and to pay for their performance of other peoples' works. The publishing of sheet music became a sizable business, and composers and publishers demanded that they be paid for the use of their songs, which they assiduously promoted and popularized. The opportunities for anonymous ballads and balladeers sharply declined, and songs that might previously have been considered "folk music" were now private property, protected by law. For example, had it not been copyrighted and widely published over a long span of time, a song such as Stephen Foster's *Old Folks at Home* would in all likelihood have qualified as folk rather than popular music.

Whether a song had been published and copyrighted was of small consequence to pioneering collectors like Helene Stratman-Thomas and Franz Rickaby. They did not collect music according to any preconceived definitions of "folk music." Rather, they sought to preserve those songs and bits of folklore that were threatened with extinction by growing commercialism and exposure to radio, recording, and publication. The musical content of the songs they collected is simple, uncomplicated in form and harmony, normally utilizing short, repeated stanzas, sometimes with an inserted refrain. Often the music plays a secondary role to the poem. An important early Wisconsin balladeer, Billy Allen of Wausau, told Franz Rickaby that he used only two or three standard tunes as the musical vehicle for many of his ballads.

By contrast, the lyrics of these songs exhibit great thematic variety. They relate the stories of real and imagined people; they deal with work and play, with marriage and politics, disasters and frolics. They touch upon all of the larger human themes: Love, Betrayal, Revenge, War, Death. Some make jokes, and some are sheerest nonsense. Taken altogether, these songs can tell us a great deal about everyday life in Wisconsin during the nineteenth and early twentieth centuries.

The songs contained in this selection are limited to those in the English language, and reflect only a portion of the rich diversity of ethnic traditions existing in the state at that time. As with immigrants from other countries, the English, Scotch, Irish, and Welsh brought their favorite old-country tunes—for example *Lord Randall* and *Paper of Pins*—to every region of America where they settled. The Irish songs, with their sparkling fantasy and wit marvelously intertwined, contain some of the most delightful lyrics of all. Similarly with the Welsh who settled around Dodgeville, whose Christmas carols and songs of faith originally inspired Helene Stratman-Thomas' interest in the preservation of Wisconsin folk music. And the Cornish, too, whose carolers solicited Christmas treats with *O, We Have Come to Your Door* and then thanked their patrons with *We Wish You a Merry Christmas.*

One group of folk songs traces an English-speaking group of people who emigrated to Wisconsin from their native Kentucky at the turn of the century. All of the collectors represented in this book encountered the songs of Appalachia in the northeastern corner of Wisconsin, near Crandon and Antigo. Perhaps these songs served as some kind of consolation to the "Kaintucks," for their move northward must have dashed many a hope and dream. Unknowingly, these people of eastern Kentucky had invested their savings in worthless, tax-encumbered land that had earlier been cut over by the lumber companies. The settlers clung to their Southern ways, tending to isolate themselves from their neighbors, and as a result their songs remained purer, and more true to the original English versions, than the songs of their counterparts in Kentucky.

To a great extent, and for a long time, Wisconsin's development was closely tied to its geographical location astride two great systems of waterways: the Great Lakes and the Mississippi River basin. Half the state's boundaries were defined by navigable waters; much of its diverse population was borne there by water; and this became a source of folk music and lore. (Testament to the importance of the Great Lakes traffic to the history of Wisconsin was a wooden signboard that once stood on the city dock at Ashland: it informed seamen in seven languages where and how they could bank their money.) Such songs as *Red Iron Ore* and *Shanty Boy on the Big Eau Claire* recall an age when pilots and raftsmen were vital figures in commerce and transportation.

Disasters were common on the Great Lakes; indeed, European immigrants came to dread the voyage from Lake Erie to Milwaukee quite as much as they did the oceanic trip from Bremerhaven or Liverpool to New York. Between 1878 and 1898, for example, almost 6,000 vessels were wrecked on the Great Lakes, of which more than a thousand sank or were totally destroyed. Some shipwrecks produced frightful losses of life. In 1847 the *Phoenix* burned and sank off Sheboygan with a loss of 250 lives, mostly Dutch immigrants at the end of a 4,000-mile journey; in 1860 the *Lady Elgin* sank off the Illinois shore, taking with her 297 persons, including a large contingent of Milwaukee Irish returning from an excursion to Chicago. "Lost on

the *Lady Elgin,* sleeping to wake no more," ran the song's mournful refrain, "numbered with those three hundred who failed to reach the shore." The theme of disaster inspired many a folk song in this collection, ranging from an accident during a log drive to such epics of horror as the Newhall House fire in Milwaukee, in which seventy hotel guests died. Life was not cheap in nineteenth-century Wisconsin, but it was frequently brief. It was the balladeer who kept the memory of disaster fresh after the newspaper headlines had faded.

Lakes and rivers were not the only waterways that figured in the folk songs of Wisconsin, for many Midwesterners put to sea and returned with sea chanties like *Reuben Ranzo* and *Sally Brown*. Franz Rickaby talked with an old sailor in 1923, who told him how the hands sang as they worked (rather than after work, as in the lumber camps), and warned him that all but a handful of sea-songs were unspeakably filthy. On some ships the "chantey man," who was often a fiddler, seated himself atop the capstan and led the others in song as they marched in step around him, turning the heavy drum on its axis. Thus, in *The Mikado* of Gilbert and Sullivan: "Man the capstan, off we go, while the fiddler swings us round."

By the last quarter of the nineteenth century rails were rapidly replacing waterways as the primary means of transport in America. Between 1868 and 1873 the track laid in Wisconsin more than doubled; in 1869 the first transcontinental line was completed; and during the decade of the 1880's more than 7,000 miles of new track were laid nationwide each year. Along with the thousands of jobs created by this enormous expansion came a small cluster of folk songs, a few of which are represented in this collection. As with songs of the waterways, it was the calamitous event—the wreck of a crack passenger train, the heroism of a brave engineer—which caught the balladeer's imagination.

As its geography affected Wisconsin's transportation routes and the influx of immigrant peoples, so did its climate and natural resources affect the growth of several important industries—notably cranberrying, mining, and lumbering. Folk songs evolved out of all three, many of them originating in Wisconsin. *The Cranberry Song* is the sole representative in this collection of an industry that developed in the bogs of central Wisconsin, where the retreat of two glacial lakes (Oshkosh and Wisconsin) left behind lake-bed swamps. The song describes the early days of cranberrying, when the berries were collected by hand in the flooded beds, cleaned, sorted, and packed for shipment. Each autumn the growers—Poles, Bohemians, and Irishmen among others—gathered to harvest the berries and to devote their evenings to gaiety and dancing.

Pick and Shovel recalls the fact that lead and zinc ore formed the mainstay of the economy of southwestern

Wisconsin throughout the territorial period. Hundreds of rugged miners, primarily "Cousin Jacks" from Cornwall in England, flocked to the lead region around Mineral Point, where, by the late 1840's, more than half the nation's lead was produced. As the song suggests, the miner's life was full of drudgery and danger; but there was also a sense of camaraderie in hardships shared:

> The mine whistle blows and the men start to sing.
> There's fear in their thinkin'. They don't say a
>   thing.
> Goin' down, down the mineshaft the echo of song
> Wipes out fear or worry. Together we're strong.

Later, in the last quarter of the nineteenth century, the lumbering industry in northern Wisconsin entered a veritable Golden Age. The lumberjacks, who labored through each winter and spring to cut and drive the white pine to sawmills downriver, were a swashbuckling group of men who created their own life style, their own legends, their own ballads.

It was a seasonal occupation; men left their wives and children in tha autumn and spent the long Wisconsin winters isolated in logging camps, snowbound and far from town. They worked hard and played hard. Generally they had little to do after supper except to sit around a stove, smoke their pipes, tell stories, and sing. As on shipboard, a fine singer was highly valued, and there are instances where an inferior sawyer or axman was tolerated because he could sing. Emery De Noyer, who recorded several lumberjack songs for Helene Stratman-Thomas, was such a man: he earned his keep in the Wisconsin lumber camps not by logging (for he had only one eye and one arm) but by singing.

Unlike sea songs, which were often sung on the job, in unison, to establish a rhythmic beat to work by, the songs of the lumberjacks were purely for entertainment. All of the popular songs of the day could be heard around the camps. Loggers liked the bawdy, the flamboyant, the unprintable songs of which *The Red Light Saloon* is a worthy representative. (Only its more acceptable stanzas are reproduced in this collection, but indeed they are bawdy enough.) Songs about barrooms and gambling and fancy women were favorites; so too were songs about legendary heroes and prodigious feats. Bull Gordon, hero of *The Little Brown Bulls,* bested his Yankee rival, McClusky, in not less than eight different versions of the song.

While logging songs flourished to the north, the circus was providing southern Wisconsin with songs as gay and colorful as its lavishly painted wagons. Although the circus originated in New York state, enterprising Yankees had their "mud shows" on the road each spring during the first half of the nineteenth century, and not long after Wisconsin attained statehood in 1848 the little town of Delavan in Walworth County had become headquarters for several itinerant

circuses. From that date the circus quite unexpectedly grew into one of Wisconsin's most celebrated industries, reaching its zenith around the time of the First World War, when the Ringling Bros. and Barnum & Bailey combined show annually sent forth some ninety double-sized railroad cars and 1,500 performers and technicians from the small city of Baraboo. Circus songs form a genre all their own. They cannot properly be called folk songs, for they were deliberately written to promote the circus; yet because of the role played by the circus in Wisconsin, and the sheer number of songs that survive, it would be a pity to exclude them. Some, such as that about the daring young man on the flying trapeze, are sung today by people who will never see a show under canvas; others, such as *Jumbo the Elephant,* were probably seldom heard except in a circus tent.

These are the songs, then—from Christmas carols and ballads of broken-hearted loneliness to calliope tunes that once electrified small-town America.

It is too much to claim that these songs comprise a social history of Wisconsin during the last century, or that they are significantly different in theme or content from those that were sung by Ohio boatmen or Kansas plowboys. Heartbreak, nonsense, and sudden death were—and are—a part of all American lives. But to read these lyrics, perhaps to pick out the tunes, is to grasp something of those who went before. We are, to be sure, the product of our own time and place, and it is unlikely that any of us will weep at the ballad of *The Fatal Oak* or laugh out loud over *Miss Fogarty's Christmas Cake.* But in their own way these songs, and others like them, are as important to an understanding of our past as any merchant's ledger or politician's letters. Like crackled photographic plates or dim, yellowing newspapers, they retain the power to move us. They remind us, with a pang, of our roots.

. . . . .

And what of the collectors of these songs? Our debt to them is sizable, for without them much of what is assembled here would probably have drifted into limbo, unnoticed and unlamented. And how tragic it would have been if the music of ordinary people had been scorned as being unworthy of preservation, or condemned to extinction out of simple apathy. To four persons in particular—two men and two women—we owe our thanks for their foresight and zeal for collecting: Asher Treat and Franz Rickaby, and Sidney Robertson and Helene Stratman-Thomas.

Asher Treat, who now lives in New Jersey, was born in Antigo, Wisconsin, in 1907. He was one of the first collectors to recognize the uniqueness of the songs that were sung by Kentuckians who had emigrated to the area of his home town, and whose second-generation children went to high school with him. In 1932, several years after graduation from the University of Wisconsin, Treat began to collect the songs of these transplanted "Kaintucks," taking care to weigh and measure the differences between the music of northern Wisconsin and that of Appalachia, where earlier collectors had recorded numerous folk songs of old England. He assumed that such songs had been modified by the influence of new surroundings and neighboring ethnic groups, as they had in Appalachia; but he discovered, to the contrary, that the Kentucky songs of northern Wisconsin were preserved in much purer form here than elsewhere. (Although the Wisconsin-Kentucky songs used in this book were transcribed from tape recordings made by Helene Stratman-Thomas, many of them are identical to those which Treat collected in the 1930's.)

Franz Rickaby was born at Rogers, Arkansas, in 1889. He was a man of rare musical and literary ability, and glimpses of his buoyant, whimsical spirit shine through in the excerpts published here of a diary he made while on a walking tour of northern Wisconsin. Of Rickaby his friend Vachel Lindsay, the poet and essayist of the 1920's, wrote: "He was a young troubadour who might have been a statesman in United States art, had he lived. . . . He had the equipment: versatility, energy, magnetism, leadership and the especial facility in poetry by which he would be called a poet, but which would have represented an interest in many United States things to a large public." Rickaby did his undergraduate work at Knox College, won a master's degree at Harvard in 1917, and soon thereafter took a job teaching English at the University of North Dakota. Six years later he removed to Pomona College in California because of ill health. Two years after, in 1925, he was dead of a rheumatic heart ailment.

Playwright, poet, fiddler, composer, and indefatigable collector of folk songs, Franz Rickaby liked nothing better than to walk and hitchhike from one small town to another, relying heavily on his skill with song and violin to pay his bed and board, alternately playing and listening, and eventually transcribing the songs that he committed to memory along the way. Over a period of years Rickaby arranged the songs by category in large notebooks: ballads of the cowboys, of the frontier, of seas and rivers, of lovers and catastrophes, relatives and Indians. He hated war, but he loved songs of the American wars, and collected more than forty during his travels. A number of the songs he collected in lumber camps of Michigan and northern Wisconsin were assembled as *Ballads and Songs of the Shanty Boy,* a staple of folk-song literature which Harvard University Press published just after Rickaby's death. Afterward, Rickaby's widow, the former Lillian Katar, married Clarence Dykstra, who became president of the University of Wisconsin in 1937. It was in this manner that a copy of the collector's seven well-ordered notebooks was given by Mrs. Dykstra to the university's School of Music.

Sidney Robertson was born in San Francisco in 1903. As a young woman she taught music in the public schools of California, where she perceived the enjoyment which folk music inspired among young people. During the Depression of the 1930's she worked in northern Wisconsin for the U.S. Resettlement Administration, helping to develop a healthier social climate among immigrant settlers in the cutover region. There she encouraged the people to draw on their own cultural resources, and especially on the music and songs that they already knew. In her free time, both then and later, she collected and recorded songs in the Rhinelander area, eventually enlarging her collection for inclusion in the Archives of Folk Song of the Library of Congress. Her principal collection, comprised of several thousand songs and their variants, she gave to the State University of New York at Cooperstown. She now lives in Shady, New York, where she is writing a book about regional wildlife and managing the sales and rental of music by her late husband, the pioneering composer Henry Cowell.

Helene Stratman-Thomas was born in Dodgeville, Wisconsin, in 1896, graduating from the University of Wisconsin with a degree in business in 1919 and thereafter spending most of her life in the state. She returned to the university, took bachelor's and master's degrees in music, and, as a member of the music faculty in Madison, taught theory, conducted the women's chorus, and was business manager for the Pro Arte string quartet. In 1940 Leland Coon, professor of music in the University of Wisconsin, instigated and arranged funding for a project to collect and record the folk songs of Wisconsin for the Library of Congress. Professor Coon administered the federal project; Helene Stratman-Thomas organized the field trips and recording sessions. In 1946 a second grant enabled her to continue the collecting which American involvement in the war had interrupted. In all, she collected 366 songs in twenty foreign languages and eighty-six songs in eleven American Indian tongues, in addition to some 250 songs in English (most of which are included in this book). She also gathered instrumental pieces, square-dance calls, poems, recitations, and reminiscences by the singers, with whom she established an extraordinary rapport. Her collected songs, recorded on discs and then transferred to tapes, were deposited with the Archives of American Folk Song in the Library of Congress. Her on-site recording equipment—a Soundscriber machine with eight-inch yellow shellac discs—now resides in the music library of the University of Wisconsin in Madison. Although she was much in demand as a speaker and participant in musical programs throughout Wisconsin, Helene Stratman-Thomas worked patiently at transcribing her recordings up to the time of her death in January 1973. Many of the songs in this book are being published for the first time, and their existence has been precarious indeed during the past thirty years.

These four collectors of Wisconsin folk songs had much in common. All were well educated; three were teachers. All possessed in good measure the personal characteristics that make a good collector: warmth, self-confidence, and a touch of humility. They dealt with plain, often reticent people in out-of-the-way places; their success or failure hinged on their ability to meet lumberjacks, fiddlers, and rural housewives on their own terms, openly and sympathetically. As the excerpted journals of Franz Rickaby and Helene Stratman-Thomas show, the collector had to be both a student of psychology and a diplomat.

Most of the songs which follow were transcribed in 1974 from the recordings of Helene Stratman-Thomas. Some which might have been included were omitted for a variety of reasons; for example, some songs that she mentions in her journals and notes could not be found on the tapes, and others were incomplete, inaudible, or partially unintelligible, either because of a faulty recorder or the frailty of an aged singer. A few songs were excluded because they were thought to be too vulgar even by today's standards. Where only a word or a phrase or two were indecipherable, a long dash indicates the gap in the lyrics.

HARRY B. PETERS

Madison, Wisconsin

Bessie Gordon of Schofield, Marathon County.
Photo by Helene Stratman-Thomas.

THE SONGS

11

THE SINGERS

... listed alphabetically, with the years of their births (where
known) and their residences in the 1940's. All but a few are
gone now. Perhaps, here and there in Wisconsin, their songs
are still sung.

Laura Avanell	b. 1866	Linden, Iowa County
Fred Bainter		Ladysmith, Rusk County
Mrs. C. A. Bishop		Madison, Dane County
Pearl Jacobs Borusky	b. 1901	Antigo, Langlade County
Fanny Boulden		Larimore, North Dakota
Charles Bowlen		Black River Falls, Jackson County
Noble B. Brown	b. 1885	Millville, Grant County
Winifred Bundy	b. 1884	Madison, Dane County
Mrs. Leslie Burton	b. 1891	Lancaster, Grant County
John Christian		Coloma, Waushara County
Lester Coffee	b. 1871	Harvard, Illinois
Emery De Noyer	b. 1878	Rhinelander, Oneida County
M. C. Dean		Virginia, Minnesota
Charles Dietz	b. 1871	Monroe, Green County
James Merrick Drew		St. Paul, Minnesota
Harry Dyer	b. 1864	Madison, Dane County
F. A. Fair		Grand Forks, North Dakota
Grant Faulkner	b. 1870	Crandon, Forest County
Ella Mittelstaedt Fischer	b. 1871	Mayville, Dodge County
Mrs. A. J. Fox		Eau Claire, Eau Claire County
Mrs. James Fowler	b. 1872	Lancaster, Grant County
Bessie Gordon	b. 1901	Schofield, Marathon County
Arthur C. Gower	b. 1852	Lake Hallie, Chippewa County
Dan Grant		Bryant, Langlade County
George M. Hankins	b. 1853	Gordon, Douglas County
Mabel Hankins		Gordon, Douglas County
Henry Humphries	b. 1865	Hancock, Portage County
Mrs. Ollie Jacobs	b. 1862	Pearson, Langlade County
Mathilde Kjorstad-Myer		Eau Claire, Eau Claire County
Mrs. J. G. Krebs		Westhope, North Dakota
Eryl Levers	b. 1922	Madison, Dane County
Hamilton Lobdell	b. 1854	Mukwonago, Waukesha County

Irene McCrady		Bemidji, Minnesota
Charles Mills	b. 1861	Marion, Waushara County
Lewis Winfield Moody	b. 1865	Plainfield, Waushara County
Moses Morgan	b. 1873	Pickett, Winnebago County
William Jacobs Morgan	b. 1870	Berlin, Green Lake County
Arthur Moseley		Black River Falls, Jackson County
Carl Nelson		Escanaba, Michigan
Bill Neupert	b. 1888	Schofield, Marathon County
Mrs. M. A. Olin		Eau Claire, Eau Claire County
Orlando Pegram		(unknown)
Miss M. E. Perley		Grand Forks, North Dakota
John Persons	b. 1859	Madison, Dane County
Mrs. Frances Perry		Black River Falls, Jackson County
Minnie Plimpton	b. 1878	Lancaster, Grant County
Mrs. Moody Price	b. 1875	Dodgeville, Iowa County
F. S. Putz	b. 1872	Almond, Portage County
Lily Richmond	b. 1862	Lancaster, Grant County
Charles Robinson	b. 1865	Marion, Waushara County
Luther Royce	b. 1913	White Lake, Langlade County
Gene Silsbe	b. 1880	Hancock, Portage County
Charles Spencer	b. 1873	Crandon, Forest County
Robert Steinback	b. 1887	Wausau, Marathon County
C. C. Talbott		Forbes, North Dakota
Dan Tanner	b. 1865	Milwaukee, Milwaukee County
Bert Taplin	b. 1857	Wautoma, Waushara County
Edward Turner		Grand Forks, North Dakota
Mrs. E. J. Vial	b. 1859	Linden, Iowa County
Robert Walker	b. 1883	Crandon, Forest County
Alfred Whitt	b. 1925	Crandon, Forest County
Myrth Whitt	b. 1902	Crandon, Forest County
D. W. Wickham		Dodgeville, Iowa County
Adolph Williams		Hayward, Sawyer County
C. A. Yoder		Bloomington, Indiana

Leslie Werner's repair shop, Black River Falls.
Photo by Charles Van Schaick.

16

1919

FRANZ RICKABY IN THE FIELD

[The following is portions of a journal which Rickaby kept on a walking tour of Michigan, northern Wisconsin, and Minnesota during the summer and fall of 1919, when he was thirty. The spelling and punctuation have been corrected here and there, and substantive omissions are indicated by ellipses. Rickaby began his trip at Charlevoix, Michigan, and the first day's entry has been retained simply because of its anecdotal charm.]

August 30

The entirely new sensation: That caused by knowing that one has no appointed time to leave, but may start whenever he is ready. Squared up affairs at Charlevoix. Sent myself $50 at Iron Mountain, Michigan. Got away a few minutes after 5:00 P.M., headed for Sequanta [a resort north of Charlevoix]. Pack rests well, and I believe will give no trouble. First ride within twenty-five minutes after I started—a farm wagon, noisy, jolty, but acceptable. A man and two children on the spring seat. "Do these little girls like gum?"

"We ain't both girls." The wee one (two years?) a boy. But the gum went just the same.

Man had lived in South Dakota. "No country for a poor man." Nonpartisan [League] business going to spread. (And again it mightn't!)

The matter of my jaunt soon the subject of conversation. The source of due surprise and fascination. "I was born in South Dakota," said the little girl between chews. The little boy took his chew out occasionally, looked at it and showed it to us.

"I'm going to make a collection of ballads, too—those songs the people sing. You've probably heard your parents sing 'em when you were a kid. 'The Fatal Wedding' and all that sort of thing."

"Yeah. I used to hear my dad sing one that there ain't nobody else but him I ever heard sing. it. Lessee—'I-Hi went up on the mount'n—that's the way it started. 'I-hi went up on the mount'n'—I've kind of forgotten now. But I never heard nobody but him sing it."

. . . . .

[Following this entry, the events of eleven days' traveling and collecting in Michigan are omitted, and Rickaby's journal resumes with a fragment written at a resort on Little St. Germain Lake, west of Eagle River in Vilas County, Wisconsin.]

September 10

I'm afraid I can't do this day justice: it has held too much, I have come through too much glory, and am in so much as I write.

September 11

The other night . . . I went up town late to mail the letters and look around. While writing to L. [Lillian, his wife] I decided to spend some of the fifty I got from the P.O. that day, on a wrist watch for her. She wants one so bad, and I don't know when I'll be better prepared to get her one than I am now.

Wednesday morning [i.e., the day before] I rolled out about 7:00 and got breakfast, and packed my stuff. Wrapped my sleeveless sweater to send on home. Went up town about 8:00 and bought the watch, a very pretty little one with a bracelet of black ribbon; I think ribbon is more comfortable, convenient, and I know one might as well buy watch instead of bracelet. The watch is fifteen-jewel, twenty-year case. Sent it on, registered, first class.

After my trip down the street I came back to the hotel, paid my bill ($2), brought my luggage down, and stepped to a garage across to ask about roads west—and the great thing happened.

A lady was talking to the garage man about routes. I came in with my map waving open. He naturally thought I was of her party, took my map and began talking to both of us about the roads to Eagle River! The lady explained that I was not of her party, and we got into a sort of conversation, the climax of which was, "Why, you might as well ride along with us." I could feel my good old horseshoe sagging my jacket down!

The party was Mr. and Mrs. Geo. M. Peck, and son Dick, of Elgin, Illinois. There was also a young lady, a Jewess, who was a friend of the family, and rather more than that of Dick's, I think. The car was a seven-passenger Stutz, but was piled full of luggage of every description, still they made room for me and mine. A most unusual occurrence. Tourists not usually so open-hearted.

The old couple and I squeezed into the back seat, the

young people in the front, and away we went about 9:00 o'clock; and we throbbed and roared along at about thirty-five miles an hour for 115 miles. They put me down about two miles outside of Eagle River. We stopped at Crandon for dinner, @ 75¢ per.

The group was a most democratic one, and all extremely pleasant. The boy had spent fifteen months in the service in France. The old gentleman was a violent Republican and several times during the day he began tirades against the present [Wilson] administration, for every conceivable sin. The Government is responsible for everything which is at present not as it ought to be. The old lady was very kind, a little of generous pride she had too. She told me of their trip to Europe at some length. The family says she runs the Highland bus line, because she picks up so many pedestrians. She herself told me they always took a big load of the halt, the maimed, and the blind home from church. Mr. Peck is in the dry goods business, and I think this is their first generation in wealth. They had along some pears which "grew in our yard at home," to which there was repeated reference. She told me she was raised in the country. They were very eager to secure some me-mentoes for little George, a grandchild. I gave them three bits of iron ore I picked up the day before. They bought some Indian moccasins at Crandon, where we spent something over half an hour.

The beauty of the ride is too much for these pages. The continually hidden road, sometimes shining out a mile or two ahead, on a hill; the touches of bright color in the trees far and near; the little lakes sparkling among the hills; the blue distance and the weil-haze over the low round hills. We stopped out among the hills somewhere and took some pictures. Of course 115 miles represents much more distance than I should have come afoot. We went N. W. to Florence, then way south to Crandon, then back north to Eagle River. The Pecks stopped at Tilldon's Resort. The resorts are a tremendous business up here, much different from Sequanta . . . as I was soon to learn.

After telling the P's good-bye, I walked on for about a mile when I was picked up by a man and a woman in a car and taken into Eagle River, when I read, "Arbor Vitae—23." I lost no time, but started right out. About a mile out I boarded a wagon and rode some little distance. I'm always fearful when I'm on these slow rides lest some speedy one come past me and leave me devoured with remorse. My sense of contract will not allow me to leave a man until the ride is over, so far as he is concerned. At one place this man stopped to step into a field and see a man who he said was his father. "I'll hold the lines," I said; and he let me. There I was! But nothing passed us, and soon we were gone again. I was beginning to take thought of the night. "Is the country much settled between here and Arbor Vitae?" I asked. "No; mighty little. They's some resorts out a ways, but

that's all." Now, while I thought it would be nice to stay at a resort, too, on this trip, I was somewhat afraid of prices and the temper of the management. However, I went on. Soon the wagon turned in, just before we crossed the Wisconsin River, and I got off again.

In a little while two fellows came by in a Ford delivery wagon and invited me on. I rode twelve miles sitting on the side of the wagon-bed: this because of their injunction, "Whatever you do, don't sit on that box." I didn't see exactly which box, so sat on no box.

"Do you fellows know about one Jackson's Resort?" I asked. Neither of them did. "I suppose you wouldn't know what he charged?" Neither of them would. I think I understood more why the silence, later.

"How far y' goin'?" one asked me.

"As far as I can get," I said. "How far can I get with you?"

"Fourteen miles out if the Ford stands up." Three miles from Arbor Vitae!

We spun along in silence, the road following the Wisconsin River. The air in the bottom was cool and fragant, and my cup was about full.

The car turned in, I looked up and saw Sisson's Resort. No wonder the men knew nothing of Jackson's! (We had passed it a short distance back, I learned—The Red Oak Resort.)

I inquired about the possibility of getting accom-modations. Such a thing was possible. I asked about prices and for the life of me I can't remember what he said. I told him what I was doing—that I couldn't pay resort rates [but] that if he and his place had any use for music I was at his service. "Come on over to the cabin, and we'll see what there is."

The resort is on the Little St. Germain Lake, and consists of five or six little cottages and a clubhouse, more or less rustic in design. The lake combines the features of a small lake and a large one, as it seems very small from only one place, but because of the endless bays, has something like forty miles of shore-line, and infinite possibilities for fishing. I saw a beautiful string of nineteen pike and one pickerel just at suppertime.

Sisson took me and introduced me to one or two others—one a Dr. Schmidt, of Chicago, who saw to it that I met everyone else who came within hailing distance. There are at present only ten or twelve people here. They are all crazy about fishing, or I suppose they would't be here. They talk nothing else.

After supper (which was a fairly good one) the moon came up over the lake. The wind sighed in the pine trees about the cottages, and the lake reflected every star in its blue depths. I went to the cabin, where I was to have a bunk, and practiced my strings a little, then went up on the clubhouse porch and played, for the benefit of any who cared to hear. Quite a number were out on the lake, on one errand or another, and I thought the music might sound well out there. According to reports, it did.

The first part of the evening I played better stuff. There was one fellow who carried on a critical conversation between tunes, on Caruso, Schumann-Heink, Gluck, McCormack, Kreisler, etc. I was going over to the cabin, thinking everyone had turned in, when I met one of the kitchen help who asked me, in a disappointed sort of voice, if I was quitting. I had forgotten those who were cleaning up supper! So I went back into the parlor this time, and played another hour, mostly popular and sentimental tunes. At ten o'clock I put my fiddle away and came out. On the porch were the husbands of the two women I had been playing for. They had been smoking and listening. One of them said, "There's one of the old tunes you haven't played."

"What is it?"

"The Last Rose of Summer."

"Now just to show you I'm right, I'll unpack and play that for you," I said.

"I ain't heard that old tune since 1890," he commented, "Not 1900, but 1890." While I was getting ready he told us of hearing Jenny Lind in Philadelphia when he was in Pittsburgh as a newsboy. He paid a dollar for S.R.O. in the "nigger heaven." He told also of seeing P.T. Barnum, brought out and introduced to the crowd at one of his own shows as "the greatest humbug of 'em all." This man and the other acted as guides for the fishermen here. The people who caught the twenty yesterday had a guide. Another fellow, who was drying his line as I washed up after coming, hadn't had a single strike all day—he had taken no guide!

There are four rooms in the cabin I am in, with a common room in the middle. The other rooms are occupied by men who come up here without family, for some fishing and general outing. The bunch sat in the common room talking last night when I cam in. I listened awhile. They were very profane, especially one named Tom Rooney—a Swede! The talk was about everything. Soon after I retired, the talk took the form of dirty stories, and I don't think I have ever heard a more complete line of rotten tales than last night. Many of them were by no means funny, the humor seeming to be merely in the distension of a situation with vulgar and obscene ideas. A night's sleep, however, seems to have washed all this mud from my mind, for I don't believe I could recall a drop of it.

This morning is fresh and cold, with a wind from the N. E. I awoke to look over across the lake into the sunrise, and hear the pines whispering louder than last night. Breakfast was good, I must admit, and all whom I met there spoke of my playing with the kindest of words. . . .

Just as I left the dining room the little red-headed girl of the proprietor, Margaret by name, and exceedingly petted and forward, greeted me thus: "Papa says when you go you owe two dollars."

After I had finished my journal yesterday morning, which I did about 9:30, I resolved to step along the row of cottages and see if I couldn't get one of my tens changed into ones. I stepped out and approached the first group I saw, one member of which was stooped over fixing the step. "Can any of you change a ten-dollar bill for me?"

"I'm sure *I* can't," replied the lady of the group superciliously, as much as to say, "Of course I'm *able* but you're foolish to ask me when I'm unprepared."

"I'll change it for you up at the house in just a moment," said the one bent over. He straightened. It was Sisson! I walked slowly toward the clubhouse, kicking myself at every step. But I let him overtake me so I could relieve my mind on the matter, as well as my purse.

"So my two hours fiddling last night wasn't worth anything? Everyone seemed to enjoy it."

I could not hear his reply, but the air around about seemed to bear me a work now and then amid a sort of mumbling. I caught, "all right," "don't owe," "square."

"I thought the little girl said you said I owed two dollars."

More mumbling, through which no individual words arrived at all. I gathered that here was a man in this business who still had some conscience left. While he was in bed and removed from my accusing presence, he was strong in his grasping; but when I appeared before him he was unable to push his point. As we stood talking, the little girl in question came up and asked me, as she had done a dozen times the evening before, "Who are you?"

"Aw, git on away from here! Git away now and ten' yore own business," exclaimed defeated papa. Oh, the glory of being angry at the innocent! The little girl was a brazen little chip, made so by continual association with the tourists and reporters. Mrs. Stearns, the lady who was sure *she* couldn't change my bill, was a prime offender, making much over her, dyking her out in ribbons, powdering her freckles out, and otherwise feeding up vanity for the ultimate slaughter. Mrs. Sisson was a picture herself, She was unco [remarkably] fat, and being a devotee of fishing, wore a suit consisting of khaki bloomers which gathered just above her shoetops, and a wee khaki coat and funny little hood-brimmed khaki hat. There were landslides on her pretty little hips every time she stepped!

I thanked my friend (?) Sisson, and prepared to get away as soon as possible, lest his strength return. I took a picture or two, and inquired about his rates, etc., religiously, as though I might be the means of getting someone out to Little Lake St. Germain:

Board and cottage,	*$18.00 per week*
Boat	*.50 per day*
Guides	*4.00 per day*

No charge for pitching tent on grounds; but such camper must rent a boat. The place is very pretty, but not so attractive as some others I have seen since. He runs usually from June 1 to December 1, but is closing up this year on account of sickness, his wife having had to go to the Mayo's at Rochester, and he himself being almost incapacitated by lumbago. I didn't see him smile once while I was there; and almost his first words to me after I came were, "I've been havin' one h—l of a time." I was amused at the bunch of dirty shreds of cloth dangling from the top of a tall pole out before the resort. They represented the necessary modicum of partiotism: the business demanded that the manager have enough of an eye to business to pull the colors up in the spring, but made no demands in the matter of caring for them from day to day. There is a lot of such partriotism. Most of the resort owners have it anyway.

I hurried away, and had to return a hundred yards or so for my walking stick, which I had forgotten. I made a mile or two amid the usual beauties of the country; before I was picked up by a tourist party; a man driving, and two ladies in the back seat. They carried me to where the ford forks a mile west of Arbor Vitae. (Manitowish, 32 miles.) We had a lively conversation, carried on mostly by me, inasmuch as they were all extremely interested in what I was doing, and what I had seen. The party was from Green Bay, Wisconsin, and were going on a few days' trip only. I regretted that they were going south instead of north. In stopped along one of the cranberry swamps and all got out to see how the berries grew and to pick a few. We had to walk on the large tufts of moss which overlay the swamps. The ladies being somewhat heavy, and not having much sole surface, punctured this in several places.

We passed lakes of all sizes, shapes, and kinds, the Arbor Vitae Lakes probably being the largest and most beautiful. I was interested to note also the moss bogs where lakes were about gone, and other large hollows among the hills which had contained lakes a good many years ago. The country is like a huge composite flower of lakes, except that there seem to be no opening buds.

Michigan would give much to have some of Wisconsin's plenty. Water without limit, and fields of almost proportionate wealth. I have seen inspiring corn fields, and smelled the odor of heavy-headed clover and timothy. But most of the country from Eagle River to the Iron Range is natural and unfarmed, much of it unarable at all, and used only by the *Summer Resort Business*. I never understood the real significance of these words in combination before.

Soon after leaving the most enjoyable companionship of my Green Bay friends, I heard behind me a noise like a cross between a twenty-horse tractor and a farm wagon on a rocky road. I turned to greet a Ford truck, with a very large box in which were a number of end-gate appliances and a skid. I rode along with the driver of this at the rate of fifteen miles an hour, for perhaps eight or ten miles (as far as Silver Lake). In

response to my question as to what he was hauling, the young fellow said "Spuds," and when I asked him if the spuds were any good here this year or not, he said, "Very good." This, aside from the usual initial questions from him, constituted our conversation. The noise was too deafening for amiable conversation.

I made the mistake of passing through Arbor Vitae, which I did about 11:30, without getting a bite of food. I decided not to walk back the mile I came beyond with the Green Bay people, trusting that I would either find a farmhouse or get a long fast lift. I did neither. There were worlds of resorts, one on every lake at least, so that I was perhaps starving in the midst of plenty. But resorts are such exclusive-looking places that I passed them up one after another. I should have suffered greatly from thirst too, had the day been hot; but it was pleasantly cool, full of momentary shadows from the flying white clouds.

Just as I dismounted from this potato wagon, a little Ford advertising Velvet Tobacco dashed past, occupied only by the driver and such Velvet as there may have been in the cabinet-bed on behind. If I might have attracted that driver, I thought, heaven only knows where I might have one—clear to Manitowish perhaps. Tough luck!

I next rode several miles with a young fellow driving an International truck with a load of concrete blocks. We had practically no conversation, as the noise and my growing fatigue prevented. My breakfast, though a good one, had been rather light for allday service. He put me down about two miles from Koerner's Spider Lake Resort, probably one of the largest resorts in Wisconsin.

After another mile or two I held up a fellow who came steaming past in a Dodge. Judging from the smell of him I should say he was a painter. He took me a few rods past Rest Lake Dam, neither of us leaving the other any wiser for our association.

Where he grounded me I saw a sign, "Manitowish, 6." Six miles around among these hills and lakes is a long distance. I got a drink from a well there to brace me up some, and saluted the sign. Wisconsin, by the way, is almost perfectly posted. In fact one man (he who lifted me in Eagle River) told me that the world is coming to Wisconsin to learn how to post the state roads. Michigan is poorly supplied in this respect. In Wisconsin it is well-nigh impossible to go wrong, and, I think, utterly impossible to get lost. The *State Trunk Highway* numbered trails are surely the work of years, but just as surely make the state a popular resort.

I was getting pretty well under the weather, about 4:20, when a car (two ladies in front and a boy behind) passed me. It passed at full speed and went on. But about thirty yards on it stopped and the boy shouted, "Wanta ride?" I did, and ran my best up to where the car was, apologizing for my lack of speed. The young lady driving said something about her brakes not working. I didn't know whether it was her brakes or her conscience which was slow to operate. In any case this machine took me clear to Manitowish, where I had decided to take the train to Mercer. The train came in as we did and I missed it by three or four minues.

There was no place I could get a room in that village, though I could have gotten a meal. As it was only 5:00 I decided to walk the R.R. to Mercer, about four miles away by that route. This was a supreme decision, but I had no desire to spend a night in Manitowish, under the existing circumstances.

Stalking up the main street of Mercer, I asked a seedy, lanky fellow about a restaurant and room. He pointed out a place for each and recommended them. I stepped across the street and mailed a card to My Angel. Then went down to the restaurant. It was a bare smelly place, with several empty showcases and an oilcloth-covered counter on which were some dirty dishes and a scattering of sugar. It was not appetizing and when the lady appeared I asked if there was any place near where I could get a meal. She referred me to Davis', three houses down the road I had just come in on. . . .

The supper was an excellent one, beautifully and appetizingly cooked; anything I wanted, any style I wanted. Everything was perfectly clean, perfectly home-like. I made up for my missed lunch. I never enjoyed a meal (away from home) so much. And the price was a dollar!

Afterward, as one of the daughters played the piano very well, we played some popular music. I did not play any alone. I talked to the lady awhile about early days. The house was a log cabin, built twenty-three years ago in the lumbering days of this country. She knew no ballads, and not a great deal of anything else, I found. The husband had died. She ran a table—and a good one I'll testify—$8 per week. The "extras" paid a dollar a meal, however.

These people guided me across the tracks to where they said I could get a room. I could arouse no one, however, and went back to see if Mrs. D. didn't have a room I might have. But I had made the mistake of mentioning that I had spent a night in a lumber camp! Accordingly she didn't have a single place of any sort where I might stay. She thought though, that the rooms at the Northern Hotel were fairly good. That was the place the seedy fellow had pointed out. It was across from the depot, however, and as I had decided to take the 5:43 train the next morning, the Northern had some attraction.

Downstairs the Northern is a bar, that is the office. We stalked in a side door to where ten or twelve loafers, in all states of intoxication, were holding forth, drinking, spitting, singing foul songs, telling fouler stories, and giving character to the place generally.

"Where do I get a room?" I asked the barkeeper.

"Right here," he said.

I asked if I could be called at 5:00, for the early train. He said I could as the place "kep' open all night." I took a ginger ale.

"D'ya want pay f'r it now?" as I moved off. "Sure do," I said, and paid him 75¢.

When I was ready mine host, called "Walker," a big fatty-soft, heavy-featured, unshaven creature who had just been singing an obscene song about a doctor, came forward. . .

"Walker" took me out a side door up an odorous stairs, and into a large corner room. When he went to strike a match, I saw that he had no fingers or thumbs. They had all been amputated close, at the first joint, I think. "Y' see, I'm a lil crippled," he said.

"Sure are," I admitted. "Get 'em frozen?"

"Lead pois'nin'," he said, as he struggled to hold the match. "I did all thish paint'n," indicating the wood-work. "Now whish room y' wan'?"

I locked the door with the thumb-catch, all the lock there was. The transom was out. The linen, which was still new, had been slept on once or twice before. The pillows both had a clean and a dirty side. I pinned my purse in my pajama jacket, and put my open hunting knife on the floor at the head of my bed. And somewhere amid the noise I dropped off to sleep.

I was awakened at midnight by a man shouting. He was in the front street, and was telling the entire country that he was drunk, and ever and anon calling on the barkeeper, or someone inside the building, and profanely inquiring if there wasn't some — — — — who could tell him how anyone could get drunk in a dry town. No one could have any difficulty in hearing him, nor I suspect in answering if he was minded to do so. He finally quit, going within to verify his opinion as to how such a thing was possible, I suppose.

I was next awakened, just as suddenly, but with something more of a start, by the sound of singing, very loud and strident, downstairs. There were women's voices. I can't remember for the life of me what the selections rendered were; but all four (I afterward learned there were four) joined in, one male voice attempting a harmony part. . . .

I was not awakened any more—not even at 5:00, according to the contract made verbally the night before. I was not bothered by bugs, though I occasionally felt something like cracker crumbs between my sheets. Perhaps the gentleman in 14 the night before had slept with his shoes on. I awoke about a quarter of five, however, and the place was in peace, except for a pronounced snoring from somewhere below stairs. I got up about 5:10, and found that there was no water in the room, and no wash basin. I was pretty peevish about this time anyway, so, finding a new towel and a pair of brand new pillow slips on the bureau, I grimly folded them in my pack. Then I wiped my eyes with my bandana (which is all the ablutions I have had this day), ran my comb through my hair, and crept out into the cold fog and the semi-dark, over toward the depot.

Here I was asked into the ticket office by the agent, whom I had met at Davis' the night before. The train was forty minutes late. In the ticket office I saw the biggest St. Bernard dog I have ever seen. It must have weighed 180 pounds at least. It was like a small lion—and must have eaten a small butcher shop at a meal too. The boys said he hung around the depot all the time and supported himself. He answered to the name of Ted, and was lovably gentle. Every time one said "Ted," he pounded a soft tattoo on the floor with his tail, without opening his eyes.

Finally the train came and I got on and slept all the way to Hurley. I had seen this country: that was the reason I was riding on the train. There will be a change in things at or near Hurley.

I notice all through this country the free flow of alcoholic beverages. 2% beer is on tap everywhere, and the beer wagon, loaded with cases and kegs, is a common sight. Whiskey evidently flowed without let or hindrance last night in my "hotel." At Hurley I sought a restaurant and had 35¢ worth of something to eat—toast, grape-nuts, fried potatoes, and cocoa. According to bill of fare, someone blundered. It should have come to 50¢, I'll swear. Then I went to the post office and mailed My Own a card.

As I stepped out of the P. O. a gentleman stopped me and asked me if I were not the university man who was tramping from somewhere in Michigan to N. Dakota. I was. He had seen the account recently in the Duluth paper. We talked pleasantly a few moments. I rather suspected him of being a school-man himself. "What is your business?" I asked him.

"I'm the Chief of Police."

I came near saying, "Why yes; that's all right. They're right here in my pack. I'll get them out and go along quietly with you." But I remembered my entertainment and remained obdurate and unconfessed. We spoke of the coming carnival and homecoming week awhile, then we shook hands and parted, he wishing me good luck and a pleasant journey. The criminal went on his way. . . .

[*Franz Rickaby's itinerary soon took him from Wisconsin to Minnesota. He traveled in all 917 miles, of which he walked 174 miles, rode on railroads for 322, and—there being no word for hitchhiking in 1919—"auto-tramped" for 421. He wrote in his journal:* "In many respects the actual hike ceased at Mercer, Wisconsin, where I began using the railroad at intervals. But I saw much country, met many people, and had many experiences in the remaining miles too. . . . In the course of this trip I met 224 people—ate with them, stayed overnight in their homes, rode with them, walked with them, or talked with them—touched them in some close way—172 men and women (about two-thirds men) and 52 children." *His expenses, recorded to the penny, amounted to $20.19 for seventeen days, of which $10.61 was for railroad fares and the balance for food and lodging.*]

1940/46

HELENE STRATMAN-THOMAS IN THE FIELD

My earliest association with folk music goes back to the days when my German grandfather used to take my brother and me to the woods near Dodgeville and sing a little German whistle song, while he tapped on the bark of a willow twig. If the bark didn't loosen, the song had to be repeated. I firmly believed that there was some magic in the little tune itself that finally made the bark loosen.

In my home, German folk songs mingled with the English game songs which my mother had learned as a small girl from the English children in the old Grove School. The Welsh and the Cornish in my little town also had their songs from the old country. I lived only a few doors from the Welsh Presbyterian Church and often listened to the Welsh hymns with their rolling bass parts. The Cornish people sang their particular Christmas carols, or "curls" as the Cornish called them. When I began teaching school in Monticello, one of the Swiss villages of southern Wisconsin, I became acquainted with Swiss yodelers and zither players.

In the summer of 1940 I was given the opportunity to be one of the field workers for the Wisconsin Folk Music Recording Project sponsored by the University of Wisconsin and the Library of Congress. Robert Draves, a University of Wisconsin music student from Oconomowoc, was selected as my recording technician. We both thought we knew our native state fairly well, but when we returned at the close of our first summer's collecting with recordings of songs from the people of Wisconsin in more than twenty different languages, we felt as though we had, for the first time in our lives, really learned to know Wisconsin.

We left Madison on August 19. The late Charles E. Brown, museum curator of the State Historical Society of Wisconsin, had provided us with a list of prospective singers and key persons in various communities throughout the state. Both Bob and I had serious doubts as to our ability to influence folks to sing for us.

However, we found the singers extremely cooperative as soon as they understood the sincere purpose of the Library of Congress and the University of Wisconsin in endeavoring to preserve both the songs and the singer's style. Sometimes an older singer needed a generous amount of convincing. "How come you want these old songs? There hasn't been anyone asked me to sing them in years. I didn't think they were any good any more."

August 19

When we started out on our collecting tour, I suggested going first into the southwestern part of the state, which I knew best. Our first stop was in Dodgeville, where we called on Dr. William Reese, a Welsh tenor. Dr. Reese, who was then in his eighties, asked one of the sopranos of the old Welsh Presbyterian choir, Miss Selina Phillips, to sing some Welsh hymns with him.

We then carried the recording equipment up three long flights of stairs to the dental office of Dr. Dan Wickham. Dr. Wickham had consented to sing a little song in Welsh brogue, *My Welsh Relation,* which had circulated through Iowa County for many years. Dr. Wickham had a patient in the chair, but when she heard our conversation with Dr. Wickham, she called out, "Go ahead, Dan, sing. I'm in no hurry!" So when we had the equipment all set up, Dr. Wickham sang for us, with his patient as the audience.

We went on to Platteville, stopping at Mineral Point, hoping that we might be able to find some Cornish songs of the early days. However, a full summer's work in 1946 was required to bring to light the old Cornish carols. Miss Dora Richards of Platteville sang a little song called *Pompey Is Dead and Laid in His Grave,* which she said must be Cornish because "I learned it from my mother and she was Cornish. She learned it from her mother and she was Cornish, so the song must be Cornish too!" I have found that this song was a great favorite both of the Cornish and those who came from other English counties to southern Wisconsin.

August 20

We arrived at New Glarus in the midst of preparations for the Wilhelm Tell play. Rehearsals for this annual Labor Day event precluded us from assembling groups of yodelers for recording, as we had planned. We were directed to a very talented Tyrolean zither player, Albert Mueller, who recorded many folk melodies, Tyrolean marches, and *laendlers.* We marveled at his dexterity. His mother too expressed her admiration and pride: "Oh *ja,* his teacher says he *hat a gut Schwung."*

August 22—23

I first learned of Bohemian music at Kewaunee through one of my former students, Dorothy Taddy (Mrs. G. D. Thoreson). At our request Mr. and Mrs. Thoreson gathered together the "Straight Eight"

Bohemian band. It was nine-thirty in the evening before they all assembled at the high school, where they played Bohemian polkas and waltzes until long after midnight. The instrumentation of this little band was typical: clarinets, cornet, flugel horn, alto, bass, and baritone. The music they played, from well-worn handwritten manuscripts, was brought to Wisconsin by the parents or grandparents of the players.

Not only the music but also the names of the players were evidence of the genuineness of this Bohemian music—Albrecht, Slatky, Kacerovsky, Pelnar, Haudek, Ramesh, Kasal. It can be said of the Bohemians of Wisconsin that they are truly a dancing people. Polkas and waltzes such as the ones in this collection are played by small bands at the community dances and are danced by young and old alike.

August 23—24

We took the ferry from Gill's Rock at the tip of Door County to Washington Island, where we were fortunate to meet Ben Johnson, the proprietor of the Washington Hotel. Mr. Johnson was not only proprietor but also a very fine cook and an excellent guide to the people on Washington Island who knew Icelandic. When we inquired of Mr. Johnson why people came to Washington Island, he replied, "Oh, they were just prospecting." We tried to narrow him down to a more explicit purpose—fishing, lumbering, farming—but each time his answer was the same: "They were just prospecting."

Mr. Johnson directed us to Mrs. Mary Richter, whose father was an early Icelandic settler on Washington Island. She decided she could sing better if she could have some more ladies sing with her. Therefore we asked Mrs. Christine Gudmundsen to join us, and she suggested that we all drive on to the home of her mother, Mrs. Karl Bjarnarson. Among the Icelandic songs recorded was the ballad of *Olafur,* the Christian knight who tried in vain to resist the charms of the pagen elfin maidens, the *hulda* folk.

All the various languages with which we came in contact were a great fascination. We never failed to try our own tongues at a bit of each one. On the return trip to her home, Mrs. Richter taught us the words of the Icelandic national anthem, which is written to the same melody as *America.* . . .

We had been directed to Al Van der Tie, a young man with a very fine voice. His songs included love songs in the Walloon dialect. A little song, *I Went to Market,* was typical of the mixture of the language from the old world with that of the new. The lines were composed of a smattering of both English and French dialect. Mr. Van der Tie had learned the song from Gust Mathey, an old resident of Brussels.

The celebration of the old Netherlands *kermesse* is still held among the Belgian people of Wisconsin in the early fall. At that time Belgians gather for two or three days of dancing and singing in the village streets. The famous Belgian fruit pies and good coffee are part of the celebration. Mr. Van der Tie sang a song which invites everyone to come to the *kermesse.* His young son was particularly interested and proud of the fact that the recordings of his father's songs would be sent to Washington, D.C.

It was almost suppertime when we arrived at the farm home of Jules Rower. Mr. Rower had been out threshing all day at a neighbor's, and had driven into the barnyard just ahead of us. We told him that we had been informed that he could sing some Belgian folk songs for us. He replied that he could. When we asked him when he wanted us to come to record them, he said, "Oh, as soon as I put the horses and get washed up." We set up the recording equipment in the kitchen and experienced a phenomenal piece of memory work. With no preparation whatsoever, Mr. Rower sang for us a song, which covered one full side of the record and half of the other side, without hesitating for a single word.

We came into Green Bay on a Saturday night. When we received our mail at the hotel, we found a letter which had been forwarded from the University. It was from Robert R. Jones of Wild Rose and told of a Welsh *Gymanfa Ganu* which was to be held the following day at Peniel Church near Pickett. . . .

August 25—26—27

We rose early on Sunday morning, hoping to be in Pickett before the *Gymanfa Ganu* started at ten o'clock, but we drove in a downpour all the way. We stopped at Moses Morgan's farm home but the dog barked in a tone which seemed to say, "Don't you know the Morgans have all been at church for hours?"

We drove on to Peniel Church, where the Morgans and all the other Welsh of that area were singing wholeheartedly the fine old Welsh hymns. We could scarcely get into the church as it was so crowded, but we soon made ourselves a part of this hymn-singing festival. Even before noon, Bob, who had been looking for Mr. Morgan, returned with the news, "Miss Thomas, we're to stay at Moses Morgan's tonight." As it turned out, the Morgans' hospitality was extended over several days.

At noon the ladies of the church served lunch to everyone, and singing was resumed at two o'clock. At about four, the afternoon meeting was closed and the men went home to do the farm chores. They returned for supper and the evening session, which lasted from about seven until ten.

During the afternoon session we recorded a number of the Welsh hymns. The beauty of Welsh singing lies not only in the voices, but also in the ability of every Welshman to sing a part. The congregational singing which our microphone picked up could well be envied by many a highly trained choir. There was something in the Welsh people's love of singing, together with their colorful language and the richness of the harmonies of the Welsh hymns, that made the *Gymanfa Ganu* an unforgettable experience. . . .

One type of folk singer for whom we were constantly looking was the true lumberjack. H. J. Kent of Wautoma, who had a great interest in local history, knew many of the older lumberjacks in Waushara and neighboring counties. He took us to visit John Christian of Coloma, Henry Humphries of Hancock, and Lewis Winfield Moody of Plainfield. Since not all lumberjack songs are intended for ladies' ears, it was sometimes suggested that I "just wait in the car!"

August 30

We drove on to Antigo, and from there to Bryant at the suggestion of Earle S. Holman to see Dan Grant, who was well-known in the community for his lumberjack ballads. Mr. Grant wasn't in the mood for singing that day, but said he would sing if we returned the next day. When we arrived the following morning at the appointed time, Mr. Grant had gone to town and his wife was not very definite about when he might come back. "Maybe some time along towards evening," she said. We were ready to wait until evening if necessary. However, it wasn't long before Mr. Grant appeared, ready to sing. We started for the house with the recording machine, but he stopped us, saying, "I'll go into the house and get my guitar and then we can go out to the barn and record the songs. The women folks are tired of hearing the same old songs." Mr. Grant sang in true lumberjack style the Wisconsin ballad, *The Little Brown Bulls.* Others were *The Flat River Girl* and *The Jam on Gerry's Rock.*

At the turn of the century, the sale of cut-over timberland brought several hundred Kentucky families to northern Wisconsin. With these new settlers came a rich heritage of folk songs and ballads, many of which had been handed down from one generation to another since the days of the early English colonies in America. In Antigo we recorded the Kentucky songs of the Jacobs family. Some years earlier these songs had been taken down in notation by Asher Treat and published in *The Journal of American Folk-Lore* (Volume LII, 1939). Now Mr. Treat's mother, Mrs. A. R. Treat, drove into the country some distance to bring Mrs. Pearl Jacobs Borusky to the Treat home so that we could have electricity for recording. Mrs. Borusky had an endless repertoire of lovely old English ballads which she had learned from her father and mother. We recorded eighteen of Mrs. Borusky's songs in one afternoon. . . .

August 31

From Antigo we went to Rhinelander and stopped at the Logging Museum. When we asked the attendant there if he knew anyone who could sing old ballads or play old dance music, his reply was, "You're looking at the man right now!" We learned that we were addressing Leizime Brusoe, who was indeed the champion old-time fiddler of the Midwest. He had earned this title in *The Chicago Herald and Examiner* old-time fiddlers' contest in 1926. A loving cup in the parlor of his home was proof of the fact. However, when we heard Mr. Brusoe play, we didn't need the loving cup to prove to us that he was unusually gifted.

Mr. Brusoe began fiddling at the age of six. He came to Wisconsin from Canada as a young man and has played for dances in the northern part of the state for fifty years. He carried an astounding number of dance tunes in his head, for he played entirely by ear and did not know one note from another. Mr. Brusoe took great pride in his playing and he was confident that if there had been a national contest of old-time fiddlers, he would have been champion of that too. He had much to tell us about how the Quadrille, the Sicilian Circle, and the French Four should be danced. He objected greatly to speeding up the tempo so that the dances lost all grace and beauty.

September 3

Our next stop was in Superior. Here we recorded Swedish songs which were sung by John G. Ostrom. One of Mr. Ostrom's songs, *Spinn, Spinn,* was chosen by Professor E. B. Gordon for a radio class, "Journeys in Music Land," conducted by the state station WHA on the University campus. The melody was transcribed from the recording. English words were adapted by Mrs. Gordon, and the song was taught by radio to some 50,000 school children.

We found some of the loveliest of folk melodies in the Finnish songs which we recorded in Superior. These were sung by Mrs. Martha Leppanenn Hayes and Jalmar Nukala. Nr. Nukala included *Tuoll' on mum kultani,* a beautiful love song which says, "My heart will break if my sweetheart does not soon return." The melody was familiar to me for it has been used by F. Melius Christiansen as the theme of his sacred choral work, *Lost in the Night.*

September 5

We came south to Black River Falls where A. P. Jones had agreed to locate some lumberjack singers for us. These were Arthur "Happy" Moseley and Charlie Bowlen. When we called on Mr. Jones, he told us Mr. Moseley was downtown somewhere, and if we would drive through the main street and listen for someone with a big voice, that would be Mr. Moseley. We had no difficulty in finding him.

We set up the equipment in the Jones's living room, and Mr. Moseley and Mr. Bowlen sang lustily. Mr. Moseley, a veritable Paul Bunyan in physique and lung power, was so delighted when we played back his own recording to him that he clapped Bob on the shoulder and exclaimed, "My boy, I never thought I would live long enough to hear myself singing." As fate would have it, Mr. Moseley lived only one month after our stop at Black River Falls. Realizing that "Happy" Moseley's songs were a definite part of Black River Falls local history, the city librarian, Mrs. Frances Perry, sent to the Library of Congress for copies of his records to be placed in the city library.

Charlie Bowlen proved to be one of our favorite lumberjack singers. When we came back to see him the following summer, he was ready and waiting to sing for us at 7:30 in the morning. He told us with pride, "My senator said he went down to that library in Washington and he got out my record and heard me singing."

We returned to Madison from our first field trip realizing that we had made a mere beginning in recording folk music in Wisconsin. We realized too that many of those who knew the songs we wanted to preserve were well along in years. On reaching Madison we immediately made a request that the recording be continued.

November 15

During the ensuing school year we made a number of recordings of folk music at Music Hall on the University campus. A student, Anthony Bacich of Eagle River, had told me about native Croatian music which he had heard in his home. He was eager to have recordings made of the Elias family of Racine. Arrangements were made and in November this group of young Croatians came to Music Hall in Madison. They were Martha, Anne, and Charles Elias, Jr., and Mary Filipovich. The father, Charles Elias, Sr., had taught his children to play the Croatian folk instrument, the *tamburica.* The *tamburicas* were of varying sizes and had fascinating names—"Bisernica," "Contrasica," "Brac," "Druga bugaria," and "Berdo." The scintillating quality of the *tamburica* music made a brilliant background for the voices as they sang dance songs, love songs, and Christmas carols.

Upon our return to Madison at the end of the 1940 field trip, we prepared a report on our collecting for the Library of Congress. We asked the secretary of the University School of Music, Winifred Bundy, to help us. As Miss Bundy was working with us, I heard her say under her breath, "Oh, I know that song," or "Hm, that's one Mother used to sing." Upon questioning Miss Bundy's songs included, among others, *Dirandel,* her mother's version of *Lord Randal, Froggy Went to Take a Ride,* Civil War songs which her mother used to sing for the G.A.R. encampments, the American ballad known as *Springfield Mountain,* and *The Homestead Strike,* an early labor song which she had learned from an older brother.

. . . . .

May 16, 1941

In the spring of '41 four Norwegian women came from McFarland with their *psalmodikons.* They were Mrs. Elsie Thompson and her daughters, Mrs. Herbert Flugstad and Mrs. Nora Brickson, and a niece, Bertha Larson. The *psalmodikon,* a one-stringed instrument played with a bow, was used originally in Norway for re-enforcing the single line of the melody of the hymns. Mrs. Thompson's father originated the idea of constructing a family of *psalmodikons* so that four-part harmony could be played. The Thompson family recorded many of the Norwegian folk songs and hymns such as *Kan du glemme qamle Norge, Peal pea Haugje,* and *Zions vogter herer Rosten.*

On the same day we were privileged to record music of another Norwegian folk instrument, the *Hardanger* violin. A Madison resident, Dr. Sverre Quisling, brought his mother, Mrs. Dagny Veum Quisling, to Music Hall. Mrs. Quisling came from Norway when about twenty. For over fifty years she has played her native dances, the *Halling* and the *Springer,* for the Norwegians of Dane County. The *Hardanger,* violin, with its set of sympathetic strings in addition to the four stopped strings, gives a weird effect. Different tunings are used, one of which Mrs. Quisling called the *Troll* tuning.

June 24

In response to a newspaper article concerning the recording project of the University of Wisconsin, we received a letter from a young woman, Mrs. Lee Lobdell, of Mukwonago, Wisconsin. Mrs. Lobdell wrote that she was sure some of the songs that her husband's grandfather sang should be preserved on records. We had gone to visit the grandfather, Mr. Hamilton Lobdell, in June of 1941. Although he was at that time eighty-seven years of age, blind and frail, he sang for us all afternoon. When we suggested that he rest now and then, he would lie back on the couch, but he kept on singing. His songs were those he had sung as a boy for entertainment at the church and school "socials" and included a great miscellany of ballads and popular songs of earlier decades: *The Girl with the Waterfall, Daisy Dean, Little Nell of Narragansett Bay,* and *Lost on the Lady Elgin.* His prize offering was *Reuben Wright and Phoebe Brown.* I have played Mr. Lobdell's recording of this yarn for many groups throughout Wisconsin since 1941. The delight of those who have heard it is proof of Mr. Lobdell's inborn ability as an entertainer. I have never found the music of *Reuben Wright and Phoebe Brown* in print, although I have found the words in an old undated advertisement for Hamlin's Wizard Oil.

Throughout the preceding months we had been planning an itinerary to visit many prospective folk singers in northern Wisconsin. A field trip for July and August was planned. Bob Draves was again selected as recording technician. Since I was scheduled to teach in summer school, Bob set out alone, going first into the lumberjack country of Waushara County. The lumberjacks whose songs he recorded were Charles Robinson, Charles Mills, Bert Taplin, Lewis Winfield Moody, Michael Leary, Henry Humphries, and F. S. Putz, whose average age was about eighty years: some of the last of the Paul Bunyans.

July 26

A return visit to the Kentucky folk in Wisconsin resulted in additional recordings of the Jacobs family. The mother, Mrs. Ollie Jacobs, was living with her daughter, Mrs. Pearl Jacobs Borusky, at Pearson. The two singers contributed many more lovely English songs which had come to Wisconsin by the way of Kentucky.

At Rhinelander Bob met Emery De Noyer, aged sixty-three, who had been an entertainer in lumber camps since he was a young boy. As he had lost his sight and an arm in an accident, he was taken by his father to the various camps on Sundays. In the camps he both learned the lumberjack ballads and sang them to the lumberjacks. Mr. De Noyer knew fine versions of *The Little Brown Bulls, Jam on Gerry's Rock The Shantyman's Life,* and a song of his own composition, *The Tomahawk Hem.* We first learned of Mr. De Noyer through Mrs. Isabel Ebert of Rhinelander, who had collected many of his songs.

July 28

At Crandon, Charlie Spencer sang two very beautiful white spirituals, *The Dying Christian* and *The Crucifixion of Christ.* In a recorded conversation Mr. Spencer told how he had conducted singing schools in Kentucky and had taken music lessons from the "music house." Another Kentuckian, Grant Faulkner, sang *The Rowan County Trouble,* which is a story of a Kentucky feud which happened when Mr. Faulkner lived in Kentucky. Speaking of the principal characters in the song, he remarked, "I know'd them as well as I know'd anybody, and every word is true, Mister."

August 1

Luther Royce of White Lake contributed another feuding song. *The Terney-Kelly Feud,* and the ballad, *The Lass of Mohee,* a song which is found in many different versions throughout the United States. His song, *Billy Vanero,* is a folk version of Eben E. Rexford's *Ride of Paul Venarez.*

August 3

In Green Bay, Desire Maes offered an astounding number of Belgian and French songs. Mr. Maes learned these songs from his father who, as a youth, had learned many of them from a blind man who sang in the public parks of the suburbs of Paris.

August 6

When Bob returned to Madison we spent an unusually interesting morning making recordings of Harry Dyer, age seventy-seven, a former logger and Mississippi riverman. Mr. Dyer provided a vast amount of information about Mississippi River rafts, log drives, and the building and piloting of lumber rafts. Mr. Dyer was not a singer, but he recited some of the lumberjack ballads and an original poem in which he listed a seemingly endless number of the names of Mississippi River rafts in rhyme.

August 11

At the close of summer school I joined Bob and we went to central Wisconsin, stopping first at Stevens Point. Bob had already met the versatile family of Adam Bartosz. Mrs. Bartosz sang Polish songs and Mr. Bartosz sang Polish, Ukrainian, Russian, and Kasshubian songs. "The Kasshubians were fisherman," Mr. Bartosz explained. "Kasshubian designated the economic status of this group rather than any particular nationality." At one time Kasshubians settled on Jones Island, Milwaukee. At the Bartosz home we also recorded Jeanette Jablonski's singing of Norwegian songs.

August 13

We were directed to Schofield to see Mrs. Bessie Gordon. Mrs. Gordon knew many of the sentimental American ballads, such as *The Baggage Coach Ahead, Prayer Meeting Time in the Hollow,* and *The Wheel of the Wagon Is Broken,* which she had learned from her mother. Mrs. Gordon would sing these songs for the entertainment of her customers at the tavern to the accompaniment of a little reed organ which she had cut down to fit under the counter.

August 14

We arrived at the home of Robert Walker in Crandon about ten in the morning. Mr. Walker was willing to sing for us but he asked us to return later in the day as he had a house full of company. When we returned in the middle of the afternoon, the guests were still there, so we suggested that perhaps they too would enjoy Mr. Walker's songs. They all agreed, and we made the recordings with some ten or fifteen listeners sitting around the room. The group included some small boys who were spellbound with the whole procedure of singing and recording. Mr. Walker's songs were all learned in the north woods. He sang his version of *The Little Brown Bulls* and many songs in Irish brogue which were typical of the songs which the lumberjacks sang for the entertainment of their fellows. One of his songs was *The Milwaukee Fire* or *The Burning of the Newhall House.* This was published shortly after the fire which occurred in the 1880's and became virtually a folk song among the lumberjacks. They sang not only the original verses but added some of their own, elaborating on the fact that the hotel had been condemned before the fire but had not been closed.

August 14

At the request of Alan Lomax of the Archives of American Folk Song, Library of Congress, we made a return trip to Rhinelander to record more of Leizime Brusoe's fiddling. Mr. Lomax had written that the records we had made of Mr. Brusoe's playing in the summer of 1940 afforded some of the best performances of old-time dance tunes that had been recorded for the national collection.

Mr. Brusoe had organized a little dance orchestra which included Mr. Brusoe, violin; Robert McLain, clarinet; Walter Wyss, string bass; and Emery Olson, accordion. The men played for us from eight-thirty in the evening to well past midnight. All of the orchestral arrangements were made by ear. Mr. Brusoe could not read music; the clarinet and string bass players were blind; the accordian player much preferred not to read music.

August 15

We drove on to Rice Lake and there we found two versatile musicians, Mr. and Mrs. Otto Rindlisbacher. Mr. Rindlisbacher had an unusual collection of folk instruments, including the Norwegian *Hardanger* violin and *psalmodikon,* lumberjack fiddles made from cigar boxes, and a lumberjack cello made from a large box fastened on a pitch fork. Mr. Rindlisbacher also made instruments fashioned upon lumberjacks' ideas. He played some genuine lumberjack dance tunes, the titles which are very meaningful— *The Couderay Jig,* which he said was from the Couderay lumber camp; *Hounds in the Woods; and The Swamper's Revenge on the Windfall.* Mrs. Rindlisbacher played a so-called ''Viking cello,'' a one-stringed instrument which was an adaptation of the lumberjack pitch fork cello.

Turning from the lumberjack instruments, the Rindlisbachers played their native Swiss instruments, the *Hand Orgelei* and the Swiss bells. Then Mr. Rindlisbacher played a number of tunes on the Hardanger violin.

August 18

On our way to the western part of the state we stopped to see our lumberjack friend, Charlie Bowlen, at Black River Falls, who was up at dawn waiting for us and ready to sing more of his songs, including his favorite, *Buck Billy Goat,* a popular stage song of the 1880 decade which had become part of the lumberjack repertoire. Mr. Bowlen said he had learned it in the woods from a red-haired Irishman named ''Sandy.''. . .

August 19

At Prairie du Chien we had solicited the aid of Dr. J. P. Scanlan, the Wisconsin historian. Dr. Scanlan and his daughter Marian had contacted singers whose songs portrayed the various strains of immigration into Prairie du Chien. Mrs. Virginia La Bonne Valley sang Canadian-French songs; Patrick Sheehy included with his Irish songs a fine old sea shanty, *On the Decks of the Baltimore,* which he had learned while sailing on an English vessel. The more recent immigration of Bohemians into Prairie du Chien was evidenced by the songs of Mrs. George McClure, Mrs. Mayme Doser, Mrs. Frank Stevens, and Albert Wachuta. In the midst of Mr. Wachuta's Bohemian song, I heard something that sounded like ''Prairie du Chenska.'' In reply to my questioning, he said, ''Yes, that's right. I'm singing about a soldier. My mother sang about a soldier of the town in Bohemia where she was born. Since I live in Prairie du Chien, I sing about the soldier from Prairie du Chien.''

. . . . .

Throughout the whole summer we were working against time, as Bob was leaving for military service. We had hoped that the little one-seated Ford in which we had traveled would hold out until the end of the trip. Bravely it did so until a short distance from Spring Green, where, weary with traveling Wisconsin highways and by-ways, a back tire blew out and fell off, and we found ourselves finishing the trip on the rim.

Due to the restrictions on transportation during the war years, we were unable to make any more extensive field trips until the summer of 1946. At that time further work in recording folk music in Wisconsin was made possible by a Rockefeller Grant to the University of Wisconsin for Studies in American Civilization. Since 1941 I had kept every possible lead that I found in newspaper articles and in conversation with those who had learned of our recording project. Throughout the state I had given numerous lectures and played recordings which we had made, hoping that members of the audience might recall other songs or singers. These lectures and radio talks did indeed bring a great many suggestions from the listeners. Our files were bulging with prospects for the full summer's field trip which was planned. Aubrey Snyder was appointed recording technician.

During our previous recording periods we had made no endeavor to collect the music of the Wisconsin Indians. The early studies and recordings by Frances Densmore were considered an adequate representation of this type of music. However, it was decided that a survey of Indian music in Wisconsin during the 1940 decade would be valuable. Chief Albert Yellow Thunder of Wisconsin Dells offered to help obtain music of the Winnebago Indians. . . .

July 24, 1946

We took our equipment to Wisconsin Dells, where we were assisted by Charles Hoffman of New York, who had come to Wisconsin for a similar purpose, and Mrs. Phyllis Crandall Connor, director of the Indian Ceremonial at Wisconsin Dells. With Mrs. Connor's permission recordings were made in the Indian village which is the summer quarters of the Indians participating in the Ceremonial.

The Winnebago music covered a wide range of religious and social significance. Chief Yellow Thunder explained the *Morning Songs,* which he sang with the accompaniment of a gourd rattle, as spiritual instructions with which the Winnebago parents wakened their children. He translated: "Do not weep anymore, my child, for I love you; the daylight of life is on its way."

Songs of friendship were contributed by Chief Yellow Thunder and by a group of Winnebago which included Sanborn and Marie White Eagle, Walking Blue Sky, Storm Walking Woman, Susie Redhorn, Bringing Home the Prisoner, Marie Sheekah, and Proud Woman.

Chief Blow Snake sang a series of songs of the old Medicine Lodge, which, explained Yellow Thunder, dealt with spiritual as well as physical matters. His translation of one of the songs reads: "You have talked about me, but upon this earth I stand with a clear conscience, with my eyes upon the Creator." John Bear Skin added other Medicine Lodge songs for which the water drum was used as an accompaniment. Both men played love calls on the Indian flute. The instrument was held in the same position as the modern clarinet. Chief Blow Snake's flute was made of wood; John Bear Skin's was made from a gun barrel.

Other religious songs were from the more recent Peyote cult, which seems to have been introduced among the Winnebago from the tribes of the Southwest. This cult is a strange mixture of Christian teachings and Indian ceremonies surrounding the power of the flower of the peyote (cactus) plant, to which not only curative powers are attributed, but also power of affording greater religious insight.

There were war dances sung by Winslow White Eagle and victory dances, which were songs of rejoicing sung by the women when the men returned from war. *The Buffalo Feast Song* sought to give understanding of the relation of animal and human life; one must be sacrificed that the other may survive. We made several recordings of songs of the moccasin game, which is a particular favorite of the Wisconsin Indians. One singer of a moccasin game song was Gerald Decorah, age sixteen. Bernard Sheeka, age twelve, sang *The Chicken Dance* and *Snake Dance.*

We value highly the recordings we were privileged to make of Indian music since we learned that many of the Indians do not have the point of view of the Winnebago historian, Chief Yellow Thunder. He felt keenly that there was a real need of somehow preserving for future generations of Winnebago children the sound of their forefathers' tribal music. Other Indians believe that the music has significance only when attached to the ceremonial for which it is intended. If, in the course of time, the ceremonial should pass into oblivion, its music should likewise be forgotten. . . .

July 30

In Dodgeville we were entertained by Mrs. Moody Price, about seventy. She had promised to sing a song, *My Grandmother Lived on Yonder Green,* which she had learned from her mother, Mrs. William Ruggles, who used to ride horseback around Iowa County to give music lessons. Mrs. Price recorded for us in her living room against a background of Mr. Price's collection of hundreds of clocks.

August 2

Another Dodgeville singer was John Persons, eighty-seven. He had moved to Madison and I called on him there. He told about the caroling in his youth by the Cornish boys in Survey Hollow near Dodgeville. The boys would sometimes blacken their faces and turn their coats inside out so the pixies wouldn't recognize them. Mr. Persons had a Cornish version of the old carol, *God Bless the Master of this House.* He could recall only a portion of *'Ark, 'ark, the 'eavenly Angels Sing,* which was a favorite carol of the Cornish around Dodgeville. In 1945 Caroline Corin, also of Dodgeville, had sung me snatches of this carol. . . .

August 3

At the celebration of the Mount Vernon Centennial earlier in the summer I had heard Mrs. Vaughn Garfoot yodel and play the Swiss accordion. We arranged to make recordings at her farm home near Verona. Mrs. Garfoot, who began yodeling at the age of six, had a repertoire not only of Swiss music which she had learned from her mother, but also Norwegian melodies which she learned from hearing her father play them on the mouth organ.

August 4

I mentioned earlier that Winifred Bundy of Madison came from a ballad singing family. At various times she spoke of her Uncle Will and said she wished we might record his songs. We planned a trip from Madison to Berlin on a Sunday so Miss Bundy could go with us. We found that William Jacob Morgan was as sweet a singer as his niece had claimed him to be. One of his songs,

Brennen on the Moor, related the story of a noted Irish highwayman of the eighteenth century. Another told of the adventures of the English highway robber, Dick Turpin.

Mr. Morgan had learned these songs from his father, James D. Morgan, who at the age of twelve came from Manchester, England, to Canada, and later to the United States where he fought in the Civil War. Miss Bundy asked her Uncle Will to sing *The Dying Wisconsin Soldier* which he did, but not without being somewhat emotionally overcome by the pathos of the song.

August 8

Through Mrs. Mary Agnes Starr of Waukesha I had learned the names of singers of French-Canadian songs in Somerset on the St. Croix River. Mrs. Starr, who is of French-Canadian ancestry and has made a study of French-Canadian songs, directed me to Donalda La Grandeur. Miss La Grandeur not only persuaded others in Somerset to sing but also invited us to stay at her home and use her living room for recording headquarters.

We came into Somerset late one evening and Miss La Grandeur enthusiastically told us of her plans to have the French people come to her home. At breakfast the following morning she recalled that she had not contacted Mrs. Rosa Marrisette Phaneuf, who was staying in the country with her daughter. We drove out to see Mrs. Phaneuf and literally took her right out of the kitchen back to Miss La Grandeur's home to record her songs. Mrs. Phaneuf needed no time for preparation, as her songs came readily. She said afterwards, ''It's as well you didn't give me time to think this over or I would have been frightened and couldn't have sung for you.''

In the evening the French singers gathered at the La Grandeur home. There were Adelord Joseph Vanasse, the village druggist, and Dr. Stanilaus Phaneuf, who included with other songs the old French *Malbrocque* as a duet in the manner to which the Somerset folks were accustomed. Mrs. C. Ciotte was persuaded to contribute a voyager song. These singers took turns with younger members of the group—Ernest Joseph Belisle, who had learned his songs from his grandfather, and Emma St. Claire, who had learned her songs from her two grandmothers. Miss La Grandeur concluded the evening with the charming little *Au Revoir* which she had often heard the French guests sing as they departed from her father's home.

August 9

John Giezendanner of Barron had been recommended as a very fine Swiss yodeler. When we arrived at his farm in the middle of the afternoon, Mr. Giezendanner was away from home helping one of the neighbors thresh. However, his wife sent one of the other men on the farm to take Mr. Giezendanner's place so that he could come home and yodel for us. Mr. Giezendanner was truly a virtuoso yodeler. His brother Albert joined him in an echo yodel. After supper with the Giezendanners, we drove on to Cumberland, where Thomas St. Angelo had arranged for the recording of Italian songs.

The Italians who settled at Cumberland came from the Abruzzi district near Rome. Many of them had been employed in building a railroad through northern Wisconsin and purchased farm land at that time. Among the songs was *L'America e tantte bella* (America is so beautiful), which Mr. St. Angelo had learned from his mother and which he had never heard anyone else sing. The St. Angelo family was joined by Mr. and Mrs. Ambrose Degidio and Michael Ranallo in singing folk hymns brought from Italy by the parents of the singers, *Salve del ciel regina, O Bambino mio divino,* a Christmas Eve hymn, and *Ecco il mio tesoro.* Good food often followed a session of recording folk songs, and this evening ended around the St. Angelo's dining table. It was early morning when we drove back to the hotel at Cumberland.

August 10

Mrs. Earle Sanford of Balsam Lake had read in a local paper of our search for folk singers. She offered to go with us to interview some of the Norwegian and Danish people in Polk County. Our first stop was at Milltown, where Mrs. Brithe Lothe, about seventy-five, had looked forward to our visit with a great deal of anticipation. She had written in answer to our inquiry: ''Received your very interesting letter, and will be very glad to assist you in any way I can. I have been living here in Wisconsin for nearly fifty years and worked plenty hard most of the time, but those folk tunes from Norway have brightened my days many a time when we were working hard in clearing land and building a home in this blessed land of opportunity by Wisconsin. I have a neighbor lady that is willing to assist me, so we are awaiting further notice from you.''

It was in this spirit that Mrs. Lothe and her neighbor, Mrs. Hannah Haug, sang *Her et det Land* (This is the homeland), *Eg veit ei liti Jente* (I know a little girl), and *Paal paa Haugje* (Paul and his chicken), and many others. Mrs. Lothe's only regret was that she became so hoarse she couldn't sing more. Her fine collection of Norwegian weaving and folk art was a counterpart to her interest in Norwegian folk music. Throughout the afternoon Mrs. Lothe's daughter kept watch over the *Rommegrod,* a wonderful Norwegian cream pudding which must cook slowly for hours.

In the rural community of West Denmark we recorded Danish songs by Mrs. Kamma Grumstrup and her daughters, Alma and Mrs. Esther Utoft. One of Mrs. Grumstrup's songs, *Fra fjerne Lande kom hun Drunning Dagmar,* told of the beloved Danish Queen who had come from the far land of Bohemia. Again we found that folk art and folk music are often preserved together, as Mrs. Grumstrup graciously showed us her Danish folk needlework.

Our next stop was Grantsburg, where Dr. Charles O. Lindberg had offered to help us locate Swedish singers. After registering at a tourist inn, "Eat and Sleep," we inquired where we might locate Dr. Lindberg. We were informed that he was in the habit of stopping at the inn for an evening lunch about 11 p.m. on his way home from the hospital.

When we introduced ourselves to Dr. Lindberg, he greeted us sorrowfully because the elderly man whose songs Dr. Lindberg hoped to have recorded had suffered a stroke a few days earlier. Dr. Lindberg was so disappointed that at first it seemed he couldn't think of another Swedish singer in Grantsburg. During the course of our conversation it became evident that Dr. Lindberg himself was a singer. After some persuading, he consented to make some recordings. This was about midnight so we asked what time in the morning he wished us to come to his home. He replied that we'd better go over to the house and start recording right then because in the morning there would probably be another baby coming and he wouldn't be available.

August 11

Several of the friends at the inn came with us to Dr. Lindberg's home where we recorded until two in the morning. About ten o'clock next morning Dr. Lindberg called and took us to the hospital to meet the old man, who could no longer sing his Swedish songs. We returned to Dr. Lindberg's home to see his unique rock garden, which is a miniature replica of a Swedish village with its quaint houses, white church, and mill.

Dr. Lindberg contacted other Swedish singers. We set up the recording equipment in the lounge of the inn where open house was held all day for those who came to sing; among them, Mrs. Ruth Olson and her sister Mrs. Alice Carlson, Orrin Olson, and the Reverend Theodore Kronberg. The recording was a novelty to all who stopped at the inn. One man was particularly interested. He said repeatedly, "I wish I knew the name of the man I heard singing in the tavern a few weeks ago. He had one of the sweetest voices I ever heard and he sang song after song." Finally, towards the middle of the afternoon, one of the patrons at the inn was able to identify the singer as someone he had known for years. He said the man was Abel Jotblod, who lived about twenty-five miles from Grantsburg on a farm near Webster. He too was enthusiastic about his friend's voice and decided that he would drive up to Webster and try to persuade Mr. Jotblod to come back with him and sing.

Mr. Jotblod, of course, was taken by surprise and he wasn't sure whether he wanted to make recordings or not, but, as he said, he reasoned with himself, "Well, I sing all the time whether anybody wants me to or not. Now somebody really wants me to sing, so I guess I better do it!" Mr. Jotblod was a second-generation Swede who had learned his songs from his parents. In an unusually lovely tenor voice, he filled several records with *I sommar kyabl* (In summer evening), *En visa vil jag sjunga* (A song I will sing), *A janta a ja* (The girl and I), and other songs.

August 12

Since Hayward was an important community in the logging industry of Wisconsin, we looked forward to finding lumberjack singers there. We hoped also that we we might record music of some of the Indians on the nearby reservation. Most of the Indian singers were away from the reservation "berrying" at the time, but with the help of my childhood friend, Mrs. Ione Levake Anderson, we were able to locate some of the lumberjacks who were not acting as fishing guides for summer tourists.

Adolph Williams, who is said to be the first white boy born in Hayward, remembered a version of *The Little Brown Bulls,* and *The Jam on Gerry's Rock.* Mr. Williams said his real name was Johnson, but as there were too many Johnsons he went by the name of Williams. Charles Ring, who in 1896 as a boy of thirteen had worked in the woods driving oxen, sang *The Shantyman's Life.* We also recorded his interesting conversation which gave a vivid picture of life in the lumber camps. . . .

August 14

At Black River Falls we had made arrangements to record music of the Winnebago Indians. Mrs. Frances Perry, city librarian, and Nancy Oestreich, an anthropologist living at the Indian mission, had consented to contact the Indians for us. During the day I received word of my brother's illness and consequently returned to Madison. However, Aubrey Snyder, the recording technician, stayed to work with Mrs. Perry and Miss Oestreich.

The recording equipment was set up in a room in the city library. Henry Thunder and Stella Stacy came from the Indian village to sing a variety of Winnebago Indian songs—war dances, moccasin game songs, peyote religious songs, love songs, lullabies, *Green Corn Song, Calumet Song,* and *Swan Song.*

Mrs. Perry has a great interest in the folk lore and local history of Black River Falls; she has learned folk songs from a variety of sources. One of her songs, *The Cranberry Song,* is of local origin, and tells of the life of the cranberry pickers around Mather. . . .

August 19

Mrs. Zida Ivey of Fort Atkinson had suggested that we record some of the square dance calls of Roy

Bicknell. Mr. Bicknell, although eighty, remembered many of the calls that dated back to his youth. As a young man he used to call for five hours straight without repeating a strain.

August 20

It was necessary to go to Harvard, Illinois, to record the songs of a very versatile singer, Lester Coffee, who had formerly lived at Pittsville, Wisconsin. Mrs. John L. Mellor had written us from Mankato, Minnesota, saying that her father, Mr. Coffee, had an endless number of old tunes and songs in his head which she thought were just what we wanted. After some correspondence back and forth, Mrs. Mellor persuaded her father to sing. She wrote, ''As long as Dad has said he would sing his songs for you, he *will*. He always keeps his word. If he had said he *wouldn't*, there would be no changing him. He is as stubborn as the donkey he sings about!''

Snyder and Phyllis were highly entertained by Mr. Coffee's singing. Mrs. Coffee aided the project by encouraging her husband and keeping his throat moistened up a bit. Mr. Coffee knew a great miscellany of old songs. Some of them, including *The Donkey,* he had learned as a small boy from hearing them sung at a circus. He recorded the tragic *Brooklyn Theatre Fire,* and *The Engineer,* which told of the wreck of the Thunder on the Elgin (Illinois) branch. *The Ramsay County Jail* was, according to Mr. Coffee, a very old song when he learned it as a young boy. There are also old English ballads, *The Broken Ring, Arise, Arise You Drowsy Sleeper,* and the Scottish *Lass of Glenshee.*

August 21

At Beloit, Wisconsin, we had planned to record the songs of Italian singers and of a Cornishman who had moved to Beloit from Mineral Point. We had been referred to the Italian singers, Joseph Accardi and Mrs. John De Noto, by Mrs. Vito Intravaia, wife of one of our former music school students. The Intravaias arranged to be present and encouraged the singers to record the songs which the intravaias had heard so often.

Mrs. De Noto sang *Signora Fortuna* (Madame Fate), *Rimpianto* (Regret), and the now popular *Torna a Sorrento* (Come back to Sorrento), which she sang as she had learned it from her parents. Mrs. De Noto's rich colorful voice evidently took the laboratory technician at the Library of Congress by surprise. On the copy of the record which was sent back to us, the technician had marked in crayon, ''Hubba-hubba!'' Mr. Accardi's songs were full of drama and comedy. As Phyllis remarked, ''Everybody in the room had such a good time; not knowing the Italian language, I couldn't tell what they were laughing about, but I laughed too.'' Among Mr. Accardi's songs were *La luna mezzo mare* (The moon over the ocean), *Tazza di cafe* (Cup of coffee), sung in Sicilian dialect; *A Zia Cicch* (Aunt

Frances), in which the humor lies both in the antics of Aunt Frances' cats and in the play on words; and *Tic ti, Tic ta,* which describes how the young lover's heart beat when he met his sweetheart.

The Cornishman, J. L. Peters, sang *How Happy Is the Sportsman,* which he had learned from his Grandfather Dobson in Mineral Point. I have since found that this was a favorite song of Cornish immigrants to southwestern Wisconsin. . . .

August 22

At Linden, Preston Willis and Mrs. Laura Avanell remembered bits of Americana. Mrs. Avanell sang the old temperance song, *Father, Dear Father, Come Home with Me Now.* This song, written by Henry C. Work in 1864, is much more generally remembered than its companion, *Father's Come Back to Us Now.* Mr. Willis recalled the days when play party games and dances were conducted to the tunes *Old Dan Tucker* and *Chase the Buffalo.* He sang his versions of the songs as they were used in Iowa County.

A University of Wisconsin music student, Elsie Taschek of Darlington, told me of the family parties at which Austrian dialect songs were still sung. Elsie's father, Richard Taschek, consented to sing and to play the zither. He arranged for a gathering of singers, among them Mrs. Laura Zenz, Louis Taschek, and Mrs. Ira Taschek. Again the evening of recording was an occasion for merriment. The list of songs recorded that night is long. It includes *Wenn ich mein Heuserl verkauf* (When I sold my house), *Wenn ich dir in Auglein schaut* (If I look in your eyes), and *Mitzel, willst mit mir auf die Alme gehen?* (Mitzel, will you go with me up the Alps).

August 23

Over a period of years I had been impressed with the interesting stories in the *Wisconsin State Journal* which had been contributed by Mrs. David Crichton of Lancaster. The stories told of the early history of Grant County and of the people who still recalled some of the incidents. I wrote Mrs. Crichton, assuming that she would know also of people who recalled old songs. Mrs. Crichton replied enthusiastically that she would help arrange the recording of several square dance callers and singers. Mrs. James H. Fowler, seventy-four, sang *The Birdies' Ball,* which her father had sung to here as a lullaby when she was a boby. This song was taught in the schools in the early days of Wisconsin, and I have heard many an elderly person mention it with a great deal of affection. From her school days, Mrs. Fowler remembered *The Hunters' Chorus,* a three-part round which, she said, was quite often used at the end of the school year at the exhibition.

Mrs. Minnie Plimpton Pendleton contributed the bits she could recall of *Tassels on Your Boots,* which the Plimpton brothers had played as a dance tune over fifty years ago. To Mrs. Pendleton this song had no particular origin but, like Topsy, just grew. From 1865 to 1875 *Godey's Lady Book* depicted the "American girls with bangs and curls and tassels on their boots." . . .

Mrs. Leslie Burton remembered *Ella Rae,* a sentimental ballad of the 1850 period. Her version of *The Young Indian Lass* or *The Lass of Mohee* was similar to the one we had gathered in 1941 from a Kentuckian who had brought it to White Lake in northern Wisconsin.

Mr. John Muench, also of Lancaster, recalled numerous square dance calls, which were used to the tunes *The Irish Washerwoman, Turkey in the Straw, Grape Vine Twist, Captain Jinks, Over the Ocean Wave, Pop Goes the Weasel,* and *Little Brown Jug.* Ralph Weide played the tunes on the accordian as Mr. Muench called, "Promenade all, 'round Beetown Hall," or ". . . Calloway Hall."

One of the last of the Negro slaves who came to the Lancaster area of Wisconsin near the close of the Civil War was Aunt Lily Richmond, age eighty-four. She was one of the Negro children brought by slave parents from Missouri. Her songs were remnants of those which had been sung in her home—the Negro spirituals, *Jordan River, I'm Bound to Cross, One More River,* the old hymn tune, *In the Cleft, Oh Rock of Ages,* and *Pretty Polly.*

August 25

Many years ago I had heard about the Bohemian bands at Yuba from my cousin at Richland Center, Mrs. Leo Dobbs. Mr. and Mrs. Dobbs were well-acquainted with many of the Yuba musicians. Snyder and I left Madison early one Sunday morning. The Dobbs joined us at Richland Center and we drove on through the hills to Yuba. Shortly after noon the Bohemian musicians began to assemble at Robert Novak's Opera House and Dance Hall. There was Joe Yansky, who was a one-man band with an accordion and drums, played the polkas *Baruska* (Barbara) and *Zvojni domu* (Home from the war). Mr. and Mrs. Joe Viagelt sang *Ochi cerny* (Black eyes) and *Virny Pravik* (True citizens of Praha [Prague]). The song asks, "What does a true citizen of Praha love?" The answer is, "Mary, Praha, and the world."

Since the Bohemians first came to Yuba, they played at dances, weddings, and funerals. Most of the members of the Yuba band which we recorded had played together for forty years. The members were Otto and Wencil Stanek, clarinet; George McGilvery and William Tydrich, cornet; Anton Stanek, horn; Nick Rott, trombone; Martin Rott, baritone; and Alford Stanek, tuba. The dances they played for us were *Litomericka polka, Popelka polka,* and *Samec gallop.*

I was particularly curious about the use of Bohemian band music at funerals. In reply to my inquiries I was told that the band would precede the hearse and march from the church to the cemetery, a distance of a mile and a half. When I asked the band if they would record one of the funeral marches, they selected *Bohemul,* which was the march played for the funeral of the uncle of one of the band members, Martin Rott, in 1932. Although this custom is passing, one elderly lady who was standing near me remarked: "When my husband died, the children didn't think we should have the band, but I insisted. I knew their father wouldn't think it right to be buried without the band marching and playing in the funeral procession." . . .

August 27

The next morning we drove to Brandon to attend a Dutch Missionfest. We had learned about this gathering from Mrs. Harman Hull of Waupun. Although she could not be present that day, she asked her sister-in-law, Miss Marion Hull, to introduce us to the Dutch people and tell them our purpose.

The Missionfest was held outdoors on the church grounds. During the course of the meetings it is still customary to sing the traditional Dutch psalms. Miss Hull had arranged with the leader of the singing that we might place our microphones to best advantage to pick up the voices. The leader, Dick Kok, seemed to sense that this was an opportunity for recording a custom which had been an inherent part of Dutch religious life in Wisconsin. The Dutch people sang fervently the slow, steady, long tunes of the familiar psalms, one verse of which filled a full side of a record.

During the noon intermission, through the courtesy of one of the neighbors, we set up the recording equipment in a home across the street and passed around word that anyone who knew a Dutch song should come over and sing it. Neither we nor the neighbor lady were prepared for the enthusiasm with which this suggestion was received. Since the noonday intermission was short, we decided to take people in turn and let them come to the microphone without even questioning them as to what the song might be. We recorded everything from an epitaph on a tombstone in Holland to *Daisy, Daisy,* which, sung in Dutch, so convulsed Snyder that he could scarcely keep his mind on the recording machine.

The epitaph was sung by Mrs. J. J. Schmedema of Randolph. It came from her mother's great-grandfather's tombstone in Holland and told how he died suddenly while leaning upon a fence. Henry Kempers contributed *Daisy.* There were children's songs, one about the mouse and the cat, by Mrs. Joe Boorsma, and *Daar kommt kleine Tomas aan* (There comes little Thomas), *Moeher, Moeder, de Beer ist los* (Mother, Mother, the bear is loose), from Anna C. Cysbers. Other religious songs were sung by John Ten Hoope, Dick Kok, Mr. and Mrs. Dorneliue Ter Beest, Mrs. Matt Redecker, Joe Koopmans, Andrew de Boer, and Mrs.

William Molder. Cora Wiersma sang *Waarheen, Pelgrims* (Whither, Pilgrims).

Following the afternoon session of the Missionfest we played from the speaker's platform all the recordings we had made during the day. As so often happened, hearing some of the old songs freshened the memory of those in the gathering; we regretted that our schedule did not permit us to stay and record more of the Dutch music.

We had arranged to call on Mrs. Ella Mittelstaedt Fischer of Mayville that evening. In response to a broadcast over WHA Mrs. Fischer's daughter, Mrs. A. G. Griesemer of Lake Mills, wrote: "The announcement that the University School of Music is looking for more old tunes awoke in me a desire to preserve some of the many songs my mother sings of the Palm Garten era."

When we arrived at Mrs. Fischer's home, she was convalescing from a serious illness, but she laughed at the thought that she was too ill to sing. Propped up in a comfortable chair, she recorded her favorite German songs which she had learned as a little girl when she went with her parents to the Schlitz Palm Garten in Milwaukee. We enjoyed Mrs. Fischer's stories of the *Gemutlichkeit* of the gatherings of the German families as expressed in her song, *Wir sitzen so frohlich beisamen* (We sit so merrily together). Mrs. Fischer not only knew the song of the *Milwaukee Fire* or *The Burning of Newhall House,* but she had also witnessed the tragedy. As a girl of twelve she had come to town the day of the fire to buy her confirmation dress. She remembered the occasion so vividly that she wept as she sang the song.

August 28

Our itinerary took us to Waukesha, where we planned to record Mrs. Mary Agnes Starr's Canadian French songs. In 1871 Mrs. Starr's grandmother and Grandfather Leroux came from the province of Ontario to settle in Oconto. Of Helene Nicholas Leroux's thirty-four grandchildren, Mrs. Starr believes she is the only one who has carried on an interest in the French songs. Her love for the songs she heard in the homes of the French people led her not only to preserve those which she had learned by rote, but also to make a study of the survival of French songs along the trails of the French explorers in America.

Out of her store of French songs she has developed fascinating lecture-song recitals which she has presented to numerous organizations, schools, and colleges in the Midwest. For recording, Mrs. Starr selected carefully those songs which were her own family heritage. Among them were *La poulette grise* (The little grey pullet), which she learned from her grandmother Leroux; *Un Canadien errant* (The Canadian wanderer), which came from her mother who had in turn learned it from her grandmother, Julienne Langlois

Nicholas; and *Michaud,* a favorite of her aunt, Eugenie Leroux Bachand. . . .

August 29

In Milwaukee, Miss Stasia Pokora, Executive Secretary of the American Relief for Poland, had enthusiastically offered to sing Polish songs. We found her in the Polish Relief Headquarters, surrounded by boxes and bundles which were ready to be shipped to Poland. We set up the recording equipment with these as a background, and Miss Pokora sang one Polish song after another. She told us that she learned a great many of her songs from the Polish immigrants who roomed at her home when she was a little girl. Among her songs were *Koraleczki* (My corals), *Bos ty jedyny* (You are the only one), *Kaczor* (The drake), and *Jabloneczka* (My apple tree).

August 30

Many of the immigrants to Wisconsin from Luxemburg settled in Ozaukee County. Near Belgium, on the farm which had been cleared by his grandfather in 1854, Jacob C. Becker, seventy-four, related stories of this immigration which he had heard from his father, Nicholas E. Becker. The father had ability at writing poetry. In his native Luxemburg dialect he penned verses which told of incidents of the life of the Luxemburgers in Wisconsin. These verses were often sung to some familiar folk melody. *Zur Errenneronk* (For remembrance) told how hard the immigrants worked when they first came here and how proud they were when they had cut their first path through the trees. *De Pier mat de gescheiten Ochsen* (Peter and his smart oxen) related an incident which took place on Nicholas Becker's farm. A farmhand, who came from Luxemburg about 1860, could drive horses but not oxen. When he got into the corner of the field, he couldn't turn the oxen around. He called to them in German and in French but to no avail. Mr. Becker, observing the difficulty, called to the oxen, "Gee! Haw! Back!" and the oxen responded. The bewildered farmhand said that he wished he understood English as well as the oxen did.

Onse Gescht fu Chicago (Our guests from Chicago) was written for a Luxemburger assembly at Port Washington. Many of the guests came from Milwaukee and Chicago. Mr. Becker's verses were sung to the tune of *Ons Hemecht,* the Luxemburg national hymn. Nicholas Becker was also alert to the American songs and made a translation of *Paddle Your Own Canoe* into the Luxemburg dialect . . . .

When Mrs. Robert Karner of Sheboygan heard one of my lectures on folk music in Wisconsin, she became enthusiastic about the wealth of folk music which was available in Sheboygan. The recording of folk music of a Wisconsin city such as Sheboygan should be a continuous municipal project. Our limited time made it necessary to select only one of the many nationalities represented there.

In the evening Mrs. Karner opened her home for the recording of a group of Lithuanian young people, who were members of the choir of the Church of the Immaculate Conception. We were told that the Lithuanians came to Sheboygan about 1890 and that Lithuanian is one of the world's oldest original languages. The names of the singers were facinating: Ruth Baranoucky, Stell and Alexander F. Skeris, Ann Belekevich, Edward Girdaukas, Mary, Lucia, and John (Jr.) Aldakauskas, Agnes Zupancich, and John Abromaitis.

The Lithuanian folk hymns were especially beautiful: *Lietuvos Himnas* (Lithuanian hymn) and *Marija, Marija* (Maria, Maria—Hymn to the Virgin) . *Subatos Vakareli* (Saturday night I saddled my black horse) told of the heartbroken lover who rode through the forest to see his sweetheart only to hear the sad singing of the bird which told him that his girl had died. To close the evening Mr. Karner, an Austrian by birth, sang two quaint little love songs in the Austrian dialect.

August 31

Some years ago I had a correspondence student in music history and counterpoint by the name of Louis Ropson, who lived on a farm between Luxemburg and Dykesville. As I was interested in locating Belgian singers in Kewaunee County, I wrote Mr. Ropson for information. He replied that he himself was Belgian and was personally acquainted with many of the local musicians. He kindly consented to accompany us on a recording expedition in the area of Luxemburg and Dykesville. Louis Ropson had played the organ in the local Catholic church for over thirty years. He began as a boy of eleven. I was so impressed by the incidents of his early study of music that I asked him to write an account, so that I might read it to my students at the University. In part, he wrote:

"I first began my studies at the age of eleven. I invested $2.25 for nine lessons. I had to walk about twelve miles back and forth to the orphan's home in Robinsville, where the nuns were giving lessons. It took me all Saturday afternoon. After my nine lessons I was appointed organist of the local church.

"When I was fourteen, my ambition to study harmony was rewarded, The Rev. M. Vanden Elsen, a master of counterpoint and a composer, was transferred from Montana to the pastorate at Fairland, which was about fourteen miles from home or twenty-eight up and back. I had no choice about it either. I had to walk it on foot in the winter too, and chances for a ride were slim, for there was at that time about five miles of timber forest with only a slight trail in it. Would leave home at about nine o'clock in the morning to be there by one o'clock. My lesson in harmony lasted from one until four o'clock and sometimes until five in the afternoon. By then it was already dark and I usually got home at eleven or midnight, as it always took me about an hour more to come home than to go.

"My teacher charged me fifty cents for a lesson of all afternoon till it was time to come home. I tell you those five miles in that forest were the longest—not a light or a house on that trail. . . ."

Mr. Ropson was also a master craftsman. He showed us several violas and violins which he had made. These fine-quality instruments have since been sold to Milwaukee and Boston musicians.

In order to have electricity, we asked permission to record in the village dance hall at Dykesville. Snyder drove around to gather Mr. Ropson's friends, Anton de Beck and Emil Boulanger, and an uncle, Theuphiel Ropson. Without Louis Ropson's help as interpreter, we would have had difficulty, for although Mr. de Beck and Mr. Boulanger had been born in Dykesville and both were nearing eighty, they did not converse in English.

Mr. de Beck and Theuphiel Ropson sang ballads of many verses, in both French and Walloon dialect. The memory of these older men for the long narratives was astounding. Our interpreter related to me the gist of the stories as they were sung. We recorded several dance tunes which Mr. Boulanger had played at dances ever since he was a boy. He too had made his own violin.

September 1

Several months before starting out on our summer field trip we had sent an article to newspapers in the various county seats, asking for information about folk singers. One reply to this article came from Mrs. I. O. Sessman of West De Pere, who told of her pleasure in hearing the Oneida Indians sing in their native language at the Oneida Methodist Church. At Mrs. Sessman's suggestion, we wrote to the pastor, Reverend J. H. Wenberg. Rev. Wenberg replied, "We have often wished we could get phonograph recording of the Oneida songs. In another generation few of the Oneida will be left who sing in their native tongue." A joint meeting was planned by Rev. Wenberg and Father William Christian of the Oneida Episcopal Church for Sunday evening, September 1st, when the Oneida would be back from cherry-picking in Door County.

Early Sunday morning we drove from Green Bay to Oneida to attend worship at Reverend Wenberg's church. Since Rev. Wenberg had written, "We hear the Oneida songs every Sunday morning," we were at first disappointed inasmuch as the choir sang an anthem in English and the congregational hymns were sung in English. However, as the offering was being taken, a single male voice, that of Wallace Smith, started an Indian hymn in which the others soon joined: *O Sayanel* (O Saviour, hear my prayer; O Lord, hear while I pray. Own my sould forever) . This thrilling music was sung in parts with no accompaniment. The parts had been learned by rote and handed down traditionally in the families of the Oneida Indians for many generations.

From Reverend Wenberg we learned that the Oneida Indians in Wisconsin do not sing any native tribal music. The hymns in the Oneida language constitute practically the only music in their native tongue. He showed us a handwritten book of translations of hymns into Mohawk, a dialect kindred to the Oneida.

In the evening the Oneidas from the Methodist and the Episcopal Churches gathered at the Methodist Church. They were very serious and co-operative. There were some beautiful voices among them, particularly the bass voice of Albert Webster. The Oneida seemed to sense that the older traditional songs were those in which we were most interested, for they sang them with an unforgettable fervor.

We recorded *O Sayanel* which we heard during the morning worship. *Tsyatkatho* (Behold what He has given to us) was sung to four different tunes. In the midst of the singing of the Oneida translation of a *Te Deum* I was certain that my ear caught the words "Cherubim" and "seraphim." I looked inquiringly towards Reverend Wenberg and he nodded in the affirmative. He explained later that the Oneida language had no equivalent for these words and thus the original words were retained by the early translator. I was startled by the melody of an Oneida Christmas carol which bore an undeniable similarity to the Danish Christmas carol which Mrs, Edwin Moll had recorded in Madison. The Oneida were enthusiastic participants; after the evening meeting had been dismissed, several of the men gathered around the microphone for more recording. . . .

September 2

Through the late Charles E. Brown, curator of the State Historical Society museum, I had become acquainted with Mrs. Ralph Kundert of Monroe, a collector of stories of early Green County. As a result of her interest in reconstructing her family history, she had discovered that her father, Charles Dietz, not only had a wealth of information and tales of pioneer days, but also remembered folk ballads of the period. Mr. Dietz had been president of the Green County Normal School for many years. It was interesting to meet a prominent educator who still had room in his mind for all of the little ditties of his boyhood days.

He had learned many English ballads from his pioneer mother who came to Wisconsin from New York state. Mr. Dietz reminisced, "She too was a school teacher. I was practically brought up in the schoolhouse, as my mother took off just enough time from her teaching for me to be born." In the style of a true ballad singer, Mr. Dietz recorded *Froggy Would A-Wooing Go*, *Young Mary*, *Three Dishes and Six Questions*, *The Old Man Came Home Again*, *Six King's Daughters*, and *Old Willis Is Dead*. He also recalled the playparties which substituted for dancing, which was frowned upon. He sang bits of songs that were used for the playparty games: *The Needle's Eye*, *King William Was King James' Son*, and *Come Philander*.

The trip to Monroe was the last of the scheduled appointments for the summer. We returned to Madison to organize our material and recording, preparatory to sending them to the Library of Congress. . . .

A COLLECTOR'S ALBUM

. . . being a selection of photographs taken by Helene
Stratman-Thomas in the 1940's, together with portraits
of herself, Sidney Robertson, Asher Treat, and Franz
Rickaby.

Helene Stratman-Thomas and Harry Dyer, Madison, ca. 1946.

Sidney Robertson, 1957.

Asher Treat, 1940.

Franz Rickaby, ca. 1920.

Singer, northern Wisconsin, 1941.

Louis J. Ropson, Dyckesville/Luxemburg

Dutch Missionfest, Brandon.

Dyckesville/Luxemburg, Kewaunee County.

Aunt Lilly Richmond, Lancaster.

Singers, ca. 1946.

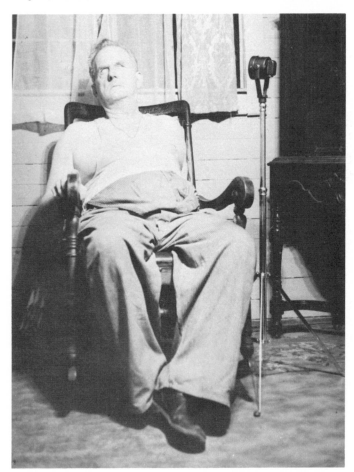

Emery De Noyer, Rhinelander.

Mrs. Otto Rindlisbacher, Rice Lake, with her "Viking cello."

40

Winnebago singers, Wisconsin Dells.

Adam Bartosz, Stevens Point.

Unknown singer.

Helene Stratman-Thomas (center) and
Swiss bell ringers, Rice Lake.

Unknown singer and recording technician.

AWAY

Immigrants en route to America, ca. 1910.
Iconographic Collection, SHSW.

AWAY TO WISCONSIN

David Peterson found the text to this song in the Fidelia Van Antwerp Papers in the Archives-Manuscripts Division of the State Historical Society of Wisconsin. Many versions of the song have been found throughout the eastern United States, sometimes under the title *The Rolling Stone.*

Since times are so hard I must tell you, sweetheart,
I've a good mind to sell both my plow and my cart,
And away to Wisconsin on a journey to go
For to double our fortune as other folks do.

Oh, husband, remember the land you must clear
Will cost you the labor of many a year.
With horses and cattle and provisions to buy,
Why you'll hardly get started before you must die.

Oh, wife, let us go now and let us not wait,
For I long to be in that wonderful state.
You'll be a fine lady and who knows, but I
May even be gov'nor some day 'fore I die.

Oh, husband, remember that land of delight
Is surrounded by Indians who murder by night.
Your house and your cowbarn will be burned to the ground.
While your wife and your children lie mangled all 'round.

Oh, wife, you've convinced me. We'll argue no more
For I've never once thought of your dying before,
And my children, I love them although they are small,
But my cattle I value most precious of all.

Away to Wisconsin

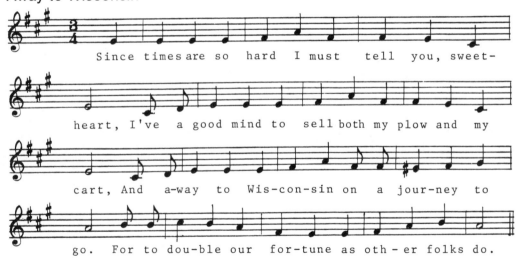

WISCONSIN AGAIN

This was a favorite melody of William N. Allen of Wausau, a composer and poet who wrote this tune as he began his return trip from the South to Wisconsin. Franz Rickaby collected the tune but not the words from Allen.

Wisconsin Again

Dancers, Black River Falls, ca. 1900.
Photo by Charles Van Schaick.

44

ETHNIC MATTERS

THE CRANBERRY SONG

Sung by Mrs. Frances Perry, Black River Falls, Wisconsin, for Helene Stratman-Thomas. This song was attributed to one Barney Reynolds of Mather, in the heart of the cranberry country in Juneau County.

You ask me to sing, so I'll sing you a song;
I'll tell how, in the marshes, they all get along,
Bohemians and Irish and Yankees and Dutch.
It's down in the shanties you'll find the whole clutch.

Did you ever go to the cranberry bogs?
There some of the houses are hewed out of logs.
The walls are of boards; they're sawed out of pine
That grow in this country called cranberry mine.

It's now then to Mather their tickets to buy,
And to all their people they'll bid them goodbye.
For fun and for frolic they plan to resign
For three or four weeks in the cranberry kline.

The hay is all cut and the wheat is all stacked.
Cranberries are ripe so their clothes they will pack,
And away to the marshes, away they will go
And dance to the music of fiddle and bow.

All day in the marshes their rakes they will pull
And feel the most gayest when boxes are full.
In the evening they'll dance 'til they're all tired out
And wish the cranberries would never play out.

The Cranberry Song

You ask me to sing, so I'll sing you a song; I'll tell
how, in the marsh-es, they all get a-long, Bo-hem-ians and
Ir-ish and Yan-kees and Dutch. It's down in the shan-ties you'll
find the whole clutch.

45

MY FATHER WAS A DUTCHMAN

Sung by Noble B. Brown, age sixty-one, Millsville, Wisconsin, in 1946.

My father was a Dutchman,
Das sprechen verstehst du?
My father was a Dutchman,
Verstehst du? Yah! Yah!

My Father Was a Dutchman

My fad-der was a dutch-man, das spreck-en for-stehs du. My
fad-der was a dutch-man, for-stehs du, yah! yah!

KITTY GRAUSE

Sung by Henry Humphries, age seventy-six, Hancock, Wisconsin, in 1941.

Oh, 'twas over on Hof Hogan one day, down by the riverside,
A-watching of the steamboat ship that went sailing down the tide.
It was there I first met me a gal, one day, she was dressed so very fine,
She had just come over from Germany on the Douglas steamboat line.

Spoken: Ya, Ya, she is the prettiest little Deutscher gal that you
ever did see. She was so pretty, I never will forget how
pretty she looked.

Standing on the steamboat dock, holding down her dress,
Waiting for the Deutscher man who was coming with her express.
She was a pretty little Deutscher gal and her name was Kitty Grause,
And now she is the new cook at the steamship boarding house.

I was just a'goin to speak mit her and say, "How do you do?"
When she gave me just an awful look that broke my heart in two.
I was just a'goin to speak with her and ask her to be mine,
When she said, "Get away or I'll break your back with the Douglas steamboat line."

Oh, she looked just like an angel, a'standing on her trunk,
Waiting for the Deutscher man, and he was pretty drunk.
Oh, they loaded up this dear girl's trunk, and she climbed on behind.
They left me there all in the firm of the Douglas Steamboat Line.

Spoken: Ya, Ya, and when they were just far enough away so I
couldn't speak to her, she threwed me one kiss and I see it.

Oh, she was standing on the steamboat dock fussing with her dress,
Waiting for the Deutscher man who was coming with her express.
She was a pretty little Deutscher gal, and her name was Kitty Grause,
And now she is a'cooking at the steamship boarding house.

46

Kitty Grause

Oh, 'twas o-ver on Hof Hogan one day, down
by the ri-ver side, A watch-ing of the
steam-boat ship that went sail-ing down the
tide. It was there I first met me a
gal one day, she was dressed so ve - ry
fine. She had just come o - ver from
Ger-man - y on the Doug-las steam-boat line.

THE ROVING IRISHMAN

Sent by M. C. Dean, Virginia, Minnesota, to Franz Rickaby in 1922.

I am a roving Irishman that roves from town to town.
I lately took a notion to view some foreign ground.
So with my knapsack on my shoulder and shillalah in my hand
I sailed away to America to view that happy land.

When I landed in Philadelphia the girls all laughed for joy.
Says one unto another, "There comes a roving boy."
One treated to a bottle and another to a dram,
And the toast went 'round so merrily, "Success to the Irishman!"

The very first night at the house where I was going to stay
The landlady's daughter grew very fond of me;
She kissed me and she hugged me and she took me by the hand,
And she whispers to her mother, "How I love this Irishman!"

It was early next morning when I was going away,
The landlady's daughter to me those words did say,
"How can you be so cruel or prove so very unkind
As to go away a-roving and leave me here behind?"

Oh, I am bound for Wisconsin. That's right among the Dutch,
And as for conversation it won't be very much.
But by signs and by signals I'll make them understand
That the spirits of good nature lies in this Irishman.

Now it's time to leave off roving and take myself a wife,
And for to live happy the remainder of my life.
Oh, I'll hug her and I'll kiss her. Oh, I'll do the best I can
For to make her bless the day that she wed with this Irishman.

The Roving Irishman

THE WELSH RELATION

Sung by Dr. D.W. Wickham, Dodgeville, Wisconsin, in 1940. This song was composed in Welsh dialect by Tom Jones of Dodgeville.

I was born not far from Cornwall
In a place called the Welsh Mountain,
When one day I and Mary
Went to ride upon the donkey.
Oh, you never did see, yes, you never did see,
Yes you never did see such a big time before.

Then we went to the railroad station
For to meet the Welsh relation,
William Jones of Cumerhan Way,
Come to see the old ——
Oh, you never did see, yes, you never did see,
Yes you never did see such a big time before.

There was John and Shawn and Mary
Eating pie and drinking sherry,
Dance away to tune of fiddle,
Up the side and down the middle.
Oh, you never did see, yes, you never did see,
Yes you never did see such a big time before.

Then we went to see the engine
It was puffin' and a brewin'.
It were made a wonderous power,
It could go three miles an hour.
Oh, you never did see, yes, you never did see,
Yes you never did see such a big time before.

It was puffin' through the whistle,
Made a noise just like old Divil.
And poor Mary was scared all over,
Thought the Old Chap had come for her.
Oh, you never did see, yes, you never did see,
Yes you never did see such a big time before.

The Welsh Relation

49

THE WILD IRISHMAN

Sung by Mrs. J. G. Krebs, Westhope, North Dakota, for Franz Rickaby in 1922.

Sure, I am a wild Irishman just come to town
For to view the green fields and the meadows around.
I went into the fair for to look about:
There was two ready fellows stood boxing it out.
Chorus: Missha tu-di-aye-ah, Whack fah-la-dah.
　　　　 Land of my father, old Erin go Braugh.

I looked 'round for a moment: not a word was there spoke.
Then says I to meself, "This is all a joke."
When up stepped a big butcher, was standing close by.
Damn me for a paddy, he'd knocked out me eye.
Chorus: Missha tu-di-aye-ah, Whack fah-la-dah.
　　　　 Land of my father, old Erin go Braugh.

I looked over my shoulder to try could I see
A paddy from Ireland that would second me,
When up stepped a brave fella that never was slack,
Saying, "Strike him, be Jabbers, I'll stand to your back."
Chorus: Missha tu-di-aye-ah, Whack fah-la-dah.
　　　　 Land of my father, old Erin go Braugh.

Sure my heart gave a leap at the word and command,
And I took my shillalah up in my right hand.
And I struck the big butcher 'long side of the head,
And I knocked him at though he'd been seven weeks dead.
Chorus: Missha tu-di-aye-ah, Whack fal-la-dah.
　　　　 Land of my father, old Erin go Braugh.

It was in one half hour I cleared the whole green,
Not the face of a butcher was there to be seen.
And while they were running, "Why don't you run quick?
Don't you see this wild Irishman wind his big stick?"
Chorus: Missha tu-di-aye-ah, Whack fal-la-dah.
　　　　 Land of my father, old Erin go Braugh.

The Wild Irishman

Sure, I am a wild I-rish-man just come to town For to view the green fields and the mead-ows a-round. I went to the fair for to look a-bout there was two read-y fel-lows stood box-ing it out. Mis-sha tu-di-i-ah, whack fah la dah, Land of my fa-ther, Old Erin go Braugh.

Outdoor dance, Black River Falls.
Photo by Charles Van Schaick.

THE RABBI'S DAUGHTER

Sung by a Miss Ewing of Pomona College in California, who told Franz Rickaby that she had heard it sung in Lansing, Michigan, in 1902.

You are a Rabbi's daughter,
And as such you must obey
Your father without question
Unto his dying day.

If a Christian you should marry
Your father's heart would break.
You are a Rabbi's daughter,
You must leave him for my sake.

The Rabbi's Daughter

You are a Rab-bi's daugh-ter And as such you must o-
bey Your fa-ther with-out ques-tion Un-to his dy-ing
day. If a Christ-ian you should mar-ry Your
fa-ther's heart would break. You are a Rab-bi's
daugh-ter, You must leave him for my sake.

DEVONSHIRE CREAM AND CIDER

Sung by Eryl Levers, age twenty-four, Madison, Wisconsin, in 1946.

I be nigh on ninety-seven, born and bred in dear old Devon,
And folks may be alone as I in other parts of England.
Oh, the Cornish seas are white but the Devon seas are whiter,
For if you be as lone as me, try Devonshire cream and cider.

Devonshire Cream and Cider

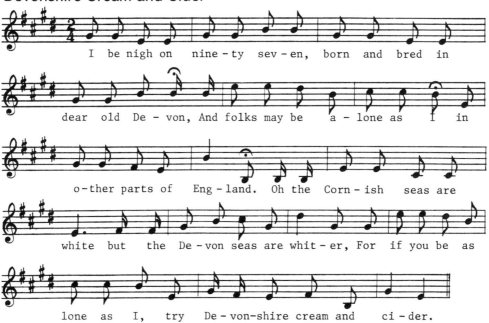

MY NAME IS McNAMARA

Sung by Robert Walker, age fifty-eight, Crandon, Wisconsin, in 1941.

My name is McNamara
And I come from County Clare.
From that darling little isle across the sea
Where the mountains and the hill
And the lakes and rippling rills
Where they sing the sweetest music all the day.

Our little farm was small.
It would not support us all.
So one of us was forced away from home.
I bade them all goodby
With a tear drop in my eye,
And I sailed for Castle Garden all alone.

For I'm an honest Irish lad.
And of work I'm not afraid.
If it's pleasures, too, I will sing or dance.
I'll do anything you say
If you'll only name the day
When they'll give an honest Irish lad a chance.

I landed in New York,
And I tried hard to get work,
And I wandered through the streets from day to day.
I went from place to place
With starvation on my face,
And every place they want no help they say.

But still I wandered on
Still hoping to find one
That would give a lad a chance to earn his bread.
But although it's just the same
And I know I'm not to blame
Still it's often times I wish that I were dead.

For I'm an honest Irish lad,
And of work I'm not afraid.
If it's pleasures, too, I will sing or dance.
I'll do anything you say
If you'll only name the day
When they'll give an honest Irish lad a chance.

But still I've one kind friend
Who a helping hand would lend
To a poor boy, and help him out at home.
I will bring my mother here
And my little sister dear,
And nevermore again from them I'll roam.

Yes I'll do whate'er is right,
Yes I'll work both day and night,
Yes I'll do the very best I can.
And they've got to help the heart
That will take a poor boy's part
And make an honest Irish lad a man.

My Name Is McNamara

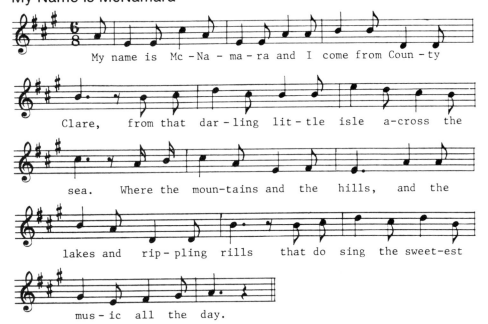

My name is Mc-Na-ma-ra and I come from Coun-ty Clare, from that dar-ling lit-tle isle a-cross the sea. Where the moun-tains and the hills, and the lakes and rip-pling rills that do sing the sweet-est mus-ic all the day.

FRIENDSHIP & FIDELITY

THE BLACK SHEEP

Sung by Robert A. Steinback, age fifty-four, Wausau, Wisconsin, in 1941.

In a country village not so many years ago,
Lived an old and feeble man whose hairs were turning grey.
He had three sons, three only sons, both Jack and Tom were sly,
And Ted was honest as could be and never told a lie.

The brothers then began to ruin Ted before the old man's eye.
The poison soon begin to work and Ted was much despised.
One day the old man said to him, "Your're heartless to the core."
And this were the worst, as Ted explained, while standing at the door.

"Don't be angry with me, Dad, don't turn me from your door.
I know that I've been weaker, but I won't be anymore.
Just give me another chance and put me through the test,
And you'll find that the black sheep loves you, Dad, far better than the rest."

Year by year kept rolling on, the father growing old,
He called to him both Jack and Tom and gave to them his gold.
All I want is a little room and a place by your fireside.
Then Jack came home one day, and brought with him a bride.

The bride began to hate the father, more and more each day.
One day he heard the three explain—the old fool is in the way.
Then, they agreed to send him to a poorhouse that was near.
And like a flash the black sheep's words cam ringing in his ear.

"Don't be angry with me, Dad, don't turn me from your door
I know that I've been weaker, but I won't be anymore.
Just give me another chance and put me to the test
You'll find the black sheep loves you, Dad, far better than the rest."

A wagon rolled up to the door, it was the poorhouse man.
The brothers pointed to their dad and said, "Here is your man."
Just then a man leaped from the road, came pushing through the crowd.
"Stop, stop," the stranger cried, "this shall not be allowed."

"They took the old man's property and all that he had saved.
They even sold a little lot containing his wife's grave.
I am his son, if you know him, from now 'til judgement day."
The old man grabbed the young man's hand, the crowd then heard him say.

"Don't be angry with me, lad, don't put me from your door.
I know that I've been foolish, but I won't be anymore.
I wish I gave to you my gold, for you have stood the test.
For I know the black sheep loves his dad far better than the rest."

The Black Sheep

In a coun-try vil-lage not so ma-ny years a-go, Lived an old and fee-ble man whose hairs were turn-ing grey. He had three sons, three on-ly sons, both Jack and Tom were sly. And Ted was hon-est as could be and nev-er told a lie.

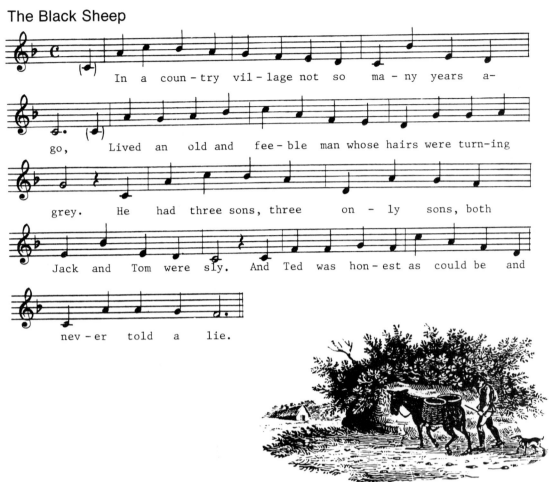

THE DONKEY SONG

Sung by Lester A. Coffee, age seventy-five, Harvard, Illinois, in 1946. Coffee learned this song as a small boy at a circus, and never heard anyone else sing it again.

I used to own a donkey,
A bob-tailed stubborn mule.
He was born about the year of forty nine.
His head was full of starch,
From stopping railroad cars.
He was raw-boned, spavined, deaf and blind.
He'd kick a steam engine,
He'd knock you for a goal.
He'd send you where Bob Ingersoll belonged.
He might have gone to Congress,
If he had only lived.
Empty is the stable, Dave is gone.
Empty is the stable, Dave is gone to rest.
He's gone where all the good donkeys go.
He died at half past four.
He's gone to the beautiful shore.
Empty is the stable, Dave is gone.

His hoof was like a slingshot,
He'd raise you through the roof.
He'd come in the house and kick you out of bed.
His feet were full of bunions,
He could eat a barrel of onions.
And go to sleep a-standing on his head.
He'd go in a saloon,
Shove his hoof through a spittoon,
Kick the bar into the gutter for a joke.
When he laid down and died,
Every mule in Jersey cried.
Empty is the stable, Dave is gone.
Dave has left the stable for the promised land.
His overshoes and saddle are in pawn.
No more hay he'll ever chew
For they've turned him into glue.
Empty is the stable, Dave is gone.

The Donkey Song

I used to own a don-key, a bob-tailed stub-born mule. He was born a-bout the year of for-ty nine. His head was full of starch From stop-ping rail-road cars.

He was raw-boned, spav-ened, deaf and blind. He'd kick a steam en-gine, He'd knock you for a goal. He'd send you where Bob In-ger-sol be-longed. He might have gone to con-gress If he had on-ly lived. Emp-ty is the sta-ble, Dave is gone. Emp-ty is the sta-ble, Dave is gone to rest. He's gone where all the good don-keys go. He died at half-past four. He's gone to the beau-ti-ful shore. Emp-ty is the sta-ble Dave is gone.

Young sports, Coleman, Marinette County.
Photo by Harry S. Boles.

RILEY AND I WERE CHUMS

Sung by Robert Walker, age fifty-eight, Crandon, Wisconsin, in 1941.

Chorus: Oh, Riley and I were chums and we always shared
Black eyes and sugar plums, a divil a hair we cared.
If there's anything nice about yah,
Take my word for whatever I done,
I handed it over to Riley.

If there was any booze to be got,
We always got a key or a pot.
I would grab up a measure and run up the block
And I'd hand it over to Riley.

One Sunday morn I went for a walk,
Me and my chum Johnny Riley.
I didn't know there was anything up
Though he acted so shyly.

Just then the cop caught me by the ear
And he said, "Young man there's a warrant here."
And I took the warrant with the greatest of fear
And I handed it over to Riley.

One Sunday morn I took me a wife,
And me best, of course, was Riley.
I thought she would be the pride of me life,
Although she acted so shyly.

I soon found out married life was no fun
When she chased me around the house with a gun.

———————————————

So I handed her over to Riley.

57

Riley and I Were Chums

If there was an-y booze to be got, We al-ways got a
keg or a pot. I would grab up a mea-sure, I'd
run up the block, And I'd hand it ov-er to Ri-ley.
Oh, Ri-ley and I were chums, And we al-ways shared
Black eyes and su-gar plums, a - di-vil a hair we cared.
If there's an-y-thing nice a-bout you,
take me word for what - ev - er I done, for I
hand - ed it ov - er to Ri - ley.

A MOTTO FOR EVERY MAN

Sung by Edward Turner, Grand Forks, North Dakota, for Franz Rickaby. Turner, a resident of a county home, told Rickaby that he learned the song from a man named Reese who had seen minstrel shows before the Civil War.

Some people you've met in your time, no doubt,
Who never look happy or gay.
But I'll tell you the way to get jolly and stout
If you'll listen a while to my lay.
I've come here to tell you a bit of my mind,
And please with the same if I can.
Advice in my song you will certainly find
And a motto for every man.

Chorus: So we will sing and banish melancholy.
Troubles may come, and we'll do the best we can
To drive care away, for grieving is folly.
Put your shoulder to the wheel is a motto for every man.

58

We cannot all fight in this battle of life;
The weak must go to the wall.
So do to each other the thing that is right,
For there's room in this world for us all.
Credit refuse if you've the money to pay,
You will find it the wiser plan;
And a penny laid by for a rainy day
Is a motto for every man.

A coward gives in at the first repulse,
A brave man struggles again
With a resolute eye and a bounding pulse
To battle his way amongst men.

For he knows he has but one chance in this life
To better himself if he can.
So make your hay while the sun doth shine
Is a motto for every man.

Economy study, but don't be mean;
A penny may lose a pound.
Through this world a conscience clean
Will carry you safe and sound.
It's all very well to be free, I will own,
To do a good turn where you can
But charity always commences at home
Is a motto for every man.

A Motto For Every Man

Some peo-ple you've met in your time, no doubt, who nev-er look hap-py or gay. But I'll tell you the way to get jol-ly and stout if you'll lis-ten a while to my lay. I've come here to tell you a bit of my mind, and please with the same if I can. Ad-vise in my song you will cer-tain-ly find And a mot-to for ev-er-y man. So we will sing And ban-ish mel-an-cho-ly. Trou-bles may come, and we'll do the best we can. To drive care a-way, for griev-ing is fol-ly. Put your shoul-der to the wheel is a mot-to for ev-ery man.

O, GLORY

ONE MORE RIVER

Sung by Aunt Lily Richmond, age eighty-four, Lancaster, Wisconsin, in 1946.

One more river and that's the river of Jordan.
One more river and that's the river to cross.
The animals came in two by two
Just one more river to cross.
The elephant and the kangaroo
That's one more river to cross.
Said the ant to the elephant, "Quit your pushing around
'Cause there's one more river to cross."

One More River

ROCK OF AGES

Sung by Aunt Lily Richmond, age eighty-four, Lancaster, Wisconsin, in 1946.

In the cleft, Oh rock of ages
Hide thou me.
Be thou my soul's eternal treasure
Hide thou me.

In the fight of Jordan's billow
Let they bosom by my pillow.
Hide me, Oh, dear rock of ages.
Faith in thee.

Rock of Ages

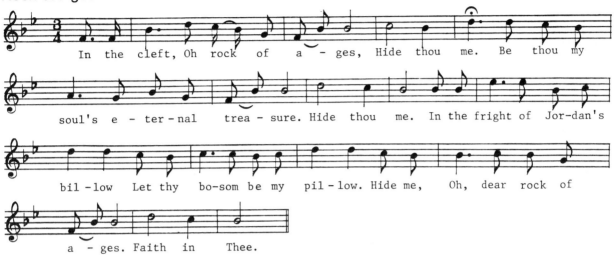

In the cleft, Oh rock of a - ges, Hide thou me. Be thou my soul's e - ter - nal trea - sure. Hide thou me. In the fright of Jor-dan's bil - low Let thy bo-som be my pil - low. Hide me, Oh, dear rock of a - ges. Faith in Thee.

COME AND I WILL SING YOU

Helene Stratman-Thomas was taught the lyrics to this Cornish carol by Mrs. E. J. Vial, age eighty-seven, Linden, Wisconsin, in 1946. Later, John Persons of Madison sang it as a question-and-answer duet with Miss Stratman-Thomas.

Come and I will sing you.
What will you sing me?
I will sing you one-oh.
What is your one-oh?
One of them is gone alone, another shall remain so.

Come and I will sing you.
What will you sing me?
I will sing you two-oh.
What is your two-oh?
Two of them are lily-white babes dressed in garland green-oh
One of them is gone alone, another shall remain so.

Come and I will sing you.
What will you sing me?
I will sing you three-oh.
What is your three-oh?

Three of them are strangers.
Two of them are lily-white babes dressed in garland green-oh.
One of them is gone alone, another shall remain so.

Four is the gospel preacher.
Five is the ferryman in his boat.
Six is the cheerful waiter.
Seven's the bright star in the sky.
Eight's the great Archangel.
Nine's the moon-shine bright and clear.
Ten is the ten commandments.
Eleven is them are gone to hell.
Twelve is the love of papa.

Come and I Will Sing You

Come, and I will sing you. What will you sing me?

I will sing you one - oh. What is your one - oh?

One of them is gone a-lone, a - no - ther shall re-

main so.

JORDAN'S RIVER I'M BOUND TO CROSS

Sung by Aunt Lily Richmond, age eighty-four, Lancaster, Wisconsin, in 1946.

Jordan's River I'm bound to cross.
Jordan's River I'm bound to cross.
Jordan's River I'm bound to cross.
Sinners fare ye well.
If you get there before I do

That's one more river to cross.
Jordan's River I'm bound to cross.
Jordan's River I'm bound to cross.
Jordan's River I'm bound to cross.
Sinners fare ye well.

Jordan's River I'm Bound to Cross

Jor - dan's ri - ver I'm bound to cross, Jor - dan's ri - ver I'm

bound to cross, Jor - dan's ri - ver I'm bound to cross,

Sin - ners fare ye well. If you get there be - fore I do that's

one more ri - ver to cross.

THE CRUCIFIXION OF CHRIST

Sung by Charlie Spencer, age sixty-eight, Crandon, Wisconsin, in 1941. Spencer learned this song in his earlier home in Kentucky. He understood that the song had been handed down for over two hundred years through the Primitive Baptist Church, and that the words and tune were written by a man named Harris in London, England. In response to the recording technician's remark that the song must have been very close to him when he was younger, Spencer replied solemnly, "Yes, sir, it was. It appealed to me from the beginnin'—from the beginnin'. The oldtimers then kept it alive as I'm a-keepin' it now. But you'll not find many oldtimers that's got it now."

A story most loving I'll tell,
Of Jesus, the wondrous surprise;
He suffered to save us from Hell,
That sinners, thou sinners might rise.
He left His exalted abode
When man by transgression was lost;
I'm telling the love of our God;
He shed forth His blood as the cause.

Oh, did my dear Jesus thus bleed,
And pity His chosen lost race;
From whence did such mercies proceed,
Such boundless compassion and grace?
His body bore anguish and pain,
His spirit 'most sunk with the load;
A short time before He was slain,
His sweat was as great drops of blood.

Oh, was it for crimes I have done,
The Savior was hailed with a kiss
By Judas, the traitor, alone?
Was ever compassion like this?
The ruffians all joined in a band,
Confined Him and led Him away,
The cords wrapped around His sweet hands.
Come, mourners, look at Him, I pray.

To Pilate's stone pillars, when led,
His body was lashed with whips.
It never was any might said,
A railing word dropped from his lips.
They made Him a crown out of thorns,
They Him and did Him abuse;
They clothed Him with crimson and scorn,
And hailed Him the King of the Jews.

They loaded the lamb of the Cross
And drove Him up Calvary's hill.
Come mourners, a moment, and pause;
All Nature looks solemn and still.
They rushed the nails through His hands,
Transfixed and tortured His feet.
Oh brethren, see passive He stands,
To look at the sight of His grave.

He cried, "My father, my God,
Forsaken, thou'st left Me alone."
The cross was all covered with blood,
The temple was bursted in twain.
He groaned His last, and He died.
The sun, it refused to shine.
They rushed the spear in His side;
This lovely Redeemer is mine.

He fought the hard battle and won
This vict'ry and gave it most free.
Oh brethren, look forward and run
In hopes that His kingdom you see,
And when He in the cloud shall appear,
With angels all at His command,
And thousands of Christians be there,
All singing, with harps in a band.

How pleasant and happy those years,
Enjoying such beams of delight.
His spirit to Christians He'll show;
Oh, Jesus, I long for the sight.
I long to mount up in the skies,
In Paradise make my abode,
And sing of salvation on high,
And rest with our glorious God.

The Crucifixion of Christ

A sto-ry most lov-ing I'll tell, Of Je-sus, the won-drous sur-

prise. He suf-fered to save us from Hell, That

sin-ners, thou sin-ners might rise. He left his ex-alt-ed a-

bode, When man by trans-gres-sion was lost. I'm

tell-ing the love of our God; He shed forth His blood as the

cause.

Photo by Charles Van Schaick, Black River Falls.

THE DYING CHRISTIAN

Sung by Charlie Spencer, age sixty-eight, Crandon, Wisconsin, in 1941. He learned this song as a schoolboy in Kentucky, where "the old school on my father's plantation had a clapboard roof, no loft, a big open fireplace. The seats that I sat on when I was attending school was made out of split logs with the rounding side down. And I remember that they did have rough carpenters at that time, because they left so many splinters on them there benches. They'd get you in bed. One reason why I kept the old-time songs is because they became part of my mind when I was a boy. You're lucky to run on these two ballads *The Dying Christian* and *The Crucifixion of Christ*, I can say that. I'm proud that you have those. You'll not find anyone around here that knows them except a Kentuckian, a Southern-born person."

My soul's full of glory, inspiring my tongue.
Could I meet with angels, I'd sing them a song.
I'd sing of my Jesus, and tell of His charms,
And beg them to guide me to His loving arms.

Methinks they're descending to hear while I sing,
Well-pleased to hear mortals a-praising their King.
Oh angels, oh angels, my soul's in a flame;
I faint in sweet raptures at Jesus's name.

Oh Jesus, Oh Jesus, Thou balm of my soul,
Was Thou, my dear Jesus, that made my heart whole.
Oh bring me to Judah, Thou precious sweet King,
In oceans of glory, Thy praises to sing.

Oh Heaven, sweet Heaven, I long to be there,
To meet all my brethren, and Jesus, my dear.
Come angels, come angels, I'm ready to fly;
Come quickly, come bade me to God in the sky.

Sweet spirits, attend me, till Jesus shall come;
Protect and defend me till I am called home.
Though worms my poor body may claim as their prey,
'Twill out-shine, when rising, the sun at noon-day.

The sun shall be darkness, the moon turned to blood,
The mountains all melt at the presence of God.
Red lightnings may flash and loud thunders may roar;
All this cannot daunt me on Canaan's blessed shore.

A glimpse of bright glory surprises my soul;
I sink in sweet raptures, to view this bright goal.
My soul, while I'm singing, is leaping to go;
This moment for Heaven, I'd leave all below.

Farewell, my dear brethren, my Lord bids me come;
Farewell, my dear, dear sisters, I'm now going home.
Bright angels now whisp'ring so sweet in my ear,
Away to my Saviour's, my spirit draws near.

I'm going, I'm going, but what do I see,
Till Jesus in glory appears unto me.
I'm going, I'm going, I'm going, I'm gone;
Oh glory, oh glory, 'tis done, it is done.

The Dying Christian

My soul's full of glo-ry, in-spir-ing my tongue. Could
I meet with an-gels, I'd sing them a song. I'd sing of my
Je-sus, And tell of his charms, And beg them to
guide me to His lov-ing arms.

65

CHRISTMAS

A CORNISH CHRISTMAS CAROL

Sung by John Persons, age eighty-seven, Madison, Wisconsin, in
1946. This beautiful carol was frequently followed by *Stille Nacht*.

Come, let us go in a childish way
With our voices praising Christ today.
To him just born, in the manger lay,
We will raise our thanks to him for aye.
Praise and honor be to Thee

Thou God's child from heav'n above.
Halleluia, Halleluia, Halleluia, we sing of love.
Praise and honor be to Thee,
Thou God's child from Heav'n above.
Halleluia, Halleluia, Halleluia, we sing of love.

A Cornish Christmas Carol

Come, let us go in a child-ish way with our voic-es prais-ing

Christ to-day. To him just born in the man-ger lay, we will

raise our thanks to Him for aye. Praise and hon-or be to Thee,

Thou God's child from Heav'n a-bove. Hal-le-lu-jah, Hal-le-lu-jah,

Hal-le-lu-jah, we sing of love. Praise and hon-or be to Thee,

Thou God's child from Hea-ven a-bove. Hal-le-lu-jah, Hal-le-lu-jah,

Hal-le-lu-jah, we sing of love.

66

Christmas time, Ellis Island, ca. 1910.
Iconographic Collection, SHSW.

'ARK, 'ARK, THE 'EAVENLY ANGELS SING

This was all that Mr. Persons could recall of a carol that he deemed one of the most popular to be sung at Dodgeville.

'Ark, 'Ark, the 'eavenly angels sing
The 'eavenly angels sing,
"Hosanna to the new-born King.
Hosanna to the new-born King.
Hosanna to the new-born King."

'Ark, 'Ark, the 'Eavenly Angels Sing

'ark, 'ark, the 'ea - ven-ly an-gels sing. The

'ea - ven -ly an - gels sing. Ho - san - na to the

new born King. Ho - san - na to the new born

King. Ho - san - na to the new born

King.

WE WISH YOU A MERRY CHRISTMAS

Cornish boys sang this song in Surrey Hollow, near Dodgeville, as late as 1876, when Mr. Persons was about seventeen. The carol is a carry-over from the familiar Cornish song *God Bless the Master of This House.*

O, we have come to your door to neither beg nor borrow,
O, we have come to your door to wash away your sorrow.
For in this Christmastide, we travel far and near,
To wish you a Merry Christmas and a Happy New Year!

68

We Wish You a Merry Christmas

Oh, we have come to your door to nei - ther beg nor bor-row. Oh we have come to your door to wash a - way your sor-row. For in this Christ-mas-tide we travel far and near, To wish you a mer-ry Christ-mas and a hap-py New Year.

ANGELS FROM THE REALMS OF GLORY

Angels from the realms of glory,
Wing your flight o'er all the earth.
Ye who sang Creation's story
Now proclaim Messiah's birth.
Come and worship, Come and worship,
Worship Christ, the new born King!
Worship Christ, the new born King!
Angels from the realms of glory,
Angels from the realms of glory,
Wing your flight o'er all the earth.
Ye who sang Creation's story,
Now proclaim Messiah's birth.
Now proclaim Messiah's birth.
Ye who sang Creation's story,
Now proclaim Messiah's birth.

Shepherds in the fields abiding,
Watching o'er your flocks by night.
God with man is now residing
Yonder shines the infant light.
Come and worship, Come and worship,
Worship Christ, the new-born King!
Worship Christ, the new-born King!
Shepherds in the fields abiding,
Shepherds in the fields abiding,
Watching o'er your flocks by night.
God with man is now residing
Yonder shines the infant light.
Yonder shines the infant light.
God with man is now residing.
Yonder shines the infant light.

Chorus: Come and worship, Come and worship,
Worship Christ, the new born King.
Worship Christ, the new born King.
Worship Christ, the new born King!

Angels From the Realms of Glory

An - gels from the realms of glo - ry, wing your flight o'er

all the earth, Ye who sang Cre - a - tion's sto - ry

Now pro - claim Mes - si - ah's birth. Come and wor - ship,

Come and wor - ship, Wor - ship Christ, the new - born King!

Wor - ship Christ, the new - born King! An - gels

from the realms of glo - ry, An - gels from the realms of

glo ry, wing your flight o'er all the earth. Ye who

sang cre - a - tion's sto - ry Now pro - claim Mes - si - ah's birth.

Now pro - claim Mes - si - ah's birth; Ye who sang Cre -

a - tion's sto - ry Now pro - claim Mes - si - ah's

birth. Come and wor - ship, Come and wor - ship,

Wor - ship Christ, the new - born King; Wor - ship Christ, the

new - born King; Wor - ship Christ, the new - born King!

ANGELS PROCLAIM

Angels proclaim the happy morn,
Their echoes fill the sky.
Their echoes fill the sky.
To you a Saviour Christ is born.
Chorus: Glory to God, Glory to God,
       Glory to God on High, Glory to God on High.

He left the shining worlds above,
And laid His glory by
And laid His glory by,
To show the wonders of His love.
Chorus: Glory to God, Glory to God,
       Glory to God on High, Glory to God on High.

"Good-will to men and peace on earth,"
Was sung to shepherds nigh.
Was sung to shepherds nigh.
Our hearts rejoice at Jesu's birth.
Chorus: Glory to God, Glory to God.
       Glory to God on High, Glory to God on High.

Angels Proclaim

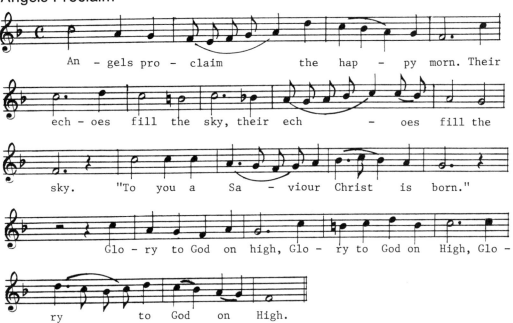

OH WELL, OH WELL

The first Noel, the angels did say
Was to certain poor shepherds in fields as they lay,
In fields where they lay keeping their sheep
On a cold winter's night that was so deep.
Oh well, oh well, oh well and oh well.
Born is the King of Israel,
Oh well, oh well, oh well and oh well.
Born is the King of Israel.

Oh Well, Oh Well

The first no - el, the an - gels did say, was to cer - tain poor shep - herds in fields as they lay. In fields where they lay, keep - ing their sheep On a cold win - ter's night that was so deep. Oh well, Oh well, Oh well and Oh well, Born is the King of Is - ra - el, Oh well, Oh well, Oh well and Oh well, Born is the King of Is - ra - el.

THE STAR OF BETHLEHEM

Lo! the eastern sages rise,
At a signal in the skies;
Brighter than the brightest gem
'Tis the star of Bethlehem;
Brighter than the brightest gem
'Tis the star of Bethlehem.

Balaam's mystic words appear
Full of light, divinely clear;
And the import wrapped in them
Is the star of Bethlehem;
Brighter than the brightest gem
Is the star of Bethlehem.

Rocks and deserts can't impede,
On they press, no aid they need.
Day and night a guide to them
Is the star of Bethlehem.
Brighter than the brightest gem
Is the star of Bethlehem.

Now the holy wise men meet at the royal Infant's feet;
Offerings rich are made by them
To the star of Bethlehem.
Brighter than the brightest gem
To the star of Bethlehem.

The Star of Bethlehem

MISS FOGARTY'S CHRISTMAS CAKE

Sung by Winfield Moody, age seventy-six, Plainfield, Wisconsin, in 1941.

Last night as I stopped at the window
A man handed through it to me,
A little gilt-edged invitation,
Saying, "Gilly come over to tea."
I hemmed and I hawed when I took it
But nothing to do but accede,
For Charlotte Fogarty sent it
Just for a friendship to seek.

The first thing they gave me to tackle
Was a slice of Miss Fogarty's cake.
Without the aid of some liquor
Found it more than a good man could take.
I chawed and I choked on a cherry
And the citron and cinnamon, too.
Tried to not make a scene over the berry
And the crust it was made of glue.

Miss Fogarty's proud as a peacock
She keeps smiling and winking this way.
When Olin came in with his brogan,
Upshot was brewing more tea.
There was caraway seed in abundance
Should've built up a fine stomach ache.
'Twould have killed a man twice, after eating one slice
Of Miss Fogarty's Christmas cake.

Miss Fogarty's Christmas Cake

Last night as I stop't at the win-dow, A man hand-ed thro' it to me, A lit-tle gilt-edged in-vi-ta-tion, Say-ing "Gil-ly come o-ver to tea." I hemmed and I hawwed when I took it, But noth-ing to do but ac-cede. For Char-o-lette Fo-gar-ty sent it, Just for a friend-ship to seek.

PROPHECY

THE GYPSY'S WARNING

DO NOT HEED HER WARNING

THE DECISION

These three related songs, all using the same melody, were taken from the notebooks of Franz Rickaby, who copied them from a leaflet in the clipping-book of George M. Hankins, Gordon, Wisconsin, in 1923. The leaflet was originally issued by H. J. Wehman, a song publisher of New York City.

Do not trust him, gentle lady, though his voice be low and sweet.
Heed not him who kneels before you, gently pleading at thy feet.
Now thy life is in its morning; cloud not this thy happy lot.
Listen to the gypsy's warning; gentle lady, heed him not.
Chorus: Listen to the gypsy's warning; gentle lady, heed him not.

Do not turn so coldly from me, I would only guard thy youth
From his stern and withering power. I would only tell the truth.
I would shield thee from all danger, save thee from all tempter's snare.
Lady, shun the dark-eyed stranger. I have warned thee; now beware.

Lady, once there lived a maiden, pure and bright, and like thee, fair,
But he wooed and wooed and won her, filled her gentle heart with care.
Then he heeded not her weeping, nor cared he her life to save.
Soon she perished, now she's sleeping in the cold and silent grave.

Keep thy gold, I do not wish it. Lady, I have prayed for this,
For the hour that I might foil him, rob him of expected bliss.
Gentle lady, do not wonder at my words so cold and wild.
Lady, in that green grave yonder lies the gypsy's only child.

Lady, do not heed her warning. Trust me, thou shalt find me true.
Constant as the light of morning I will ever be to you.
Lady, I will not deceive thee; fill thy guileless heart with woe.
Trust me, lady, and believe me; sorrow thou shalt never know.

Stranger, I've been thinking sadly how you promised, wooed and won;
How her innocent love gladly heard fair words, built hopes thereon.
Now she's in the cold ground sleeping by the river's moaning wave,
And the willows now are weeping o'er that maiden's early grave.

Warnings from that grave do tell me, and a living voice I hear,
Of a wooer who would seek me, pleading by a love sincere,
That without me life is sorrow: take this hand and heart of mine,
Promise bliss for every morrow, then forsake me, let me pine.

Stranger, I will heed the warning coming from the river's side.
Flowers you strew there in the morning, I'll renew at eventide.
There we'll walk, but not together, for the gypsy tells me true,
Mourns her child in tears that smother every kindly thought of you.

Lady, every joy would perish, pleasures all would wither fast
If no heart could love and cherish in this world of storm and blast.
E'en the stars that gleam above thee shine the brightest in the night;
So would he who fondly loves thee, in the darkness be thy light.

Down beside the flowing river where the dark green willow weeps;
Where the leafy branches quiver, there a gentle maiden sleeps.
In the morn a lonely stranger comes and lingers many hours.
Lady, he's no heartless ranger, for he strews her grave with flowers.

Lady, heed thee not her warning; lay thy soft white hand in mine,
For I seek no fairer laurel than the constant love of thine.
When the silver moonlight brightens, thou shalt slumber on my breast.
Tender words thy soul shall lighten, lull thy spirit into rest.

Down beside yon flowing river, there bereft where willows weep,
There must lie that fair one ever. Stranger, why these vigils keep?
Why go there alone and early, all those mornings, flowers to strew?
Did you love, in truth, so dearly? Do you grieve as others do?

The Gypsy's Warning

Do not trust him, gen-tle la-dy, Though his
voice be low and sweet. Heed not him who kneels before you, gen-tly plead-ing at thy feet. Now thy
life is in its morn-ing, Cloud not this thy hap-py
lot. Lis-ten to the gip-sy's warn-ing; gen-tle
la-dy heed him not.

MOTHER SHIPMAN'S PROPHECY

Sung by Miss M.E. Perley, Grand Forks, North Dakota, for Franz Rickaby in 1923. Rickaby recorded in his notebook: "Learned song from her father and grandmother, the latter born in 1803. Mother Shipman supposed to be contemporary with the grandmother. Everything Mother Shipman foretold came true except the last."

Carriages without horses shall go,
And accidents fill the world with woe.
Men in the air shall be seen
In blue and black and white and green.
Through the desert man shall ride
And no horse nor ass be at his side.
Under the water men shall walk,
Shall work and think and talk.
The world to an end shall come
In eighteen-hundred-eighty-one.

Russian peasant woman.
Iconographic Collection, SHSW.

AT WORK

PICK AND SHOVEL

Obtained from Carl Nelson, Escanaba, Michigan, by David Peterson. In 1965 Nelson, a man of about fifty, approached Professor Peterson with the score of a musical show that he hoped might be produced. The story line was based on the early history of Upper Michigan. Peterson felt that he could not produce the drama just then, so Nelson left his manuscript and disappeared. Later on, Peterson came upon *Pick and Shovel* in Nelson's abandoned score.

The pick and the shovel are all that I know.
I'm workin' the day-shift away down below.
A mile under ground I keep pickin' all day.
I work for a livin' but not for much pay.

Chorus: From Cornwall we have come to explore.
Yes, we are the men with an eye for ore.
We've got to find ore and plenty much more,
Or we'll be hittin' the road.

The mine whistle blows and the men start to sing.
There's fear in their thinkin'. They don't say a thing.
Goin' down, down the mine-shaft the echo of song
Wipes out fear or worry. Together we're strong.

Chorus: Since laddies of six, we've worked with picks
Learnin' all of mining's deceiving tricks.
And so we dig ore and plenty much more
Or we'll be hittin' the road.

The air-blast is li'ble to come any day,
And when it comes blowin', it goes its own way.
It snatches your breath, lays you out in your tomb.
A sociable death, we all lie in one room.

Chorus: From Cornwall we have come to explore.
Yes, we are the men with an eye for ore.
We've got to find ore and plenty much more,
Or we'll be hittin' the road.

To my wife I'm a hero she pieces my pay,
Takes care of the children the long workin' day.
She says I'll be foreman, but that won't be so.
The pick and the shovel are all that I know.

Chorus: Since Laddies of six, we've worked with our picks
Learnin' all of mining's deceiving tricks.
And so we dig ore and plenty much more
Or we'll be hittin' the road.

Pick and Shovel

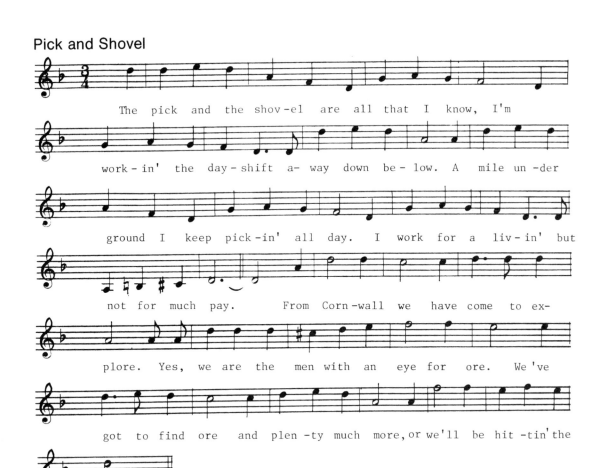

The pick and the shov-el are all that I know, I'm

work-in' the day-shift a-way down be-low. A mile un-der

ground I keep pick-in' all day. I work for a liv-in' but

not for much pay. From Corn-wall we have come to ex-

plore. Yes, we are the men with an eye for ore. We've

got to find ore and plen-ty much more, or we'll be hit-tin' the

road.

THE TOMAHAWK HEM

Sung by Emery De Noyer, age sixty-three, Rhinelander, Wisconsin, in 1941.

Now boys, if you will listen to my few lines of care
Although heart-broken in sorrow we came here.
We could curse the day that we were born or ever forced to go
And camp out on the Tomahawk where evergreens do grow.

'Twas on the tenth of March, my boys, the weather being fair,
We finished up the shanties and left the skid we bear.
'Twas then we got the orders to start without delay
And haul from section seventeen, though stormy was the day.

We pitched our tents that evening while the stormy winds did blow
While camping on the Tomahawk where evergreens do grow.

Oh, here's to our jolly teamsters we do recall of you.
The first is Robert Eckerson, the playboy of the crew,
He's never in a hurry but drives his cattle slow
And always makes his landing where evergreens do grow

79

Oh, here's to our noble scaler. His name I'll tell you all,
His name is Mister Webster, the jolliest in the crew.
He's never in a hurry nor seldom ever swears,
But he loads and scales and separates, and he does it on the square.

Oh, here's to our noble landing man, his name I'll tell to you;
His name is Marcel Duceps and from Kennedy he came.
He landed safe at Merrill without a friend or foe
And soon struck Mike Dolan's camp, where evergreens do grow.

Oh, here's to Joseph Stappard, our great merchant boy,
Who left behind his sweetheart. It caused for her to cry,
She says, "My dearest Joseph, I hope you will not go
And camp out on the Tomahawk where evergreens do grow."

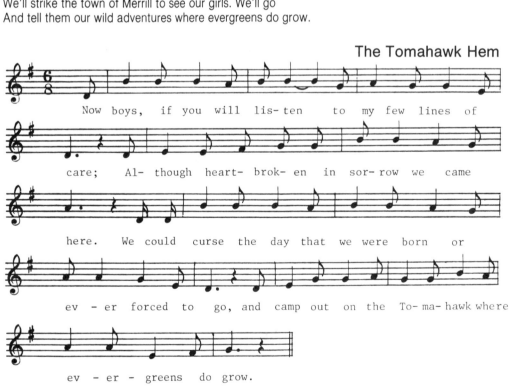

"Oh, it's goodbye my lovely Maggie, I must go away.
My comrades are awaiting and no longer can I stay.
But I'll think of you, dear Maggie, wherever I may go.
Yes, even on the Tomahawk where evergreens do grow."

Oh, here's to Jimmy Robinson, we'll say a word or two.
He is the only favorite that we have in the crew.
He's never in a passion or seldom ever swears
But he cooks for us poor shanty boys where evergreens do grow.

Oh, spring is now a'coming, the robin soon we'll see.
The small birds seem to sing so sweet on the branches of the tree.
And as they fly around and sing so cheerfully,
It tells to us poor shanty boys our time is short to stay.

But when we gain our freedom, it's homeward we will steer,
We'll strike the town of Merrill to see our friends so dear.
We'll strike the town of Merrill to see our girls. We'll go
And tell them our wild adventures where evergreens do grow.

The Tomahawk Hem

Now boys, if you will lis-ten to my few lines of
care; Al-though heart-brok-en in sor-row we came
here. We could curse the day that we were born or
ev-er forced to go, and camp out on the To-ma-hawk where
ev - er - greens do grow.

80

THE SHANTYMAN'S LIFE (1)

Sung by Henry Humphries, age seventy-five, Hancock, Wisconsin,
in 1940. This is what might be termed the "standard version" of a
widely popular song. Another version follows.

The shantyman's life is a worrisome one,
Though some call it free from care.
It's the ringing of the ax from morning 'til night
In the middle of the forest fair.

While life in the shanties, bleak and cold;
While the wintry winds do blow,
As soon as the morning star does appear,
To the wild woods we must go.

Then far are we ever from the pretty maidens fair,
On the bank of Wisconsin's streams
Where the wolves and the owls with terrifying howls
Disturb our nightly dreams.

About three in the morning the early cook cries,
"Boys, 'tis the break of day."
When broken slumber thus we pass
Long winter nights away.

It is then in the spring when the hardships begin,
When the waters are piercing and cold.
Our limbs are almost frozen, and dripping wet our clothes,
And our oars we can scarcely hold.

Now the rapids that we run, we think them only fun,
Devoid of all slavery and fear.
And the rocks, shoals and sands give employment to all hands,
Our well-banded rafts to steer.

Had we ale, wine, or beer our spirits for to cheer
Whilst in the forests alone,
Not a friend have we here to wipe away a tear
When our troubles and trials come on.

The Shantyman's Life

THE SHANTYMAN'S LIFE (2)

Sung by Emery De Noyer, age sixty-three, Rhinelander, Wisconsin, in 1941. This version, sung by a blind, one-armed logging-camp entertainer, has a different modal melody and gives a keener portrait of the logger at work.

All you jolly fellows, come listen to my song;
It's all about the pinery boys and how they got along.
They're the jolliest lot of fellows, so merrily and fine,
They will spend the pleasant winter months in cutting down the pine.

Some would leave their friends and homes, and others they love dear,
And into the lonesome pine woods their pathway they do steer.
Into the lonesome pine woods all winter to remain,
A'waiting for the springtime to return again.

Springtime comes, oh, glad will be its day!
Some return to home and friends, while others go astray.
The sawyers and the choppers, they lay their timber low.
The swampers and the teamsters they haul it to and fro.

Next comes the loaders before the break of day.
Load up your sleighs, five thousand feet to the river, haste away.
Noon time rolls around, our foreman loudly screams,
"Lay down your tools, me boys, and we'll haste to pork and beans."

We arrive at the shanty, the splashing then begins,
The banging of the water pails, the rattling of the tins.
In the middle of the splashing, our cook for dinner does cry.
We all arise and go, for we hate to lose our pie.

Dinner being over, we into our shanty go.
We all fill up our pipes and smoke 'til everything looks blue.
"It's time for the wood, me boys," our foreman he does say.
We all gather up our hats and caps, to the woods we haste away.

We all go out with a welcome heart and a well-contented mind
For the winter winds blow cold among the waving pines.
The ringing of saws and axes until the sun goes down.
"Lay down your tools, me boys, for the shanties we are bound."

We arrive at the shanties with cold and wet feet,
Take off our overboots and packs, the supper we must eat.
Supper being ready, we all arise and go
For it ain't the style of a lumberjack to lose his hash, you know.

At three o'clock in the morning, our bold cook loudly shouts,
"Roll out, roll out, you teamsters, its time that you are out."
The teamsters they get up in a fright and manful wail:
"Where is my boots? Oh, where's my pack? My rubbers have gone astray."
The other men they then get up, their packs they cannot find
And they lay it to the teamsters, and they curse them 'til they're blind.

Springtime comes, Oh, glad will be its day!
Lay down your tools, me boys, and we'll haste to break away.
The floating ice is over, and business now destroyed.
And all the able-bodied men are wanted on the Pelican drive.

With jam-pikes and peavys those able men do go
Up all those wild and dreary streams to risk their lives, you know.
On cold and frosty mornings they shiver with the cold,
So much ice upon their jam-pikes, they scarcely them can hold.

Now whenever you hear those verses, believe them to be true.
For if you doubt one word of them, just ask Bob Munson's crew.
It was in Bob Munson's shanties where they were sung with glee
And the ending of my song is signed with C. D. F. and G.

Ole Emerson's logging camp near Cable, Bayfield County.
Iconographic Collection, SHSW.

KEEP THE WORKING MAN DOWN

Sung by Henry Humphries, age seventy-six, Hancock, Wisconsin, in 1941.

Kind friends your attention I'll ask for awhile.
Some facts I'll endeavor to show.
This world is a network which very small,
But holds us as through life we go.

Of trials and troubles we all have our share.
Oft'times heartless men gain renown.
But the way that they do it, I'll now tell to you
It's by keeping the working man down.

A man who is working, his wages he'll spend
To his comrades so happy and gay.
And scarcely before the week comes to an end
His wages is all passed away.

But if he would lay by a dollar or so,
And place it in some bank in town.
He could then wink his eye to his boss on the sly
They can't keep the working man down.

And hold up your head, and this world never dread.
Don't care for its sneers or its frowns.
Store faith in its face if your heart's in its place
They can't keep the working man down.

Take this house as it stands here tonight
And compare it; for that is my plan.
The roof is our stock and so are the walls;
The foundation—the hard-working man.

You take off the roof and the walls still remain
Take the walls, the foundation is sound.
But you take the foundation the working man made,
The structure then falls to the ground.

Then hold up your head and this world never dread
Don't care for its sneers or its frown.
Store faith in its face, if your heart's in its place,
They can't keep the working man down.

Keep the Working Man Down

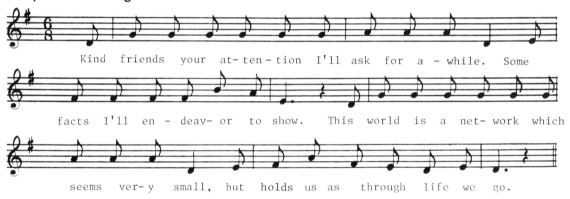

Kind friends your at-ten-tion I'll ask for a-while. Some

facts I'll en-deav-or to show. This world is a net-work which

seems ver-y small, but holds us as through life we go.

84

A-LUMBERING WE WILL GO

Sung by Lewis Winfield Moody, age seventy-five, Plainfield, Wisconsin, in 1940.

On the banks of the Wisconsin where the limpid waters flow,
We'll tell our wild adventures and once more a-lumbering go.
And we'll tell our wild adventures and once more a-lumbering go.

With the music of our axes, we'll make the woods resound,
And often times we laugh so hard we tumble to the ground.
And at night around our good campfire we'll sing while the wild winds blow,
And we'll tell our wild adventures and once more a-lumbering go.
And we'll tell our wild adventures and once more a-lumbering go.

And we'll talk about our pastimes, our pleasures and our place,
But we think of us as lumbermen while dashing in our sleighs.
We have no better pastimes than the local buckards do
But we'll tell our wild adventures and once more a-lumbering go.
And we'll tell our wild adventures and once more a-lumbering go.

And when we find we're getting old and our pockets getting worn
We'll each one take a little wife and settle on a farm.
With enough to eat, to drink, to wear, content through life we'll go
And tell our wild adventures and no more a-lumbering go.
And tell our wild adventures and no more a-lumbering go.

A-Lumbering We Will Go

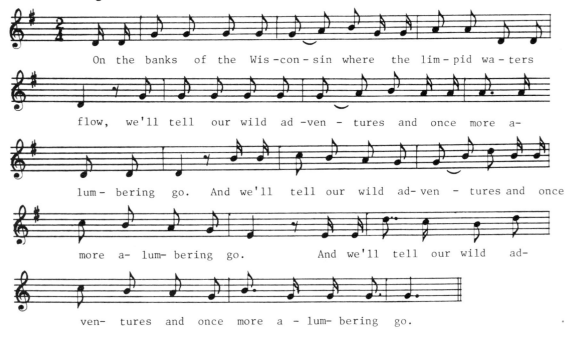

On the banks of the Wis-con-sin where the lim-pid wa-ters flow, we'll tell our wild ad-ven-tures and once more a-lum-bering go. And we'll tell our wild ad-ven-tures and once more a-lum-bering go. And we'll tell our wild ad-ven-tures and once more a-lum-bering go.

OLD-TIME LUMBERJACKS

Sung by Dan Grant, Antigo, Wisconsin, for Asher Treat in the 1930's.

We sit around the camp at night when the daily work is o'er
And listen to the lumberjacks who logged in days of yore.
They fell more trees in camp at night, 'twould put ol' Paul to shame.
Why they'd never have to work if they got paid for what they claim.
When they start fellin' pine at night we get prepared to jump.
They measured one the other night ten feet across the stump.
I must admit we smile a bit to hear them make such cracks.
But then we've come to expect it from those old-time lumberjacks.

We love to hear of how they logged some forty years ago.
Some people claim that we've advanced but that may not be so.
For one man then did more than ten men in the woods today,
And what we take for train loads now, they hauled up on a sleigh.
Their logging roads were perfect then and how they used to haul.
It's a wonder that there's any timber left for us at all.
They ate salt pork and pea soup then for which they thanked the Lord.
An' now no matter what they get, they kick about the board.

They slept like hunks in wooden bunks and did not mind the lice.
And now you hear them tell of how it was so very nice.
I'm half inclined to think their minds were weaker than their backs
When list'ning to the fairy tales of old-time lumberjacks.
But perhaps in twenty years or so we'll tell the younger men
How we logged pine and hemlock twenty million feet back then.
The young men then may think that we exaggerate the facts,
And then they may be right for we're the old time lumberjacks.

Iconographic Collection, SHSW.

THE SHANTY BOY AND THE FARMER

Sung by Fred Bainter, Ladysmith, Wisconsin, for Franz Rickaby in 1923; and by Charles Mills, Marion, Wisconsin, for Helene Stratman-Thomas in 1941.

As I walked out one evening just as the sun went down,
I strolled along quite leisurely 'til I came to Trenton town.
It was there I heard two maids discoursing as I slowly passed them by,
One said she loved a farmer's son, the other, a shanty boy.

The one that loved the farmer's son, those words I heard her say.
The reason that she loved him was at home with her he'd stay.
He'd stay at home in the winter, to the woods he would not go,
And when the spring it did set in, his land he'd plow and sow.

"All for to plow and sow your lands," I heard the other say,
"If your crops would prove a failure, your debts you couldn't pay
If your crops would prove a failure, the grain market being low
Oftimes the sheriff sells your grain to pay the debts you owe."

The paying of our little debts, I'm not in the least alarmed.
For what is the use of being in debt when you're living on a good farm?
You raise your bread right on your land, don't work through storms or rain
Your shanty boy works hard each day, his family to maintain.

I shall dearly love my shanty boy when he goes up at fall.
He's rugged, stout and healthy and fit to stand the squall.
With pleasure I'll receive him in the spring when he comes down.
And his money with me he'll spend quite free, while your farmer's son has none.

Oh, how you praise your shanty boy, who to the woods must go.
Your shanty boy is ordered out before daylight to work through every squall.
Whilst my farmer's son to stay at home and with me he will comply.
And tell to me sweet tales of love as the stormy winds blow by.

I care not for the soft talk that the farmer's sons do say
For most of them they are so green that the cows would eat for hay.
How quickly it is noticed whenever they come to town
The little boys all gather about saying, "Mossy, are you down?"

Now all you've said of your shanty boy, I hope you'll pardon me.
And from that ignorant farmer's son, I soon will be free.
And if ever I make another change to a shanty boy I'll go
I'll leave the farmer broken-hearted, his land to plow and sow.

The Shanty Boy and the Farmer

As I roved out one eve - ning just as the sun went
down, I walked a - long quite lei -sure -ly till I
came near a twink - ling town. I heard two girls con-
vers- ing so slow- ly as I pass'd by. One said she loved a
farm- er's son, and the oth- er a shan -ty - boy.

MANSON'S CREW

Sung by Bert Taplin, age eighty-seven, Wautoma, Wisconsin, in 1941. Taplin himself wrote this song about 1894.

It's on the Tomahawk River, a stream you all know well;
It's of a crew of shanty boys, a story I would tell.
From north, from south, from east, from west, those jolly boys do go
To brave a Wisconsin winter and work in frost and snow.

Our company's name was Manson, for honesty they're renowned.
They are two honest lumbermen who lived in Wausau town.
Though George is —— as Tony sure he got there just as hard.
And the son he runs the sawmill and he tends to the lumberyard.

Old R. P. is the old man, he greets you with a smile;
He's a fatherly way about him, and in fact, I like his style.
He never has gone back on the boys as I've been often told.
For in his prime he used to work out in the frost and cold.

Our foreman's name was Furness, a fact you all know well.
He is a jolly good fellow, the truth to you I'll tell.
He is as good a logger as in Tomahawk can be found
Here's luck to Billy Furness, now let this toast go 'round.

Terry Kennedy, the little bull puncher, he drives a little white bull,
And it would make you smile, my boys, to see him take from them some pulls.
He is a veteran woodsman, then, they say that in his prime
'Twas his delight from morn 'till night, to tumble down the pine.

There was Billy Durer, his partner, a fellow I'm sure you know.
He's worked in old Wisconsin through many a winter's snow.
He's a quiet boy in the shanty, and for skidding he can't be beat.
And when the social glass goes 'round; he always stands his treat.

There was Banks and there was Murphy; they were driving the other two teams.
They are two quiet fellows and good teamsters, too, it seems.
Between the four fine punchers and the white Norway pine
They keep the sleighs well-loaded the entire wintertime.

We've got a boy in the shanty, who's a boss upon this book.
He is the king of wrestlers and he's a dandy cook.
For keeping things up tidy, Eddy Wall, he can't be beat,
And he is the jolliest boy, my lads, that you'll meet on Wausau's street.

As to our choppers and sawyers, they are the best of men
And for handling logs with cant hooks, you can't beat Oscar and Ben.
They're Manson's dandy loaders, and they top load all the team.
And to beat them handling saw logs, you'd have to do it by steam.

As to our jolly horse teamsters, there are thirteen in this mob.
There ain't a sneak among them, nor a son-of-a-gun of a snob.
They never take on saw logs, for thousands we have hauled
But for making miles on log roads we'd rather have them small.

Here's luck to young George Manson, here's luck to the old man, too.
Here's luck to Billy Furness, here's luck to this whole crew.
Here's luck unto the drivers who drive the saw logs down
And when the month of June sets in, may they all reach Wausau town.

Manson's Crew

It's on the To-ma-hawk riv-er, a stream you all know well; It's of a crew of shanty boys, a sto-ry I would tell. From north, from south, from east, from west those jol-ly boys do go to brave a Wis-con-sin win-ter and work in frost and snow.

OLD HAZELTINE

Sung by Bert Taplin, age eighty-seven, Wautoma, Wisconsin, in 1941. Taplin composed this song about a tyrannical lumberman and sang it for the amusement of his fellow loggers. One night, he told Helene Stratman-Thomas, "I was in a saloon singin' while I was drunk. Along came Hazeltine—God, how I hated him—and I had to sing this song. They stood by the door, the boys, and they wouldn't let him out. He had to stay and listen. I was drunk that night—oh, God!"

It's of the Eau Claire River, a stream I'm sure you know.
It's of a crew of shanty boys who worked through the snow.
And as to old Hazeltine, he's a lousy son-of-a-bitch,
For it is from the poor man that he has grown rich.
For the cheating, and the robbing, and the stabbing of his crew,
I think he's an old screw.

Old Hazeltine

THE JAM ON GERRY'S ROCK

Sung by Emery De Noyer, age sixty-three, Rhinelander, Wisconsin; Dan Grant, Bryant, Wisconsin; and Bert Taplin, age eighty-four, Wautoma, Wisconsin—all in 1941, and all for Helene Stratman-Thomas.

Come all ye true born shanty boys, whoever that ye be.
I would have you pay attention and listen unto me,
Concerning a young shanty boy so tall, genteel, and brave.
'Twas on a jam on Gerry's Rock he met a watery grave.

It happened on a Sunday morn as you shall quickly hear.
Our logs they piled up mountain high, no one to keep them clear.
Out boss he cried, "Turn out, brave boys. Your hearts are void of fear.
We'll break that jam on Gerry's Rock and for Agonstown we'll steer."

Some of them were willing enough, but others they hung back.
'Twas for to work on the Sabbath they did not think 'twas right.
But six of our brave Canadian boys did volunteer to go
And break the jam on Gerry's Rock with their foreman, young Monroe.

They had not rolled off many logs when the boss to them did say,
"I'd have you be on your guard, brave boys. That jam will soon give way."
But scarce the warning had he spoke when the jam did break and go
And it carried away these six brave youths and their foreman, young Monroe.

When the rest of the shanty boys these sad tidings came to hear,
To search for their dead comrades to the river they did steer.
One of these a headless body found, to their sad grief and woe,
Lay cut and mangled on the beach, the head of young Monroe.

They took him from the water and smoothed down his raven hair.
There was one fair form amongst them; her cries would rend the air.
There was one fair form amongst them, a maid from Saginaw town.
Here sighs and cries would rend the skies for her lover that was drowned.

They buried him quite decently, being on the seventh of May.
Come all the rest of you shanty boys, for your dead comrade pray.
'Tis engraved on a little hemlock tree that at his head doth grow,
The name, the date, and the drowning of this hero, young Monroe.

Miss Clara was a noble girl, likewise the raftsman's friend,
Her mother was a widow woman lived at the river's bend.
The wages of her own true love the boss to here did pay,
And a liberal subscription she received from the shanty boys next day.

Miss Clara did not long survive her great misery and grief.
In less than three months afterwards death came to her relief.
In less than three months afterwards she was called to go
And her last request was granted, to be laid by young Monroe.

Come all the rest of ye shanty men who would like to go and see,
On a little mound by the river's bank there stands a hemlock tree.
The shanty boys cut the woods all round; these lovers they lie low.
Here lies Miss Clara Dennison and her shanty boy, Monroe.

The Jam on Gerry's Rock

Come all ye true born shan-ty boys who-ev-er that ye

be. I would have you pay at-ten-tion and lis-ten un-to

me. Con-cern-ing a young shan-ty boy so tall, gen-teel and

brave. 'Twas on a jam on Gerry's rocks he met a wat-'ry

grave.

THE PINERY BOY

Sung by Mrs. M. A. Olin, Eau Claire, Wisconsin, for Franz Rickaby in the early 1920's. Mrs. Olin said that she learned this song from a neighbor boy soon after coming to Wisconsin in 1867.

Oh, a raftsman's life is a wearisome one,
It causes many fair maids to weep and mourn.
It causes them to weep and mourn
For the loss of a true love that never can return.

"O father, O father, build me a boat,
That down the Wisconsin I may float,
And every raft that I pass by
There I will inquire for my sweet Pinery Boy."

As she was rowing down the stream
She saw three rafts all in a string.
She hailed the pilot as they drew nigh,
And there she did inquire for her sweet Pinery Boy.

"O pilot, O pilot, tell me true,
Is my sweet Willie among your crew?
Oh, tell me quick and give me joy,
For none other will I have but my sweet Pinery Boy."

"Oh, auburn was the color of his hair,
His eyes were blue and his cheeks were fair.
His lips were of a ruby fine;
Ten thousand times they've met with mine."

"O honored lady, he is not hers.
He's drownded in the dells I fear.
'Twas at Lone Rock as we passed by,
Oh, there is where we left your sweet Pinery Boy."

She wrung her hands and tore her hair,
Just like a lady in great despair.
She rowed her boat against Lone Rock
You'd a-thought this fair lady's heart was broke.

"Dig me a grave both long and deep,
Place a marble slab at my head and feet;
And on my breast a turtle dove
To let the world know that I died for love.
And at my feet a spreading oak
To let the world know that my heart was broke."

The Pinery Boy

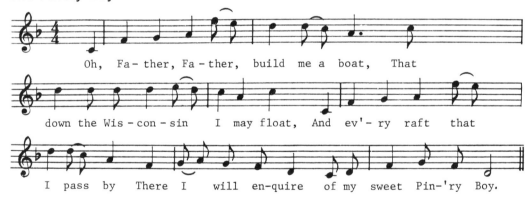

Oh, Fa-ther, Fa-ther, build me a boat, That down the Wis-con-sin I may float, And ev'-ry raft that I pass by There I will en-quire of my sweet Pin-'ry Boy.

Unknown man with home-made violin.
Iconographic Collection, SHSW.

ON THE BANKS OF THE LITTLE EAU PLEINE

This song was written by William N. Allen of Wausau, who sang it for Franz Rickaby in the 1920's. Rickaby recorded that Allen could not remember exactly when the song was composed—"perhaps in the seventies sometime, he thought. This song, like the shanty-boy on the Big Eau Claire, has no historical basis, other than the character of Ross Gamble, who was a well-known pilot on the Wisconsin River at that time."

One evening last June as I rambled
The green woods and valleys among,
The mosquito's notes were melodious,
And so was the whip-poor-will's song.
The frogs in the marshes were croaking,
The tree-toads were whistlin' for rain,
The partridges 'round me were drumming
On the banks of the Little Eau Pleine.

The sun in the west was declining
And tinging the tree-tops with red.
My wandering feet bore me onward,
I not caring whither they led.
I happened to see a young school-ma'am.
She mourned in a sorrowful strain;
She mourned for a jolly young raftsman
On the banks of the Little Eau Pleine.

Saying, "Alas, my dear Johnnie has left me.
I'm afraid I shall see him no more.
He's down on the lower Wisconsin;
He's pulling a fifty-foot oar.
He went off on a fleet with Ross Gamble
And has left me in sorrow and pain
And 'tis over two months since he started
From the banks of the Little Eau Pleine."

I stepped up beside this young school-ma'am,
And thus unto her I did say:
"Why is it you're mourning so sadly
While all nature is smiling and gay?"
She said, "It is for a young raftsman
For whom I so sadly complain.
He has left me alone here to wander
On the banks of the Little Eau Pleine."

"Will you please tell me what kind of clothing
Your jolly young raftsman did wear?
For I also belong to the River,
And perhaps I have seen him somewhere.
If to me you will plainly describe him,
And tell me your young raftsman's name,
Perhaps I can tell you the reason
He's not back on the Little Eau Pleine."

"His pants were made out of two meal-sacks,
With a patch a foot square on each knee.
His shirt and his jacket were dyed with
The bark of a butternut tree.
He wore a large open-faced ticker
With almost a yard of steel chain,
When he went away with Ross Gamble
From the banks of the Little Eau Pleine.

"He wore a red sash 'round his middle,
With an end hanging down at each side.
His shoes number ten were of cowhide
With heels about four inches wide.
His name it was Honest John Murphy,
And on it there n'er was a stain.
And he was as jolly a raftsman
As was e'er on the Little Eau Pleine.

"He was stout and broad-shouldered and manly.
His height was about six feet one.
His hair was inclined to be sandy,
And his whiskers as red as the sun.
His age was somewhere about thirty,
He neither was foolish nor vain.
He loved the bold Wisconsin River
Was the reason he left the Eau Pleine."

"If John Murphy's the name of your raftsman,
I used to know him very well.
But sad is the tale I must tell you:
Your Johnny was drowned in the Dells.
They buried him 'neath a scrub Norway,
You will never behold him again.
No stone marks the spot where your raftsman
Sleeps far from the Little Eau Pleine."

When the school-ma'am heard this information,
She fainted and fell as if dead.
I scooped up a hat-full of water
And poured it on top of her head.
She opened her eyes and looked wildly,
As if she was nearly insane,
And I was afraid she would perish
On the banks of the Little Eau Pleine.

"My curses attend you, Wisconsin!
May your rapids and falls cease to roar.
May every tow-head and sand-bar
Be as dry as a log school-house floor.
May the willows upon all your islands
Lie down like a field of ripe grain,
For taking my jolly young raftsman
Away from the Little Eau Pleine.

"My curses light on you, Ross Gamble,
For taking my Johnny away.
I hope that the ague will seize you
And shake you down into the clay.

May your lumber go down to the bottom,
And never rise to the surface again.
You had no business taking John Murphy
Away from the Little Eau Pleine.

"Now I will desert my vocation,
I won't teach district school anymore.
I will go to some place where I'll never
Hear the squeak of the fifty-foot oar.
I will go to some far foreign country,
To England, to France, or to Spain;
But I'll never forget Johnny Murphy,
Nor the banks of the Little Eau Pleine."

On the Banks of the Little Eau Pleine

The sun in the west was de-clin-ing, And tinge-ing the tree tops with red. My wan-d'ring feet bore me on-ward Not car-ing whith-er they led. I hap-pened to see a young school ma'am, She mourned in a sor-row-ful strain, She mourned for a jol-ly young rafts-man, On the banks of the Lit-tle Eau Pleine.

AFLOAT

RED IRON ORE

Sung by M. C. Dean, Virginia, Minnesota, for Franz Rickaby. Dean used the same tune and refrain as is often used for *The Little Brown Bulls.* Death's Door is the treacherous passageway between the tip of Door County and Washington Island, a place greatly (and justifiably) feared by Great Lakes sailors and pilots of the nineteenth century.

Come all you bold sailors that follow the Lakes
On an iron ore vessel your living to make.
I shipped in Chicago, bid adieu to the shore,
Bound away to Escanaba for red iron ore.
    Derry down, down, down derry down.

In the month of September, the seventeenth day,
Two dollars and a quarter is all they would pay,
And on Monday morning the Bridgeport did take
The *E. C. Roberts* out in the Lake.
    Derry down, down, down derry down.

The wind from the southard sprang up a fresh breeze,
And away through Lake Michigan the *Roberts* did sneeze.
Down through Lake Michigan the *Roberts* did roar,
And on Friday morning we passed through death's door.
    Derry down, down, down derry down.

This packet she showled across the mouth of Green Bay,
And before her cutwater she dashed the white spray.
We rounded the snad point, and anchor let go,
We furled in our canvas and the watch went below.
    Derry down, down, down derry down.

Next morning we have alongside the *Exile,*
And soon was made fast to an iron ore pile,
They lowered their chutes and like thunder did roar,
They spouted into us that red iron ore.
    Derry down, down, down derry down.

Some sailors took shovels while others got spades,
And some took wheelbarrows, each man to his trade.
We looked like red devils, our fingers got sore,
We cursed Escanaba and that damned iron ore.
    Derry down, down, down derry down.

The tug *Escanaba* she towed out the *Minch,*
The *Roberts* she thought she had left in a pinch,
And as she passed by us she bid us good-bye,
Saying, "We'll meet you in Cleveland next Fourth of July!"
    Derry down, down, down derry down.

Through Louse Island it blew a fresh breeze;
We made the Foxes, the Beavers, the Skillageles;
We flew by the *Minch* for to show her the way,
And she ne'er hove in sight till we were off Thunder Bay.
    Derry down, down, down derry down.

Across Saginaw Bay the *Roberts* did ride
With the dark and deep water rolling over her side.
And now for Port Huron the *Roberts* must go,
Where the tug *Kate Williams* she took us in tow,
   Derry down, down, down derry down.

We went through North Passage—O Lord, how it blew!
And all 'round the Dummy a large fleet there came too.
The nigh being dark, Old Nick it would scare.
We hove up next morning and for Clevelend did steer.
   Derry down, down, down derry down.

Now the *Roberts* is in Cleveland, made fast stem and stern,
And over the bottle we'll spin a big yarn.
But Captain Harvey Shannon had ought to stand treat
For getting into Cleveland ahead of the fleet.
   Derry down down, down derry down.

Now my song it is ended, I hope you won't laugh.
Our dunnage is packed and all hands are paid off.
Here's a health to the *Roberts,* she's staunch, strong and true;
Nor forgotten the bold boys that comprise her crew.
   Derry down, down, down derry down.

Red Iron Ore

Come all ye bold sail-ors that fol-low the Lakes On an
I - ron ore ves-sel your liv-ing to make. I shipp'd in Chi-
ca - go, bid a-dieu to the shore, Bound a - way to Es-ca-
na - ba for red i-ron ore. Der-ry down, down,
down, der - ry down.

A YANKEE SHIP CAME DOWN THE RIVER

Sung by Noble B. Brown, age sixty-one, Millsville, Wisconsin, in 1946. Brown was a seaman for eight years, beginning at the age of twenty; prior to that he had worked in Midwestern lumber camps for five years. He sailed in various ships—the *Eliza,* out of Genoa, Italy; the *Donna Francisca,* a four-masted vessel out of London; the *Drummuir,* another four-master out of Victoria; and finally a British freighter which ran between the state of Washington and Dublin, Ireland. It was on the latter vessel that he learned this song.

A yankee ship came down the river.
Blow, boys, blow.
A yankee ship came down the river.
Blow, boys, bonnie boys, blow.

Oh, how do you know she's a yankee clipper?
Blow, boys, blow.
Oh, how do you know she's a yankee clipper?
Blow, boys, bonnie boys, blow.

The stars and bars that flew behind her,
Blow, boys, blow.
The stars and bars that flew behind her,
Blow, boys, bonnie boys, blow.

And who do you think was the skipper of her?
Blow, boys, blow.
A blue-nosed Nova Scotia hard case.
Blow, boys, bonnie boys, blow.

And who do you think was the first mate of her?
Blow, boys, blow.
A loud-mouthed disbarred Boston lawyer,
Blow, boys, bonnie boys, blow.

And what do you think we had for breakfast?
Blow, boys, blow.
The starboard side of an old sou'wester,
Blow, boys, bonnie boys, blow.

Then what do you think we had for dinner?
Blow, boys, blow.
We had monkey's heart and shark's liver
Blow, boys, bonnie boys, blow.

Can you guess what we had for supper?
Blow, boys, blow.
We had strong salt jerk and weak tea water,
Blow, boys, bonnie boys, blow.

Then blow us out and blow us homeward,
Blow, boys, blow.
Oh, blow today and blow tomorrow,
Blow, boys, bonnie boys, blow.

Blow fair and steady, mild and pleasant,
Blow, boys, blow.
Oh, blow us into Boston harbor,
Blow, boys, bonnie boys, blow.

We'll blow ashore and blow our payday,
Blow, boys, blow.
Then blow aboard and blow away,
Blow, boys, bonnie boys, blow.

We'll blow until our blow is over,
Blow, boys, blow.
From Singapore to Cliffs of Dover,
Blow, boys, bonnie boys, blow.

A Yankee Ship Came Down the River

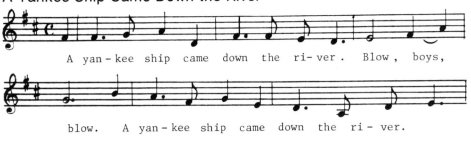

A yan-kee ship came down the ri-ver. Blow, boys,

blow. A yan-kee ship came down the ri-ver.

Blow, boys, bon-nie boys, blow.

ONE SHIP DRIVES EAST

Sung by Eryl Levers, age twenty-four, Madison, Wisconsin, in 1946.
This is usually sung as a round.

One ship drives east and one ship drives west,
By the south-same winds that blow.
Yet the set of the sails and not the gale,
The set of the sails and not the gale
Determines the way-i-aye-i-aye,
That determines the way she goes.

One Ship Drives East

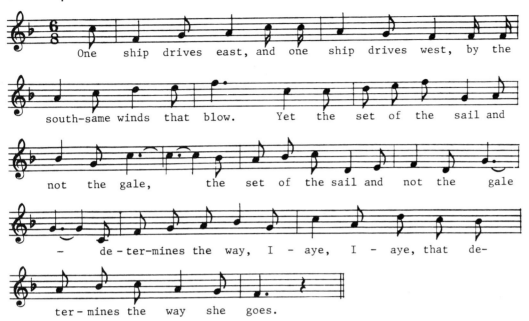

One ship drives east, and one ship drives west, by the
south-same winds that blow. Yet the set of the sail and
not the gale, the set of the sail and not the gale
- de-ter-mines the way, I - aye, I - aye, that de-
ter-mines the way she goes.

THE BIGLER'S CREW

Sung by M. C. Dean, Virginia, Minnesota, for Franz Rickaby.

Come all my boys and listen, a song I'll sing to you.
It's all about the *Bigler* and of her jolly crew.
In Milwaukee last October I chanced to get a sight
In the schooner called the *Bigler* belonging to Detroit.
Chorus: Watch her, catch her, jump up on her juber ju.
        Give her the sheet and let her slide, the boys will push her through.
        You ought to seen us howling, the winds were blowing free,
        On our passage down to Buffalo from Milwaukee.

It was on a Sunday morning about the hour of ten,
The *Robert Emmet* towed us out into Lake Michigan;
We set sail where she left us in the middle of the fleet,
And the wind being from the southard, oh, we had to give her sheet.

Then the wind chopped round to the sou-sou'west and blew both fresh and strong
But softly through Lake Michigan the *Bigler* she rolled on,
And far beyond her foaming bow the dashing waves did fling,
With every inch of canvas set, her course was wing and wing.

But the wind it came ahead before we reached the Manitous.
Three dollars and a half a day just suited the *Bigler's* crew.
From there unto the Beavers we steered her full and by,
And we kept her to the wind, my boys, as close as she could lie.

Through Skillagalee and Wabble Shanks, the entrance to the Straits,
We might have passed the big fleet there if they'd hove to and wait;
But we drove them on before us, the nicest you ever saw,
Out into Lake Huron from the Straits of Mackinaw.

We made Presque Isle Light, and then we boomed away,
The wind it being fair, for the Isle of Thunder Bay.
But when the wind it shifted, we hauled her on her starboard tack
With a good lookout ahead for the Light of the Point Au Barques.

We made the light and kept in sight of Michigan North Shore,
A-booming for the river as we'd oftimes done before.
When right abreast Port Huron Light our small anchor we let go
And the *Sweepstakes* came alongside and took the *Bigler* in tow.

The *Sweepstakes* took eight in tow and all of us fore and aft,
She towed us down to Lake St. Clare and stuck us on the flats.
She parted the *Hunter's* tow-line in trying to give relief,
And stem and stern went the *Bigler* into the boat called *Maple Leaf*.

The *Sweepstakes* then she towed us outside the River Light,
Lake Erie for to roam and the blustering winds to fight.
The wind being from the southard we paddled our own canoe,
With her nose pointed for the Dummy she's hell-bent for Buffalo.

We made the Oh and passed Long Point, the wind was blowing free.
We howled along the Canada shore, Port Colborne on our lee.
What is it that looms up ahead, so well known as we draw near?
For like a blazing star shone the light on Buffalo Pier.

And now we are safely landed in Buffalo Creek at last,
And under Riggs' elevator the *Bigler* she's made fast.
And in some lager beer saloon we'll let the bottle pass,
For we are jolly shipmates and we'll drink a social glass.
Chorus: Watch her, catch her, jump up on her juber ju.
        Give her the sheet and let her slide, the boys will push her through.
        You ought to seen us howling, the winds were blowing free,
        On our passage down to Buffalo from Milwaukee.

SALLY BROWN

Sung by Orlando Pegram for Franz Rickaby, ca. 1920. Pegram was an old sailor who had been at sea from 1879 to about 1885. He described this song as a "tops'l halyards chantey—one for a long pull."

O Sally Brown, I love your daughter.
Ho, hey, roll and go!
I love that place across the water.
Spend my money on the girls down town!

The Bigler's Crew

Come all my boys and lis - ten, a song I'll sing to you. It's all a - bout the Big - ler and of her jol - ly crew. In Mil - wau - kee last Oct - o - ber I chanc'd to get a sight In the schoon - er called the Big - ler be - long - ing to De - troit. Watch her, catch her, jump up on her ju - ber - ju. Give her the sheet and let her slide, The boys will push her through. You ought to seen us howl - ing, the winds were blow - ing free. On our pas - sage down to Buf - fa - lo from Mil - wau - kee.

Sally Brown

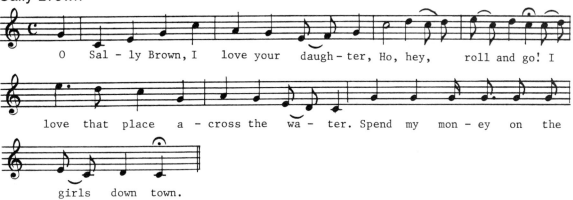

O Sal - ly Brown, I love your daugh - ter, Ho, hey, roll and go! I love that place a - cross the wa - ter. Spend my mon - ey on the girls down town.

REUBEN RANZO

Sung by Noble B. Brown, age sixty-one, Millsville, Wisconsin in 1946. Brown learned this song while on a freighter running from San Francisco to Falmouth, England.

Oh, pity poor Reuben Ranzo.
Ranzo, boys, Ranzo.
Oh, poor old Reuben Ranzo,
Ranzo, boys, Ranzo.

Oh, Ranzo was no sailor,
Ranzo, boys, Ranzo.
So he shipped aboard a whaler.
Ranzo, boys, Ranzo.

Oh, Ranzo was no beauty,
Ranzo, boys, Ranzo.
He couldn't do his duty.
Ranzo, boys, Ranzo.

So they took him to the gangway,
Ranzo, boys, Ranzo.
And gave him five and thirty.
Ranzo, boys, Ranzo.

Now the captain was a good man,
Ranzo, boys, Ranzo.
He took him to the cabin.
Ranzo, boys, Ranzo.

He took him to his cabin,
Ranzo, boys, Ranzo.
And gave him wine and brandy.
Ranzo, boys, Ranzo.

And he taught him navigation,
Ranzo, boys, Ranzo.
To fit him for his station.
Ranzo, boys, Ranzo.

And he married the captain's daughter,
Ranzo, boys, Ranzo.
And still he sails blue water.
Ranzo, boys, Ranzo.

And now he's Captain Ranzo,
Ranzo, boys, Ranzo.
Hurrah for Captain Ranzo.
Ranzo, boys, Ranzo.

Reuben Ranzo

Oh, pi-ty poor Reu-ben Ran - zo, Ran -zo, boys, Ran- zo, Oh,

poor old Reu- ben Ran- zo, Ran -zo, boys, Ran-zo.

Photo by Matthew Witt, Cross Plains, ca. 1930.

THE SHIP THAT NEVER RETURNED

Sung by Noble B. Brown, age sixty-one, Millsville, Wisconsin, in 1946. Brown learned this song from his mother, who was of Dutch and Scottish extraction.

'Twas a summer's day and the waves were rippled
By a soft and gentle breeze,
When a ship set sail with a cargo ladened
For a port beyond the sea.

There were fond farewells, loving demonstrations
By the ones who were most concerned.
Though they little knew 'twas the fatal voyage
Of the ship that never returned.

Did she ever return? No, she never returned,
And her fate is yet unlearned.
Though for years and years there were fond hearts watching
For the ship that never returned.

Said the feeble lad to his anxious mother,
"I must cross the deep blue sea,
For they say, perchance, in some foreign climate
There is help and strength for me."

'Twas a gleam of hope in the midst of danger
And her heart for her youngest yearned.
But she sent him forth with a smile and a blessing
On the ship that never returned.

"Only one more trip," said a gallant seaman
As he kissed his weeping wife.
"Only one more bag of the gold and treasure
And 'twill last us all through life.

"Then we'll settle down in our cosy cottage
And enjoy the rest we've earned."
But alas, poor man, for he sailed commander
Of the ship that never returned.

Did she ever return? No, she never returned,
And her fate is yet unlearned.
Though for years and years there were fond hearts watching
For the ship that never returned.

The Ship That Never Returned

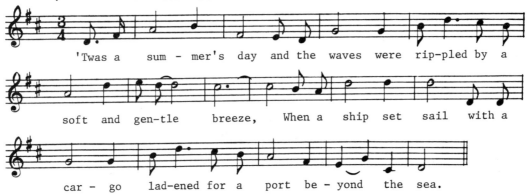

'Twas a sum-mer's day and the waves were rip-pled by a soft and gen-tle breeze, When a ship set sail with a car-go lad-ened for a port be-yond the sea.

SO MERRY, SO MERRY ARE WE

Sung by Noble B. Brown, age sixty-one, Millsville, Wisconsin, in 1946.

So merry, so merry, so merry are we.
There is no one more merry than the sailor on sea.
Oh I dare say, I do say, as we sail along
Give a sailor his grog, but no salt meat too strong.

We're pulling, we're hauling and heaving away
In all kinds of weather, by night and by day.
Oh I can say, I will say, as we sail along
Give a sailor his grog and he won't think it wrong.

Tho' blowing or snowing the elements wild
A sailor on duty is cheerful and mild.
Oh I still say, I must say, as we sail along
Give a good glass of rum and a good shanty song.

So Merry, So Merry Are We

So mer-ry, so mer-ry, so mer-ry are we. There is no one more mer-ry than the sail-or on sea. Oh I dare say, I do say, as we sail a-long, give a sail-or his grog but no salt meat too strong.

THERE WERE ONCE THREE BROTHERS

Sung by Fred Bainter, Ladysmith, Wisconsin, for Franz Rickaby in 1923.

Three loving brothers in merry Scotland,
And three loving brothers were they,
And they did cast lots to see which of the three
Would sail Robin around the salt sea.

The lot it fell on Andrew Bartan,
The youngest one of the three,
That he should go robbing around the salt sea
To maintain his two brothers and he.

They had not sailed more than three long winters' nights,
Till a ship they espied,
A-sailing far off, a-sailing far off,
'Till at length it came sailing 'longside.

"Who's there? Who's there?" says Andrew Bartan,
"Who's there that sails so nigh?"
"It's the three merchant vessels of old England's shore,
And please will you let us pass by?"

"Oh no, oh no," says Andrew Bartan,
"That thing it never can be.
Your ships and your cargoes I'll have my brave boys,
And your bodies I'll sink in the sea."

The news it straight to old England came,
King Henry a-wearing the crown;
His ships and his cargoes were taken away
And his merry men they were all drowned.

"Go build me a boat," says Captain Charles Stores,
"Go build it both safe and sure,
And if I don't bring you young Andrew Bartan,
My life I shall never endure."

The boat was built at his command,
It was made both safe and sure,
And Captain Charles Stores was placed on the front
To take the whole command.

They had not sailed more than three long summer's nights
Till a ship they espied,
A-sailing far off, a-sailing far off,
Till at length it came sailing 'longside.

"Who's there? Who's there?" says Captain Charles Stores,
"Who's there that sails so nigh?"
"It's the little Scotch robber of merry Scotland,
And please will you let us pass by?"

"Oh no, oh no," says Captain Charles Stores,
"That thing it never can be.
Your ships and your cargoes I'll soon take away,
Your bodies I'll carry with me."

"Come on, come on," says Andrew Bartan,
"I value not a pin,
For if you can show brass buttons without,
I'll show you good steel within."

So now the battle has begun,
And loud the cannons roar.
They fought for five hours, five hours or more,
Till Captain Charles Stores gave o'er.

"Go back, go back," says Andrew Bartan,
"Go and tell King Henry for me.
That he can reign king on all the dry lands,
But I will reign king of the sea."

There Once Were Three Brothers

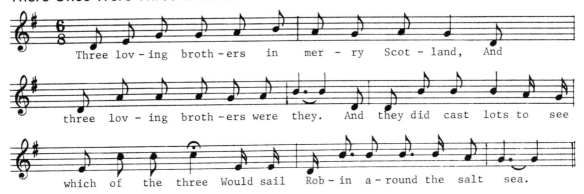

Three lov-ing broth-ers in mer-ry Scot-land, And
three lov-ing broth-ers were they. And they did cast lots to see
which of the three Would sail Rob-in a-round the salt sea.

A SHIP SET SAIL FOR NORTH AMERICA

Sung by Mrs. Ollie Jacobs, age seventy-nine, Pearson, Wisconsin, in 1941. A printed version of this seventeenth-century ballad begins: "Sir Walter Rawleigh has built a ship/ In the Neatherlands/ And it is called The Sweet Trinity,/ And was taken by the false gallaly,/ Sailing in the Low-lands." In Mrs. Jacobs' version (printed below), Captain Raleigh's treachery is gallantly rebuked by the heroic shipboy.

A ship set sail for North America
And she went by the name of the *Turkish Reveille,*
As she sailed along the lonesome lowlands low,
As she sailed along the lowland sea.

There was another ship in the north country,
And she went by the name of the *Golden Willow Tree,*
As she sailed upon the lonesome lowlands low,
As she sailed upon the lowland sea.

"Captain, oh captain, what will you give me
If I overtake her and sink her in the sea,
If I'll sink her in the lonesome lowlands low,
If I'll sink her in the lowland sea?"

"I have a house and I have land,
And I have a daughter that will be at your command
If you'll sink her in the lonesome lowlands low,
If you'll sink her in the lowland sea."

"I have a little tool just fitted for the use,
Boring for salt water, letting in the sluice,
As she sails upon the lonesome lowlands low,
As she sails upon the lowland sea."

He fell upon his back and away swam he,
Until he'd overtaken the *Golden Willow Tree,*
As she sailed upon the lonesome lowlands low,
As she sailed upon the lowland sea.

Some with their hats and some with their caps,
Trying to stop the salt water gaps,
As she sailed the lonesome lowlands low,
As she sailed along the lowland sea.

He fell upon his back and away swam he
Until he'd overtaken the *Turkish Reveille,*
As she sailed along the lonesome lowlands low,
As she sailed along the lowland sea.

"Captain, oh captain, take me on board,
And be to me as good as your word,
For I've sunk her in the lonesome lowlands low,
For I've sunk her in the lowland sea."

"Neither will I take you on board,
Nor be to you as good as my word,
Though you've sunk her in the lonesome lowlands low,
Though you've sunk her in the lowland sea."

"If it wasn't for the love I have for your men,
I would serve you as I've served them.
I would sink you in the lonesome lowlands low,
I would sink you in the lowland sea."

A Ship Set Sail for North America

A ship set sail for North A - mer - i - ca, And she
went by the name of the Turk - ish Re - veil - le, As she
sailed a - long the lone-some low - lands low, As she
sailed a - long the low - land sea. There was an oth - er ship in the
north coun - try, And she went by the name of the
Gold - en Wil - low Tree, As she sailed u - pon the lone - some
low - lands low, As she sailed up - on the low - land sea.

WELL MET, WELL MET, MY OLD TRUE LOVE

Sung by Pearl Jacobs Borusky, age thirty-nine, Antigo, Wisconsin, in 1940. Three generations of Jacobses have sung this song, going back to Mrs. Borusky's grandmother in Kentucky. This version differs from most collected variants, which say "my *own* true love."

"Well met, well met, my old true love,
Well met, well met," said he.
"I have just returned from the salt, salt sea;
And it's all for the sake of thee.

"I once could have married a king's daughter fair,
And she would have married me;
But I refused that rich crown of gold,
And it's all for the sake of thee."

"If you could have married a king's daughter fair
I'm sure you are much to blame,
For I am married to a house carpenter,
And I think he's a fine young man."

"If you'll forsake your house carpenter
And go along with me,
I will take you where the grass grows green,
On the banks of the Sweet Willee."

"If I forsake my house carpenter
And go along with thee,
What have you got for my support,
And to keep me from slavery?"

"I have six ships upon the sea,
and the seventh one at land,
And if you'll come and go with me
They shall be at your command."

She took her babe into her arms
And gave it kisses three,
Saying, "Stay at home, my pretty little babe
To keep your father company."

She dressed herself in rich array
To exceed all others in the town,
And as she walked the streets around
She shone like a glittering crown.

They had not been on board more than two weeks,
I'm sure it was not three,
Until one day she began to weep
And she wept most bitterly.

"Oh, are you weeping for your houses or your land,
Or are you weeping for your store,
Or are you weeping for your house carpenter
You never shall see any more?"

"I'm not weeping for my houses or my land,
Nor I'm not weeping for my store,
But I am weeping for my pretty little babe
I never shall see any more."

They had not been on board more than three weeks,
It was not four I'm sure,
Until at length the ship sprung a leak,
And she sunk to arise no more.

"A curse, a curse to all sea men;
And a curse to a sailor's life!
For they have robbed me of my house carpenter
And have taken away my life."

Well Met, Well Met, My Old True Love

"Well met, well met my old true love. Well met, well met, said he. I have just re-turned from the salt, salt sea And it's all for the sake of thee. And it's all for the sake of thee.

A SHIP WAS BECALMED IN A TROPICAL SEA

Sung by Noble B. Brown, age sixty-one, Millsville, Wisconsin, in 1946. Of this song and singer, Helene Stratman-Thomas recorded: "Mr. Brown, a sailor who had rounded Cape Horn three times, was actually becalmed on the Atlantic for three weeks. They caught rainwater for drinking. . . . The first time he rounded Cape Horn the wind changed and threw the ship into the trough of the sea. The lee rail was awash, and they had to shift the cargo to the other side of the ship. The captain and mate were so frightened that they cried; whereupon the boatswain took charge, ordered the yards boxed, and not one man was lost."

A ship was becalmed on a tropical sea.
Away, away, blow the man down.
For three long weeks no wind had she.
Oh, give us some time to blow the man down.
Blow the man down, bullies, blow the man down,
Heave away, away, blow the man down.
For three long weeks no wind had she.
Oh, give us some time to blow the man down.

The wheel had been lashed; all the crew were asleep.
Away, away, blow the man down.
The skipper ———— watch and deck keep.
Oh, give us some time to blow the man down.
Blow the man down, bullies, blow the man down,
Heave away, away, blow the man down.
The skipper ———— watch and deck keep.
Oh, give us some time to blow the man down

Her canvas hung limply from not being fed.
Away, away, blow the man down.
Had no strength to carry the vessel ahead.
Oh, give us some time to blow the man down.
Blow the man down, bullies, blow the man down
Heave away, away, blow the man down.
Had no strength to carry the vessel ahead.
Oh, give us some time to blow the man down.

The skipper leaned over the poop afterrail.
Away, away, blow the man down.
He wished that a fair wind was filling his sail.
Oh, give us some time to blow the man down.
Blow the man down, bullies, blow the man down,
Heave away, away, blow the man down.
He wished that a fair wind was filling his sail.
Oh, give us some time to blow the man down.

He prayed to King Neptune, the ruler of seas.
Away, away, blow the man down.
He prayed to King Neptune to send him a breeze.
Oh, give us some time to blow the man down.
Blow the man down, bullies, blow the man down,
Heave away, away, blow the man down.
He prayed to King Neptune to send him a breeze.
Oh, give us some time to blow the man down.

A porpoise appeared with a kink in his tail.
Away, away, blow the man down.
He looked at the skipper and winked at the sail.
Oh, give us some time to blow the man down.
Blow the man down, bullies, blow the man down
Heave away, away, blow the man down.
He looked at the skipper and winked at the sail.
Oh, give us some time to blow the man down.

It then disappeared and a whale took his place.
Away, away, blow the man down.
It spouted and seemed to be eager to race.
Oh, give us some time to blow the man down.
Blow the man down, bullies, blow the man down
Heave away, away, blow the man down.
It spouted and seemed to be eager to race.
Oh, give us some time to blow the man down.

The flying fish soared as though offering aid.
Away, away, blow the man down.
The skipper believed, and was glad he had prayed.
Oh, give us some time to blow the man down.
Blow the man down, bullies, blow the man down
Heave away, away, blow the man down.
The skipper believed, and was glad he had prayed.
Oh, give us some time to blow the man down.

The Captain could hardly his senses believe.
Away, away, blow the man down.
Such an answer so soon he'd not thought to receive.
Oh, give us some time to blow the man down.
Blow the man down, bullies, blow the man down
Heave away, away, blow the man down.
Such an answer so soon he'd not thought to receive.
Oh, give us some time to blow the man down.

But he roused and he called all the hands out on deck.
Away, away, blow the man down.
For on the horizon appeared a black speck.
Oh, give us some time to blow the man down.
Blow the man down, bullies, blow the man down
Heave away, away, blow the man down.
For on the horizon appeared a black speck.
Oh, give us some time to blow the man down.

They trimmed all the yards and she sailed right along.
Away, away, blow the man down.
The wind on the quarter blew steady and strong.
Oh, give us some time to blow the man down.
Blow the man down, bullies, blow the man down.
Heave away, away, blow the man down.
The wind on the quarter blew steady and strong.
Oh, give us some time to blow the man down.

The skipper then said with a smile on his face,
"Away, away, blow the man down.
All hands will lay aft and we'll splice the main brace."
Oh, give us some time to blow the man down.
Blow the man down, bullies, blow the man down
Heave away, away, blow the man down.
All hands will lay aft and we'll splice the main brace.
Oh, give us some time to blow the man down.

A Ship Was Becalmed in a Tropical Sea

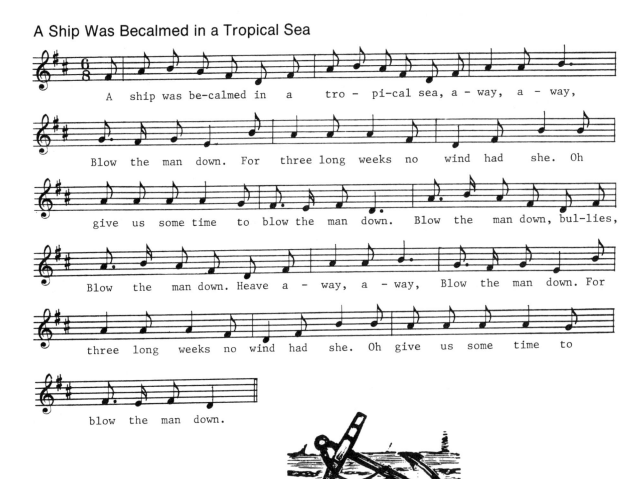

A ship was be-calmed in a tro - pi-cal sea, a - way, a - way,

Blow the man down. For three long weeks no wind had she. Oh

give us some time to blow the man down. Blow the man down, bul-lies,

Blow the man down. Heave a - way, a - way, Blow the man down. For

three long weeks no wind had she. Oh give us some time to

blow the man down.

112

Joe Yansky, one-man band of Yuba, Richland County.
Photo by Helene Stratman-Thomas.

LONGING

THE PRETTY MAHMEE

Sung by Mrs. Leslie Burton, age fifty-five, Lancaster, Wisconsin, in 1946. Song collectors disagree about the origins of this song and the meaning of the word "Mahmee" (variously given as Mauhee, Mohea, Mawhee, Mauiee, Mohee, and Mowhee). Some believe that the song is of American origin and the word a corruption of the Indian tribal name Miami; others believe that the song originated with English whaling men and derives from the Hawaiian island of Maui. The Wisconsin versions of the song reflect these two schools; one tells of the lass of Mowhee, the other (printed here) of the pretty Mahmee.

As I was a'walking for pleasure one day
To view recreation and pass time away,
As I was amusing myself on the grass,
Who chanced to step up but a young Indian lass?

She sat down beside me and she gave me her hand,
Saying, "You are a stranger, but not of this land.
If you will be tempted to go live 'long with me,
I will teach you the language of the pretty Mah-mee."

So, early next morning, at the break of the day,
I almost broke her poor heart, by the words I did say:
"I'm going to leave you; farewell, my dear,
For the ship lies a-waiting, and for home I must steer."

The Pretty Mahmee

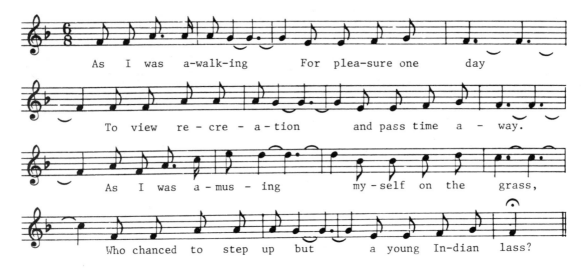

As I was a-walk-ing For plea-sure one day

To view re - cre - a-tion and pass time a - way.

As I was a - mus - ing my-self on the grass,

Who chanced to step up but a young In-dian lass?

114

THERE WAS A RICH OLD FARMER

Sung by Pearl Jacobs Borusky, age forty, Pearson, Wisconsin, in 1941.

There was a rich old farmer lived in the country high.
He had an only daughter on whom I cast an eye.
She was so tall and slender, so delicate and so fair,
No other girl in the country with her I could compare.

I asked her if it made a difference if I crossed over the plains.
She said, "It made no difference if you come back again."
She promised she'd be true to me until our parting time,
So we kissed, shook hands and parted, and I left my girl behind.

Straightway to old Missouri, to Pikesville, I did go,
Where work and money were plentiful and the whiskey it did flow.
Where work and money were plentiful and the girls all treated me kind.
But the girl I left behind me was always on my mind.

One day while I was out walking down by the public square
The mail boat had arrived and the postman met me there.
He handed me a letter which gave me to understand
That the girl I left behind me was married to another man.

I advanced a few steps forward, full knowing these words to be true.
My mind being bent on rambling, I didn't know what to do.
My mind being bent on rambling this wide world to see o'er,
I left my dear old parents, perhaps to see no more.

There Was a Rich Old Farmer

There was a rich old farm-er, lived in the coun-try nigh. He had an on-ly daugh-ter on whom I cast my eye. She was so tall and slen-der, so del-i-cate and so fair. No o-ther girl in the coun-try with her I could com-pare.

SADIE RAE

Sung by Mrs. Leslie Burton, age fifty-five, Lancaster, Wisconsin, in 1946.

Near a green and shady woodland
Where the rippling stream must flow
Dwelt a maiden fair and lovely.
But 'twas in the long ago.

Oft I kissed her and caressed her
As we danced the hours away.
Oft I told her that I loved her.
Now she's dead, my Sadie Rae.

When at eve, a golden sunset
Ushers in the moon and stars
Arm in arm we walk together
To the gate called Chestnut Bars.

There we talked of future pleasures.
There I named the wedding day.
But alas, 'twas long in coming
For she's dead, my Sadie Rae.

In my dreams I see her smiling
Far above the clear blue skies.
She is kneeling with the angels,
Who in groups are standing by.

Then again, I hear her calling
"Come my darling, come," I say.
"There is room here for another
Come and kiss your Sadie Rae."

Sadie Rae

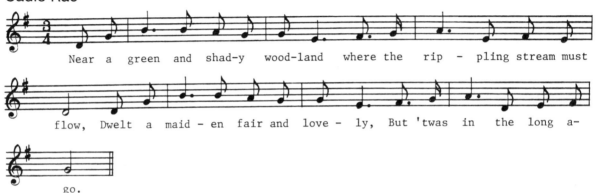

Near a green and shad-y wood-land where the rip - pling stream must flow, Dwelt a maid - en fair and love - ly, But 'twas in the long a- go.

THE DREARY BLACK HILLS

Sung by Lewis Winfield Moody, age seventy-five, Plainfield, Wisconsin, in 1940.

Kind friends, pay attention to a very sad tale;
I'm an object that's needy, a-looking quite stale.
I left off my trade, boys, selling rat traps and pills
For to go and dig gold in the dreary Black Hills.
Then don't you go, boys; stay, stay away if you can,
Far from the city they call Cheyenne,
Where the great Walafee and the great comrade Bill,
They'll take off your scalps in the dreary Black Hills.

When I got to the Black Hills no gold could I find,
But I thought of the free lunch I left far behind.
Oh, the rain, hail and snow, boys, soak up to the gills
And they call you the — boys of the dreary Black Hills.
Then don't you go, boys; stay, stay away if you can,
Far from the city they call Cheyenne.
Where the great Wallafee and the great comrade Bill,
They'll take off your scalps in the dreary Black Hills.

116

This Cheyenne, that outhouse, is filled every night
With bummers of every description and plight.
Not a rag on their backs, in their pockets no bills,
But still they'll keep striking out for the dreary Black Hills.
Then don't you go, boys; stay, stay away if you can,
Far from the city they call Cheyenne.
Where the great Wallafee and the great comrade Bill,
They'll take off your scalps in the dreary Black Hills.

The Dreary Black Hills

Kind friends, pay at-ten-tion to a ver-y sad

tale; I'm an ob-ject that's need-y, a-look-ing quite

stale. I left off my trade, boys, sell-ing rat traps and

pills, for to go and dig gold in the drear-y Black

Hills. Then don't you go, boys, stay, stay a-way if you

can, Far from the cit-y they call Chey-enne, Where the

great Wall-a-fee, and the great com-rade Bill, They'll

take off your scalps in the drear-y Black Hills.

117

ROBIN

Sung by William J. Morgan, age seventy-six, Berlin, Wisconsin, in 1946. Morgan sang this song from verses copied by his wife forty-six years earlier from Mrs. Mark Shackleton of Milwaukee.

Oh Robin, they tell me you're going away
And you've come to bid me goodbye.
I can see every word that your dear lips would say
By the dim light that beams from your eye.
Perhaps you'll forget me, Oh say you will not.
I'll try and believe you are true.
And I'll come every night to this dear little spot
And dream, my dear Robin, of you.

There'll be others that's fairer, in satin and lace.
There'll be smiles that will beam for your sake.
And maybe, dear Robin, some pretty girl's face
Will cause you your promise to break.
Perhaps you'll forget me, Oh say you will not,
I'll try to believe you are true.
And I'll come every night to this dear little spot
And dream, my dear Robin, of you.

Robin

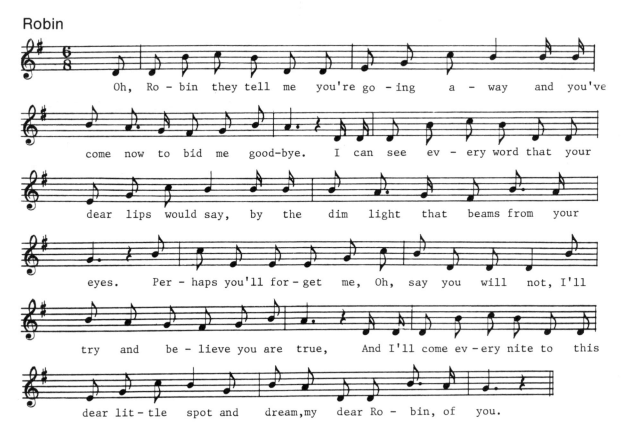

Oh, Ro-bin they tell me you're go-ing a-way and you've

come now to bid me good-bye. I can see ev-ery word that your

dear lips would say, by the dim light that beams from your

eyes. Per-haps you'll for-get me, Oh, say you will not, I'll

try and be-lieve you are true, And I'll come ev-ery nite to this

dear lit-tle spot and dream,my dear Ro-bin, of you.

Photo by Charles Van Schaick, Black River Falls.

ELLA REA

Sung by Mrs. Leslie Burton, age fifty-five, Lancaster, Wisconsin, in 1946.

Oh Ella dear, so kind and true
In the little church yard lies.
Bright drops of dew upon her grave,
And brighter were her eyes.
Then carry me back to old Tennessee
There let me live and die
Among the fields of yellow corn
In the land where Ella lies.

Ella Rea

Oh El-la dear, so kind and true, In the lit-tle church-yard lies. Bright drops of dew up-on her grave, and bright-er were her eyes. Then car-ry me back to old Ten-nes-see. There let me live and die A-mong the fields of yel-low corn in the land where El-la lies.

GREEN MOUNTAIN

Sung by Winifred Bundy, age fifty-seven, Madison, Wisconsin, in 1941. Miss Bundy believed this song was of English origin as it was one of the favorites of her grandfather, a soldier's son who was born in the army barracks at Manchester, England, in 1837—the year of the queen-to-be Victoria's birth. The song came with her father from England to Canada, and thence to the United States when he enlisted in the Union army during the Civil War.

There is a lovely mountain called the Mountain of Green,
All things on this mountain are fair to be seen,
At the top of this mountain the ivy doth grow,
At the foot of this mountain, the river doth flow.

On the top of this mountain a castle doth stand,
All decked in green ivy from the top to the strand,
Fine arches, fine porches, and the marble so white,
'Tis a warning to sailors on a dark stormy night.

At the foot of this mountain where the tides ebb and flow,
Ships from the East Indies to Madeira doth go,
With their red flags a-flying and the beating of drums
Sweet instruments of music and the firing of guns.

Come all ye little small streams that murmur and flow,
Come carry me now to my true love you know,
For his eyes are so enticing though his lips they say "No,"
Some good angel direct me to where shall I go.

120

Green Mountain

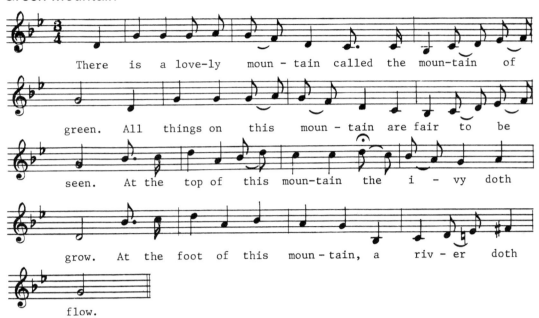

There is a love-ly moun - tain called the moun-tain of green. All things on this moun - tain are fair to be seen. At the top of this moun-tain the i - vy doth grow. At the foot of this moun - tain, a riv - er doth flow.

THE SHIP CARPENTER

Sung by Dan Tanner, age seventy-five, Boyne City, Michigan, in 1941. The melody and lyrics were transcribed from a recording made by Mr. Tanner's grand-nephew. Tanner learned this song from Joseph Ross, blacksmith in a lumber camp in Marquette County, Michigan.

Oh, I've just returned from the salt, salt sea,
My true love for to see
And she was married to a ship carpenter
And a jolly little lad was he, was he,
And a jolly little lad was he.

"Oh, if you will forsake your ship carpenter
And go along with me,
I will take you to a spot where the grass grows green
On the banks of a sweet valley, valley,
On the banks of a sweet valley."

"Oh, if I should forsake my ship carpenter
And go along with thee,
What have you, sir, for to maintain me
Or to keep me from slavery, 'ery,
Or to keep me from slavery?"

"Oh, I've seven ships all in the port,
And seven more at sea,
Four hundred twenty sailor boys
And they're all for to wait on me, on me,
And they're all for to wait on me."

Then she took her babes upon her knee
And gave them kisses three,
Saying, "Stay at home, you dear little ones,

For to keep your pa's company, 'any,
For to keep your pa's company."

Oh, she had not been on board two weeks,
I'm sure it was not three,
When she was sitting by her cabin door.
And she wept most bitterly, 'erly,
And she wept most bitterly.

"Oh, is it for gold you weep,
Or is it for fear,
Or is it for the ship carpenter,
That you left when you came on here, on here,
That you left when you came on here?"

"Oh, it is not for gold I weep,
Nor it is not for fear
But it is for the two little ones
That I left when I came on here, on here,
That I left when I came on here."

Oh, she had not been on board three weeks,
I'm sure it was not four,
When she threw her body overboard
And her weeping was heard no more, no more,
And her weeping was heard no more.

The Ship Carpenter

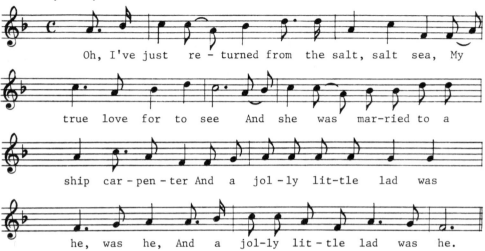

Oh, I've just re - turned from the salt, salt sea, My

true love for to see And she was mar-ried to a

ship car -pen - ter And a jol-ly lit-tle lad was

he, was he, And a jol-ly lit-tle lad was he.

THE LITTLE LOG CABIN BY THE STREAM

Sung by Lester A. Coffee, age seventy-five, Harvard, Illinois, in 1946.

There was a happy time for me not many years ago,
When the townfolks used to gather on the green.
And the fiddle and the banjo, they could make a forest ring.
In that little old log cabin by the stream.
Chorus: Then hang up the fiddle and banjo on the wall,
    And we'll lay aside the bones and the tambourine.
    Since death did come and claim my Rose,
    The only flow'r that grows,
    In that little old log cabin by the stream.

The footpath's all grown over now that leads around the hill
And the fences am a-goin' to decay.
And the brook is all dried up where I used to go to swim,
For in time it's changed its course another way.

The chimbly tumbled down and it killed the brindled cow,
And I 'spect to break my head, if I remain.
But the angels they watch o'er me while I lay me down to sleep
In that little old log cabin by the stream.

The Little Log Cabin by the Stream

There was a hap-py time for me not ma - ny years a-
go, When the town folks used to ga - ther on the
green. And the fid-dle and the ban - jo they would
make the for - est ring. In that lit - tle old log
cab - in by the stream. Then hang up the fid-dle and the
ban - jo on the wall, And we'll lay a - side the
bones and tam - bour - ine. Since death did come and
claim my rose, the on - ly flow'r that grows, In that
lit - tle old log ca - bin by the stream.

ON THE BANKS OF THE OLD MOHAWK

Sung by Lester A. Coffee, age seventy-five, Harvard, Illinois, in 1946.

It's all about my sweetest Julia,
And she looked just as natural as she lie.
And they buried her deep, deep down among the rocks
On the banks of the old Mohawk.
On the banks of the old Mohawk.
Where my love and I spent many an hour.
Just as happy as the birds
That soared among the flowers,
On the banks of the old Mohawk.

123

One day sweet Julia sat a-sewing
When death came knocking at the door.
And that very same day death stole her away
On the banks of the old Mohawk.
On the banks of the old Mohawk
Where my love and I spent many an hour.
Just as happy as the birds
That soared among the flowers,
On the banks of the old Mohawk.

On the Banks of the Old Mohawk

It's all a - bout my sweet-est Ju-lia, And she looked just as

nat - ural as she lie. And they bur-ied her deep, deep

down a - mong the rocks, On the banks of the old Mo-hawk. On the

banks of the old Mo - hawk, Where my love and I spent ma-ny an

hour. Just as hap-py as the birds that soared a - mong the

flowers, on the banks of the old Mo - hawk.

JOHANNA SHAY

Sung by Mrs. A. J. Fox, Eau Claire, Wisconsin, in 1922, for Franz
Rickaby.

In the Emerald Isle so far from here across the dark blue sea
There lives a maid that I love dear, and I know that she loves me.
With roguish eyes of Irish blue, her cheeks like dawn of day,
Oh, the sunshine of my life she is, my own Johanna Shay.

Oh, Johanna is tall and lovely, and like a lily fair.
She is the prettiest girl that can be found in the county of Kildare;
And if I have good luck, me boys, I'll make her Mrs. O'Day,
For my bundle I'll pack and I'll sail right back to my own Johanna Shay.

124

There's a bird in yonder garden singing from a willow tree
That makes me think of Johanna when she used to sing to me,
When side by side o'er the mountains or by the lake we strolled,
And her cheeks would flush with an honest blush whenever a kiss I stole.
Though the ocean rolls between us, if harm was in her way,
I'd jump right in and boldly swim to my own Johanna Shay.

Johanna Shay

Jo - han - na's tall and love - ly, she's like the lil - ies fair. She's the hand-som - est girl that can be found in the coun - ty of Kil - dare, And if I have good luck, me boys, she will soon be mis-sus O' - Day. For me bun - dle I'll pack and I'll sail right back to my own Jo-han - na Shay.

KITTY WELLS

Sung by Lester A. Coffee, age seventy-five, Harvard, Illinois, in 1946.

You ask what makes this darky weep?
And why, like others, am not gay.
What makes the tears roll down my cheek
From early morn 'til close of day.
My story, darky, you shall hear
For in my memory fresh it dwells.
'Twill cause you all to shed a tear
On the grave of my sweet Kitty Wells.
Refrain: The birds were singing in the morning
The myrtle and the ivy were in bloom.
The sun on the hilltop was a-shining,
It was then we laid her in the tomb.

I never shall forget the day
When we together roamed the dells.
I kissed her cheek and named the day
That I should marry Kitty Wells.

But death came to my cabin door
And took from me my joy and pride.
And when I found she was no more
I laid my banjo down and cried.

I often wish that I were dead
And laid beside her in the tomb.
The sorrow that bows down my head
Is deeper than the midnight doom.

Springtime has no charm for me
Though flowers are blooming in the dells,
For that bright form I cannot see
Is the form of my sweet Kitty Wells.

Refrain: The birds were singing in the morning
The myrtle and the ivy were in bloom.
The sun on the hilltop was a-shining,
It was then we laid her in the tomb.

Kitty Wells

You ask what makes this dark-y weep And why, like
o-thers, am not gay; What makes the tears roll down my
cheek From ear-ly morn 'til close of day. My sto-ry,
dark-y, you shall hear, For in my mem-ory fresh it
dwells. 'Twill cause you all to shed a tear On the
grave of my sweet Kit-ty Wells. The birds were
sing-ing in the morn-ing; The myr-tle and the I-vy were in
bloom. The sun on the hill-top was a'-shin-ing. It was
there we laid her in the tomb.

Photo by Charles Van Schaick, Black River Falls.

THE VERY FIRST TIME I SAW MY LOVE

Sung by Pearl Jacobs Borusky, age thirty-nine, Antigo, Wisconsin, in 1940.

The very first time I saw my love
I was very sick in bed;
And the only request I asked of her
Was to tie up my head.
O, love it is a killing thing,
Did you ever feel the pain?
Did you ever see a man so sick as I
For to get well again?

I wish my love was a rose so red
And in yon garden grew,
And if I was a gardener
Great care I'd take of you.
There would not a month in the year roll 'round
But what I would renew,
I'd garnish you all around and about
With sweet William, thyme and rue.

The Very First Time I Saw My Love

The ver-y first time I saw my love I was ver-y sick in

bed; And the on-ly re-quest I asked of her was to tie up my

head. Oh, love it is a kill-ing thing, Did you ev-er feel the

pain? Did you ev-er see a man so sick as I? for to get well a-

gain?

128

RISE, MY TRUE LOVE

Sung by an unknown voice on a tape recording made by Helene Stratman-Thomas.

Rise, my true love, and present to me your hand,
And we'll take a pleasant ramble through some far and distant land.
Where Jim Hawkins shot Jim Buzzard, and Jim Buzzard shot Jim Crow,
And we'll rally 'round the wild woods and chase the buffalo.
And chase the buffalo, and chase the buffalo.
We'll rally 'round the wild woods and chase the buffalo.

Rise, My True Love

THE WHITE CAPTIVE

Sung by Gene Silsbe, age sixty-one, Hancock, Wisconsin, in 1941.

At the foot of a mountain Amanda did sigh
At the hoot of the owl or the catamount's cry,
Or the howl of the wolf in some deep lowly dell,
Or the crash of some dead forest tree as it fell.

At the foot of the hemlock the wild game was flung,
While above from its branches a crude hammock swung.
While from the land's plunder each would repose
From the toils of the day 'til the evening should close.

The watch fires kindled, 'twas fanned by the breeze
'Til the red embers shown through the evergreen trees.
And fierce was the look of that old savage scene
As the light on the face of each warrior did gleam.

They brought in their captive, all friendless, forlorn,
Her face stained with blood and her garments all torn.
And she counted with vengeance each merciless foe
And sighed for the hour when her suffering might close.

The pile was constructed, the red light did glare;
Amanda was bound with her white bosom bare.
Whil'st around her stood gazing that merciless throng
Impatient to dance in the war dance and song.

Then up steps young Alvin, the prince of them all,
His eye like an eagle, his step like a deer.
He —— to scorn his own freedom to crave
Aside from her suffering until —— the grave.

"Forbear," cries young Alvin, "your tortures forbear."
"This maid shall live, by my wampum I swear.
And tonight if a victim must burn at the tree,
Young Alvin, your leader, that victim shall be."

So early next morning, at the break of the day
A birch bark canoe was seen gliding away.
And swift as the wild duck that swam by their side,
Young Alvin and Manda together did ride.

At the close of that evening a white cottage seen,
And the blue curling smoke over the willows so green.
And great was her joy when she came to the shore
And beheld her kind father and mother once more.

Young Alvin stood by them, he saw them embrace.
His heart overflowed and tears rolled down his face.
And all that he asked was protection and food
From the father of Amanda to the chief of the wood.

The White Captive

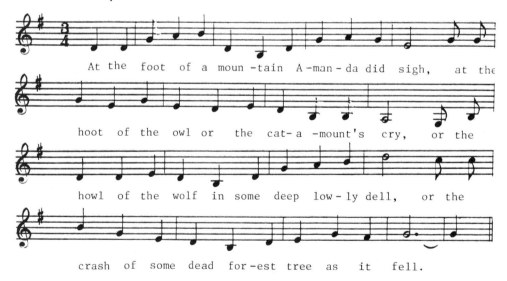

At the foot of a moun-tain A-man-da did sigh, at the
hoot of the owl or the cat-a-mount's cry, or the
howl of the wolf in some deep low-ly dell, or the
crash of some dead for-est tree as it fell.

ONCE I COURTED A PRETTY LITTLE GIRL

Sung by Pearl Jacobs Borusky, age thirty-nine, Antigo, Wisconsin, in 1940.

Once I courted a pretty little girl,
As pretty a little girl as ever you did see.
But she loved another man far better than me,
And she'd taken her flight and was gone.
She had taken her flight and was gone.

I ran up street and I ran down
In search of my bonny little girl.
I whooped and I hollered and I played on my flute,
But my bonny little girl, she was gone.
But my bonny little girl, she was gone.

I looked east and I looked west
As far as the eye could discern,
And there I saw my bonny little girl
Standing locked in another man's arms,
Standing locked in another man's arms.

She waved her lily white hand at me
As if she had once been my own;
But I passed on by and I never cast an eye
Though I brought out a sigh and a moan,
Though I brought out a sigh and a moan.

Oh now you have got my bonny little girl
You must treat her as well as you can.
And if you don't keep her safely at home
I will walk with her now and again,
I will walk with her now and again.

Once I Courted a Pretty Little Girl

THE SHANTY-BOY ON THE BIG EAU CLAIRE

This version was sung in 1923 for Franz Rickaby by Mathilde Kjorstad-Myer, who said that she had learned it thirty-five years before, "right here in Eau Claire."

Come all ye jolly shanty-boys, come listen to my song.
It's one I've just invented, it won't detain you long.
It's about a pretty maiden, a damsel young and fair,
Who dearly loved a shanty-boy upon the Big Eau Claire.

This young and artful maiden with a noble pedigree,
Her mother she kept a milliner's shop 'way down in Mosinee.
She sold waterfalls and ribbons and bonnets trimmed with lace
To all the high-toned people in this gay and festive place.

This shanty-boy was handsome, there were none so gay as he.
In the summer time he labored at the mills of Mosinee,
Till stern keen winter came along with cool and blistering breeze,
He went upon the Big Eau Claire to fell the big pine trees.

He had a handsome black mustache and a curly head of hair.
A finer lad than he was not upon the Big Eau Claire.
He loved this milliner's daughter, he loved her long and well,
Till circumstances happened, and this is what I tell.

The milliner swore her daughter the shanty-boy never to wed.
But Sally, seeming not to care for what her mother said,
So she packed down her waterfalls and bonnets by the stack,
And started another milliner shop 'way down by Fond du Lac.

It was in her occupation she found but little joy.
Thoughts came rushing through her mind about the shanty-boy.
Till one fine autumn came along to ripen all the crops,
She then went down to Baraboo and went to picking hops.

Sal is broken-hearted and tired of her life.
She's thinking of the shanty-boy, and wished to be his wife.
She caught the scarlet fever, was sick a week or two
Down in a shabby pest-house, 'way down in Baraboo.

It was oftimes in her raving she tore her auburn hair.
And talked about her shanty-boy, upon the Big Eau Claire.
The doctors tried, but all in vain; her life they could not save.
And now this weeping willow stands drooping o'er her grave.

When the shanty-boy heard this sad news, he became a lunatic.
He acted just as others do when they become love-sick.
He hid his saw in a hollow log and traded off his axe,
And hired out to pull an oar a fleet for Sailor Jack.

He fell off from a rapids-place at the falls of Mosinee,
Which put an end to his career and all his misery.
The bold Wisconsin River is waving o'er his bones;
His friends and his companions are weeping for him at home.

The milliner now is bankrupt; her shop is gone to wrack.
She's thinking now of some fine day to move from Fond du Lac
Her pillow sobbed every night in spite of her daughter fair,
And by the ghost of the shanty-boy upon the Big Eau Claire.

Come all ye young and pretty fair maids, come take an advice of me,
Not be too fast to fall in love with everyone you see;
For the shanty-boys are rowdyish, which everybody knows.
They dwell in the mighty pine woods where the mighty pine tree grows.

Stealing logs or shingle booms, telling each other lies,
Playing cards, or swearing, is all their exercise.
But if you want to marry for comfort or for joy,
I advise you to get married to an honest farmer's boy.

The Shanty-Boy on the Big Eau Claire

Come all you jol-ly shan-ty boys, Come lis-ten to my
song. It's one I've just in-vent-ed, It won't de-tain you
long. It's of a pret-ty maid-en, a dam-sel young and
fair Who dear-ly loved a shan-ty boy up-on the Big Eau
Claire.

POLLY OLIVER

Sung for Franz Rickaby by Mary Sands, Allanstand, North Carolina, in 1916.

So early one morning pretty Polly she rose
And dressed herself in a suit of men's clothes.
Now down to the stable pretty Polly's just gone
To view out a gelding to travel her ground.

In riding all day and riding in speed
The first thing she came to was her captain indeed.
She stepped up to him. What news do you bear?
Here's a kind, loving letter from Polly your dear.

In breaking this letter ten guineas he found.
He drunk his own health with the soldiers all round;
And reading the letter, he sit and did cry,
Not a-thinking Polly was nigh.

Polly Oliver

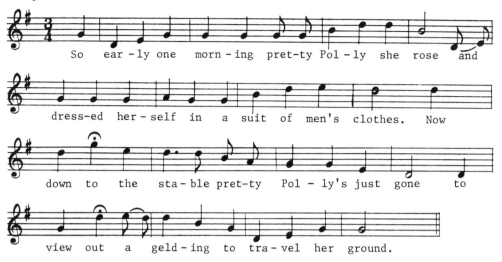

So ear-ly one morn-ing pret-ty Pol-ly she rose and
dress-ed her-self in a suit of men's clothes. Now
down to the sta-ble pret-ty Pol-ly's just gone to
view out a geld-ing to tra-vel her ground.

ON THE LAKES OF PONTCHARTRAIN

Sung by Mrs. Frances Perry, Black River Falls, Wisconsin, in 1946.
Mrs. Perry said that this song came from the mountain people of
Georgia.

Through swamps and alligators I wend my weary way;
O'er railroad tracks and crossings my weary feet did stray,
Until the shades of evening some higher ground did gain,
'Twas there I met the Creole girl, on the lakes of Pontchartrain.

On the Lakes of Pontchartrain

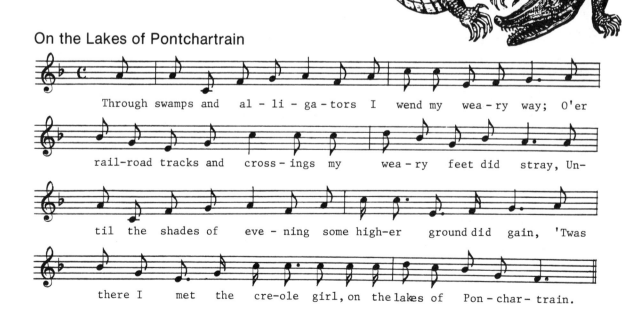

Through swamps and al-li-ga-tors I wend my wea-ry way; O'er
rail-road tracks and cross-ings my wea-ry feet did stray, Until the shades of eve-ning some high-er ground did gain, 'Twas
there I met the cre-ole girl, on the lakes of Pon-char-train.

134

Photo by Charles Van Schaick, Black River Falls.

I ONCE KNEW A LITTLE GIRL

Sung by Pearl Jacobs Borusky, age thirty-nine, Antigo, Wisconsin, in 1940.

I once knew a little girl,
A charming beauty bright,
And to make her my wife
Was my own heart's delight.
Oh, was my own heart's delight.

I took her by the hand,
And I led her to the door,
And I held her in my arms,
And I asked her once more.
Oh, I asked her once more.

She looked me in the eye,
With scorn and disdain,
And the answer that she gave me was,
"You can't come again.
Oh, you can't come again."

I stay'd away six weeks,
Which caused her much pain,
And she wrote me a letter saying,
"Do come again.
Oh, love, do come again."

I answer'd her letter,
Just for to let her know,
That young men oft-times venture,
Where they ort not to go.
Oh, where they ort not to go.

Come, all you young men
And warning take by me.
Never place your affections
On a green growing tree.
Oh, on a green growing tree.

For the leaves they will wither,
And the roots they will decay,
And the beauty of a fair girl
Will soon fade away.
Oh, will soon fade away.

I Once Knew a Little Girl

I once knew a lit-tle girl a charm-ing beau-ty bright, and to make her my wife was my own heart's de-light. Oh was my own hearts de-light.

x

x

THE FLYING TRAPEZE

Composed by George Leybourne. Lyrics supplied by the Circus World Museum, Baraboo, Wisconsin.

Once I was happy but now I'm forlorn
Like an old coat that is tattered and torn;
Left on this world to fret and to mourn,
Betrayed by a maid in her teens.
The girl that I loved she was handsome;
I tried all I knew her to please
But I could not please her one quarter so well
As the man upon the trapeze.

Chorus: He'd fly through the air with the greatest of ease,
That daring young man on the flying trapeze.
His movements were graceful, all girls he could please,
And my love he purloined away.

This young man by name was Signor Bona Slang,
Tall, big and handsome, as well made as Chang.
Where'er he appeared the hall loudly rang
With ovation from all people there.
He'd smile from the bar on the people below
And one night he smiled on my love.
She wink'd back at him and she shouted "Bravo,"
As he hung by his nose up above.

Her father and mother were both on my side
And very hard tried to make her my bride;
Her father he sighed, and her mother she cried,
To see her throw herself away.
'Twas all no avail, she went there every night,
And would throw him bouquets on the stage,
Which caused him to meet her; how he ran me down,
To tell you would take a whole page.

One night I as usual went to her dear home,
Found there her father and mother alone.
I asked for my love, and soon they made known,
To my horror that she'd run away.
She'd packed up her box and eloped in the night
With him, with the greatest of ease;
From two stories high he had lowered her down
To the ground on his flying trapeze.

Some months after this I went to the Hall;
Was greatly surprised to see on the wall
A bill in red letters, which did my heart gall,
That she was appearing with him.
He'd taught her gymnastics and dressed her in tights,
To help him live at his ease,
And made her assume a masculine name,
And now she goes on the trapeze.

Chorus: He'd fly through the air with the greatest of ease,
That daring young man on the flying trapeze.
His movements were graceful, all girls he could please,
And my love he purloined away.

The Flying Trapeze

Once I was hap-py, but now I'm for-lorn, Like an old

coat that is tat-ter'd and torn; Left on this wide world to

fret and to mourn, Be-tray'd by a maid in her teens. The

girl that I loved, she was hand-some, I tried all I

knew, her to please. But I could not please her one

quar-ter so well, Like that man up-on the tra-peze.

He'd fly thro' the air with the great-est of ease, That

dar-ing young man on the fly-ing tra-peze; His move-ments were

grace-ful, All girls he could please, And my love he

pur-loined a-way.

Schulte's Reed and String Band, Racine.
Iconographic Collection, SHSW.

FLAT RIVER GIRL

Sung by Dan Grant, Bryant, Wisconsin, in 1940.

I'm a heart-broken raftsman from Gransville I came.
All joys are departed, all virtues the same,
Since the clear skies of Cupid have caused me my grief,
My heart's well nigh broken, I can ne'er find relief.

My occupation, I'm a raftsman where the Flat River flows.
I've printed my name on both rocks and the shore.
In shops, farms and households I'm very well known,
They call me Jack Haggarty, the pride of my town.

My story I'll tell you without much delay.
A neat little lassie my heart stole away.
She was a miller's daughter, close by riverside
And I always intended to make her my bride.

Her form, like a lily, was slender and neat.
Her hair hung in ringlets to her tiny white feet.
Her voice was as sweet as the wind on a leaf.
Her skin like the breast of the white smiling sea.

I took her to supper, to parties and balls.
Sunday morning went riding from the first time I call.
I called her my darling, what a gem for a wife!
When I think of her treachery, I could forfeit my life.

I dressed her in the finest of muslins and lace
And the finest of jewels that I could encase.
I gave her my wages, the same to keep safe.
I begrudged her of nothing I had on the place.

I worked on the river and saved a lot of stake.
I was steadfast and steady and ne'er played the rake.
I was buoyant and smiling on the stiff boiling stream.
Her face was before me, it haunted my dream.

One day on the river a note I received.
She said from her promise herself she released.
She'd wedded a lover she long since delayed
And the next time I'd see her she'd not be a maid.

Now getting this note sure caused some surprise.
When I think of her now it brings tears to my eyes.
For it filled me with anger and made me half mad.
I'm weary and heartsick and wish myself dead.

But it were on her mother I lay on the blame,
She'd wrecked both our lives and blackened my name.
She'd thrown off the rigging that God would soon tie
And made me a loner 'til the day that I die.

On the banks of Flat River I no more can rest,
So I told them my feeling and pulled for the west.
I will go to Muskegon, a new job to find.
I'm leaving Flat River and a false love behind.

Come all jolly raftsmen, so brave and so true
Don't love a young girl, you'll be beat if you do.
When you see a sweet lassie with bright golden hair
Then remember Jack Haggarty and his Flat River girl.

Flat River Girl

I'm a heart-brok-en rafts-man from Grans-ville I came. All joys are de-part-ed, all vir-tues the same. Since the clear skies of Cu-pid have caused me my grief, My heart's well neigh bro-ken, I can ne'er find re-lief.

WILLIE AND MARY

Sung by Noble B. Brown, age sixty-one, Millville, Wisconsin, in 1946. Mr. Brown learned this ballad in central Wisconsin from his mother. There is evidence that the earliest printing of the song was in England in 1794.

As Willie and Mary strolled by the seaside,
A fond farewell there to take,
"Should you never return, dear Willie," said she,
"I'm sure that my poor heart would break."
"Oh, do not despair, little Mary," he said,
As he pressed his fair maid to his heart,
"In my absence don't mourn, for when I return,
We'll marry and never more part."

Three years passed away, when the news came at last,
As she stood by her own cottage door;
An old beggar came by with a patch on his eye,
Sad, ragged, forlorn, and poor.
"If your kind charity upon me you'll bestow,
It's your fortune I'll tell you beside;
The lad you mourn for, he will never return,
To make little Mary his bride."

"Oh!" she started, surprised and excited exclaimed,
"All the money I have I'll give you,
If you'll tell me the truth, that is all I ask you,
If my Willie still is alive?"
"He is living," said he, "but in dire poverty,
Shipwrecked, but still has his pride.
And he'll never return because he's too poor
To make little Mary his bride."

"Oh, the high heavens known the great joy that I feel;
And as for his misfortune I mourn.
If in riches I'm rolled or was covered with gold,
He should make little Mary his bride,
For I love him so dearly, so sincere and true,
That no other will I have in his place,
He'd be welcome to me in deep poverty,
For poverty is no disgrace."

Then the old beggar threw by the patch from his eye,
His old coat and crutches beside,
And with cheeks of roses, and his jacket of blue,
It was Willie stood by Mary's side.
"Oh, do not despair, precious Mary," he said,
As he clasped the fair maid in his arms.
To the church they repaired, it was not far away,
Was enriched by the loyal maid's charms.

Willie and Mary

As Wil-lie and Ma-ry strolled by the sea-side, a
fond fare-well there to take, "Should you
nev-er re-turn, dear Wil-lie," said she, "I'm
sure that my poor heart would break." "Oh,
do not de-spair, lit-tle Ma-ry," he said as he
pressed this fair maid to his heart, "In my
ab-sence don't mourn, for when I re-turn we'll
mar-ry and nev-er-more part.

THE DARK BRITISH FOES

Sung by Fred Bainter, Ladysmith, Wisconsin, for Franz Rickaby. Bainter learned this song from his mother, who had come to Wisconsin from Scotland by way of Indiana. Presumably the song originated during the War of 1812.

The dark British foes was invading our soil
And pressing our young men in slavery and war.
Young Edwin he bade his fair Mary adieu,
And they said when they parted their love would prove true.

Then this young warrior undaunted and brave,
Put on his tarpolian to fight on the waves,
To fight on the deep waters where the loud cannons roar,
To fight for his country and his dear native shore.

He had not been gone more than weeks two or three
When Mary no tidings from Edwin could hear.
She asked of each breeze as they blew gently by
If they'd brought her no tidings from her sailor boy.

142

To add to her misfortunes, her parents both died,
Which left her abandoned on life's flowing tide.
It seemed her misfortune that caused her to roam
From the scenes of her childhood, her juvenile home.

He had not been gone more than years two or three
Until the war ended and peace smiled again.
He landed at Hudson on the banks of the stream
Where the banks were all covered and clothed in green.

The thoughts of his Mary still ran in his mind.
He says, I will go and my Mary will find.
He sought her with love, oh, he sought her with care,
For it's long had she wandered and no one knew where.

One evening on the banks as he strayed
Where the wild songsters sang and their notes were displayed,
The sun was declining and the evening drew near,
When the voice of his Mary enchanted his ear.

He saw her declining from the shade of a tree,
Where the wild branches wove at the sigh of the breeze.
Her cheeks were growing pale, she was fairer than the sun
And those were the accents that fell from her tongue.

"Oh pity, kind heavens, and soothe my sad state,
And why was I doomed from my Edwin to part?
Oftimes in the shadow of yonder tall pine
Have I smoothed down his hair with those fingers of mine.

"Perhaps he is drowned in some ocean dark wave
Where thousands have met with their watery graves;
Perhaps he has died in some far distant land
Where his death-bed is soothed with no true lover's hand.

"I wish he was entombed in some graveyard near home;
This moment it's I to his grave I would roam.
With the finest of laurels I'd entwine round his bier,
And I'd moisten his grave with an affectionate tear."

Young Edwin no longer his feelings could contain.
He rushed from the ambush, he seized her fair hand.
"O Mary, dear Mary, the joys of my heart,
Through life until death nevermore shall we part."

The Dark British Foes

The dark Brit-ish foes was in-vad-ing our soil And press-ing our young men in slav-ery and war. Young Ed-win he bade his fair Ma-ry a-dieu, And they said when they part-ed their love would prove true.

THE BLUSHING ROSE

Sung by Myrth Whitt, age thirty-nine, Crandon, Wisconsin, in 1941.
Mrs. Whitt heard this beautiful song from relatives of her husband
in Kentucky, and never heard it sung elsewhere. She said, "My first
and only sweetheart sang it to me when I was sixteen."

Hold me to you, closely, darling;
As you did in days of old.
Place your lips upon my forehead
Then I see the golden shore.

Life is from me fastly fleeting,
Then I be in sweet repose.
When I'm dead I'll ask a favor
Place my head beneath a rose.

Oftimes we have roamed together
Down beside the moonlight sea.
There you told me you'd be mine, love,
Said you'd love no one but me.

I've been dreaming of you, darling,
Dreaming of your eyes so blue.
Take me back for I am dying,
I can love no one but you.

They may tell you I'm unworthy,
They may tell you I'm untrue,
Believe them not, my dearest darling,
For I love no one but you.

I'll send back to you your letter
And the ring I love so well.
Now I know we'll meet as strangers
But I can never say farewell.

Let my grave be like your cheeks, Love,
Covered with a blushing rose.
Lay me where sweet flowers mingle,
Where the downing lillies blow.

The Blushing Rose

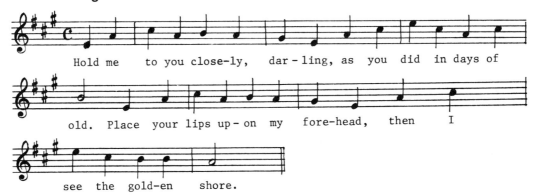

WHEN SHE GOT THERE

Sung by Pearl Jacobs Borusky, age thirty-nine, Antigo, in 1940.

My mother shall crave it,
My daddy shall have it,
If you will go with me
To yonder green tree.
But when she got there
She was highlee mounted,
She looked him scornfullee
Right in the face, saying,
"I know what you mean,
But you're highlee mistaken."
And away she went galloping
Down the long lane.

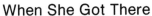

When She Got There

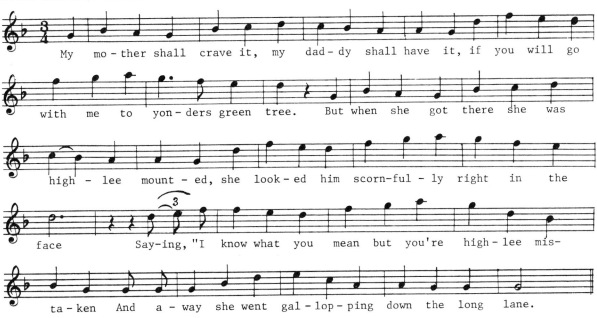

COURTSHIP

THE PAPER OF PINS

Sung by Mary Laycock, Grand Forks, North Dakota, at a date unknown. This courtship song, which is widely sung in many variants, was collected by Franz Rickaby. Frequently it is sung by alternating a male and a female voice on every other verse, though a solitary singer can also mimic the alternate voice.

I'll give to you a paper of pins,
If that is the way that love begins,
If you will marry me, me, me,
If you will marry me.

No, I'll not accept of your paper of pins,
If that is the way that love begins,
And I'll not marry you, you, you,
And you'll not marry me.

I'll give to you a crown of green
That you may look like any queen,
If you will marry me, me, me,
If you will marry me.

No, I'll not accept of your crown of green
That I may look like any queen,
And I'll not marry you, you, you,
And you'll not marry me.

I'll give to you a dress of red
All bound 'round with a golden thread.

No, I'll not accept of your dress of red
All bound 'round with a golden thread.

I'll give to you a coach and six
With every horse as black as pitch.

No, I'll not accept of your coach and six
With every horse as black as pitch.

I'll give to you the key to my heart,
That you and I will never part.

No, I'll not accept of the key to your heart,
That you and I will never part.

I'll give to you the key to my chest,
That you may have money at your request.

Oh yes, I'll accept the key to your chest,
That I may have money at my request.
And I will marry you, you, you,
And you will marry me.

No, you'll not accept the key to my chest,
That you may have money at your request.
And you'll not marry me, me, me,
And I'll not marry you.

The Paper of Pins

I'll give to you a pa-per of pins, If that is the way that love be-gins, If you will mar-ry me, me, me. If you will mar-ry me.

OSSIAN'S SERENADE

Sung by Winifred Bundy, age fifty-seven, Madison, Wisconsin, in 1941. The singer told Helene Stratman-Thomas that although she had learned the song from her English mother, she believed that it was of Irish origin. "Ossian was a legendary Gaelic bard," she said. "His poetry was called Fenian poetry, and Fenian is a name for the old inhabitants of Ireland. In Gaelic legend the name signified one of a band of heroes forming a kind of soldiery or chivalric order."

Oh come with me and be my love
For thee, the deepest depths, I vow.
Oh come with me for I long to go
To the Isle where the mango apples grow.
Chorus: Oh, I'll chase the antelope over the plain
And the tiger's cub I'll bind with a chain.
And the wild gazelle with the silvery feet
I'll give thee, love, for a playmate sweet.

I'll climb that palm for the bayou's nest,
Red peas I'll gather to deck thy breast.
I'll pierce the coco's cup for its wine
And — to thee, if thou be mine.

Then come with me in my little canoe
When the sea is bright and the sky is blue.
For should we linger another day
— may rise and love decay.

Ossian's Serenade

OH YAH, AIN'T DAT BEEN FINE

Sung by Minnie Pendleton, age sixty-eight, Lancaster, Wisconsin, in 1946.

Now Katryn, my darling, come sit by my side
I'll tell you somethin' that open your eyes wide.
I love you so much I can't tell you how
And I's goin' to ask you, "Won't you be my frau?"
"Oh, shame yourself Scharlie, don't speak out like that.
Although ist was fine what you say.
I love you mit all the love what I got
And Ich bin your frau right away."
Yah, yah, Ich das bin fine.
Katryn she told me she's goin' to be mine.
Yah, yah, Ich das bin fine.
Scharlie, he's told me he's goin' to be mine.

Now when we get married won't we put on style?
We'll chump on a streetcar and ride all the while.
We've got plenty of sauerkraut always on hand,
And live chust as good as der king of der land.
Den I get some dresses what schtick out behind
And drag about a yard in der schtreet.
And a nice liddle hat, chust the best I can find.
Oh, Scharlie, den von't I look schweet?
Yah, Yah, Ich das bin fine,
Katryn she told me she's goin' to be mine.
Yah, Yah, Ich das bin fine,
Scharlie, he's told me he's goin' to be mine.

Oh Yah, Ain't Dat Been Fine

THE DEMON LOVER

The melody and text of this song were extracted by Franz Rickaby from a copy of William Motherwell's *Ancient and Modern Scottish Ballads* that he found in the Duluth public library.

"O where have you been, long, long love,
This long seven years and mair?
O I'm come to seek my former vows
Ye granted me before."

"O hold your tongue of your former vows,
For they will breed sad strife;
O hold your tongue of your former vows,
For I am become a wife."

He turned him right and round about,
And the tear blinded his e'e.
"I wad ne'er hae trodden on Irish ground
If it had not been for thee.

"I might have had a king's daughter,
Far, far beyond the sea;
I might have had a king's daughter
Had it not been for love of thee."

"If ye might have had a king's daughter,
Yer self ye had to blame;
Ye might have taken the king's daughter,
Fer ye kend that I was nane."

"O false are the vows o' womankind,
But fair is their false bodie;
I ne'er wad hae trodden on Irish ground
Had it not been for love o' thee."

"If I was to leave my husband dear,
And my two babes also,
O what have you to take me to,
If with you I should go?"

"I have seven ships upon the sea,
The eighth brought me to land;
With four-and-twenty bold mariners
And music on every hand."

She has taken up her two little babes,
Kissed them baith cheek and chin:
"O fare ye well, my ain two babes,
For I'll ne'er see you again."

She set her foot upon the ship,
No mariners could she behold;
But the sails were of the taffetie,
And the masts of the beaten gold.

She had not sailed a league, a league,
A league but barely three,
When dismal grew his countenance
And drumlie grew his e'e.

The masts that were like the beaten gold
Bent not on the heaving seas;
And the sails that were o' the taffetie
Filled not in the eastland breeze.

They had not sailed a league, a league,
A league but barely three,
Until she espied his cloven foot,
And she wept right bitterlie.

"O hold your tongue of your weeping," says he,
"Of you weeping now let me be;
I will show you how the lillies grow
On the banks of Italy."

"O what hills are yon, yon pleasant hills,
That the sun shines sweetly on?"
"O yon are the hills of heaven," he said,
"There you will never win."

"O whaten a mountain is yon," she said,
"All so dreary wi' frost and snow?"
"O yon is the mountain of hell," he cried,
"Where you and I will go."

And aye when she turned her round about,
Aye, taller he seemed to be;
Until that the tops of the gallant ship
Nae taller were than he.

The clouds grew dark and the wind grew loud,
And levin filled her e'e;
And waesome wailed the snow-white sprites
Upon the girlie sea.

He strack the tapmast wi' his hand.
The foremast wi' his knee;
And he brake that gallant ship in twain
And sank her in the sea.

The Demon Lover

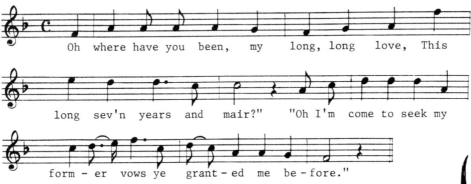

Oh where have you been, my long, long love, This long sev'n years and mair?" "Oh I'm come to seek my form-er vows ye grant-ed me be-fore."

ONE MORNING, ONE MORNING, ONE MORNING IN SPRING

Sung by Mrs. Ollie Jacobs, age seventy-nine, Pearson, Wisconsin, in 1941. Mrs. Jacobs said that she used to think that "kallamaking" was some kind of bush or tree, and that it was only by looking up a published version of the song that she found it meant "cow a-milking." She continued, however, to sing it her way.

One morning, one morning, one morning in spring
I heard a fair damsel so gallantly sing
As she sat under her kallamaking,
"Please God, I'll be married next Sunday!"

"Fourteen years is too young to get married.
A girl of your age is apt to get sorry.
For seven long years I'd have you tarry.
Put off your wedding next Sunday!"

"Old man, old man, you talk on a cheap scale.
That's seven long years against my will.
My mind is to marry and I mean to fulfill.
I wish that tomorrow was Sunday."

"My shawl and my gown lies under the press.
My love will be here before I can dress
With a bunch of blue ribbons tied round my waist
To make me look neat against Sunday.

"Saturday night will be all my care
To feeble my locks and curl my hair,
And two little maidens to wait on me there
To dress me up neat against Sunday.

"Saturday night to dance all around
With a bunch of blue ribbons and new fashioned gown,
Invite all the ladies from Barbersville town
To be at my wedding next Sunday."

One Morning, One Morning, One Morning in Spring

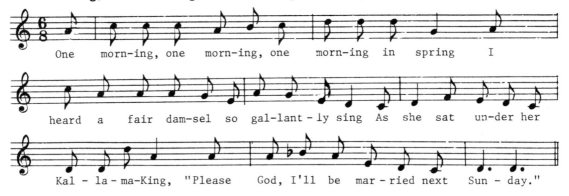

One morn-ing, one morn-ing, one morn-ing in spring I heard a fair dam-sel so gal-lant-ly sing As she sat un-der her Kal-la-ma-King, "Please God, I'll be mar-ried next Sun-day."

150

THREE DISHES AND SIX QUESTIONS

Sung by Charles Dietz, age seventy-five, Monroe, Wisconsin, in 1946. This old riddle song was handed down in Mr. Dietz's family; his version lacks the story of the courtship which leads to the asking of the riddles, but most of the riddles found in early printings of the song are present here. A different version of the song was included in the *Franklin Square Song Collection* of 1881, a popular songbook in the public schools of Wisconsin.

"Oh go away, you silly man,
And do not bother me.
Before that you can lie with me,
You must cook me dishes three.
Three dishes you must cook for me,
And I will eat them all.
Then you and I in the bed will lie,
And you'll lie next to the wall.

"For my breakfast you must cook
A bird without any bones.
And for my dinner you must cook
A cherry without any stones.
And for my supper you must cook
A bird without a gall.
Then you and I in the bed will lie,
And you'll lie next to the wall."

"Oh, while the bird is in the shell,
It surely has no bones;
And while the cherry is blossoming
It surely has no stones;
The dove is a gentle bird
And flies without a gall.
Now you and I in one bed will lie,
And you'll lie next to the wall."

"Oh go away, you silly man,
And do not me perplex,
Before that you can lie with me,
You must answer questions six.
Six questions you must answer me,
As I repeat them all.
Then you and I in the bed will lie,
And you'll lie next to the wall.

"What is rounder than a ring?
What's higher than a tree?
What is worse than a woman's tongue?
What's deeper than the sea?
What bird sings first and what one best,
And where does the dew first fall?
Then you and I in the bed will lie,
And you'll lie next to the wall."

"This world is rounder than a ring,
Heaven's higher than a tree.
The devil's worse than a woman's tongue.
Hell's deeper than the sea.
The lark sings first, the sparrow best,
And out does the dew first fall.
Now you and I in the bed will lie,
And you'll lie next to the wall."

Three Dishes and Six Questions

"Oh, go a-way, you sil-ly man, and do not both-er me. Before that you can lie with me, you must cook me dish-es three. Three
dish-es you must cook for me, and I will eat them all. Then
you and I in the bed will lie, and you'll lie next to the wall.

SING LAY THE LILY LOW

Sung by Pearl Jacobs Borusky, age thirty-nine, Antigo, Wisconsin, in 1940.

My Jack has gone a-sailing, and trouble's on his mind,
A-leaving of his country, his darling girl behind.
Sing lay, sing lay, sing lay the lily low.

He went down to the store and he bought him a suit of grey,
And off to battle field my dear Jack was marched away.
Sing lay, sing lay, sing lay the lily low.

"Your waist, it is too slender, your fingers, they're too small,
Your face too red and rosy to face a cannon ball."
Sing lay, sing lay, sing lay the lily low.

"My waist, it may be slender, my fingers may be small,
But it does not harm me, darling, to see ten thousand fall."
Sing lay, sing lay, sing lay the lily low.

She went up on the battle field and searched the battle ground.
Among the dead and wounded, her darling Jack she found.
Sing lay, sing lay, sing lay the lily low.

She took him in her arms and she carried him to the town,
Calling for a doctor to cure his bloody wound.
Sing lay, sing lay, sing lay the lily low.

This couple, they got married, so well did they agree.
This couple, they got married, so why not you and me?
Sing lay, sing lay, sing lay the lily low.

Sing Lay the Lily Low

My Jack has gone a - sail - ing and trou-ble's on his mind. A - leav-ing of his coun - try, his dar-ling girl be-hind Sing lay, sing lay, sing lay the li - ly low.

Unknown singer, northern Wisconsin, ca. 1946.
Photo by Helene Stratman-Thomas.

I'M IN LOVE WITH A TIPPERARY MISS

Sung by Lester Coffee, age seventy-five, Harvard, Illinois, in 1946.

I'm in love with a flip of a tip-tip-typical Tipperary Miss.
She's a regular flip with a rosy lip you would dearly love to kiss.
From the tip of her toes to the tip-tip-top of her nose I love her so.
I'd like to just take her and squeeze her, I know that it wouldn't displease her,
But she lives in Tipperary many miles away from here.
If I could just see her and meet her and greet her
I'm thinking I'd eat her, my darling.
But she's many miles away from here and so I wait, I fear,
'Til I take a notion and sail o'er the ocean to Ireland.
Chorus: Faith, and it's me that's nearly crazy
From that Tipperary daisy.
All the day me heart's uneasy,
But the thing I find that's on my mind
Is the darling girl I left behind.
Far off in dear old Tipperary.

I will give you a tip aboard the ship when I start the trip away.
I'd be there with a yell when they ring the bell, and I'd shout, "Hip, Hip, Hurray."
And the whistle would toot and away we'd shoot with the choo-choo down the bay.
And I'd wave a bye-bye when we're sailing, from over the top of the railing,
Then across the briny ocean to the tiny Emerald Isle.
I'd give my last penny, if I hadn't any, begorry, or many, to see her smile
As she used to when she sat with me down beside the stile.
But I was a rover, be gad, and came over from Ireland.

I'm In Love With a Tipperary Miss

I'm in love with a flip of a tip tip-ty-pi - cal
Tip-pe-ra-ry miss. She's a reg - u -lar flip with a
ro - sy lip you would dear - ly love to kiss. From the
tip of her toes to the tip-tip top of her nose, I love her

so. I'd like to just take her and squeeze her, I

know that it would - n't dis - please her, but she

lives in Tip - pe - ra - ry ma - ny miles a - way from

here. If I could just see her and meet her and

greet her, I'm think-ing I'd eat her, my darl-ing. But she's

ma - ny miles a - way from here and so I wait, I fear, 'til

I take a no - tion and sail o'er the o - cean to Ire-

land. Faith, and it's me that's near-ly cra - zy.

From the Tip-pe-ra-ry dai - zy. All the day me

heart's un - eas - y, But the thing I find that's

on me mind is the darl-ing girl I left be - hind, Far

off in dear old Tip-pe-ra - ry.

LAST SATURDAY NIGHT I ENTERED A HOUSE

Sung by Pearl Jacobs Brousky, age thirty-nine, Antigo, Wisconsin, in 1940. In other versions the young man is called Johnny McCardner and Jamieson Wilks. Mrs. Borusky's mother, Ollie Jacobs, brought the song with her from Kentucky.

Last Saturday night I entered a house
And through the dark way I crept like a mouse.
I opened the door and went straightway
Into a room where the girls all stay.
And it's hard times!

Such laughing and chatting as we did keep!
We waked the old widder all out of her sleep,
And in a few words she did address me,
"Such an impudent fellow before me I see!"
And it's hard times.

"O, widder, O, widder, you'd better keep calm
Until you find out who I am.
I'm Johnny the Carpenter I go by that name.
A-courting your daughter, for the purpose I came."
And it's hard times!

"O daughter, O, daughter, O, daughter," said she.
"To think that my daughter would go before me
When I am so old and you are so young.
You can get sweethearts and I can get none."
And it's hard times!

"O, widder, O, widder, O, widder at large,
If you are an old widder you are a great charge.
O, widder, O, widder, O, widder by name."
She up with a broomstick and at me she came.
And it's hard times!

Such fighting and scratching! At last I got clear,
I mounted my horse and for home I did steer,
The blood running down, my head being sore.
There stood the old widder with a broom in the door.
And it's hard times!

Come all young men, take warning by me,
And never a widder's daughter go see.
For is you do, t'will be your doom.
They'll fight you like Satan and beat you with a broom.
And it's hard times!

Last Saturday Night I Entered a House

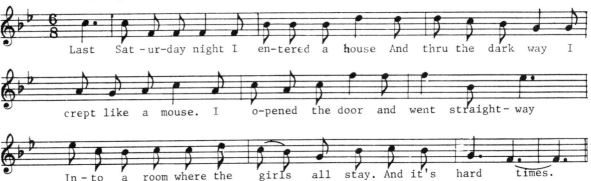

Last Sat-ur-day night I en-tered a house And thru the dark way I crept like a mouse. I o-pened the door and went straight-way In-to a room where the girls all stay. And it's hard times.

MY GRANDMOTHER LIVED ON YONDER GREEN

Sung by Charles Dietz, age seventy-five, Monroe, Wisconsin, in 1946.

My grandmother lived on yonder little green,
As fine an old lady as ever was seen.
She often cautioned me to take care—
Of all false young men to beware.
Timmy I, Timmy I, Timmy I, pata—
Of all false young men to beware.

And now, dear daughter, don't you believe,
For they will fib and cunningly deceive.
They will cruelly deceive you before you're aware,
Then away goes poor granny's care.
Timmy I, Timmy I, Timmy I, pata
Then away goes poor granny's care.

The first to come courting was honest young Green,
As fine a young gentleman as ever was seen,
But the words of my granny so rang in my head
I couldn't pay heed to a word he said.
Timmy I, Timmy I, Timmy I, pata
I couldn't pay heed to a word he said.

The next to come courting was honest young Grove,
And with him I fell in a joyful love.
Such a joyful love as you needn't be afraid,
For 'tis better to get married than to die an old maid.
Timmy I, Timmy I, Timmy I, pata
For 'tis better to get married than to die an old maid.

Oh, dear, what a fuss our old grannies make.
Thinks I to myself, there must be some mistake.
For if all old ladies of young men were afraid.
Why Granny herself would've died an old maid.
Timmy I, Timmy I, Timmy I, pata
Why Granny herself would've died an old maid.

My Grandmother Lived on Yonder Green

157

TASSELS ON HER BOOTS

By an unknown singer on a tape recording made by Helene Stratman-Thomas.

'Twas at a fancy ball, I met my charmer fair,
'Midst waltzing swells and dashing belles, the prettiest dancer there.
I watched her while the music played the latest waltz of Cootes.
And fell in love, no not with her, but the tassels on her boots. Oh yes,

Refrain: Those tassels on her boots, a style I'm sure that suits
    The Yankee girls with hair in curls, those tassels on her boots.

I watched her up the stairs, when we to supper went,
Upon those tassels on her boots, my soul was so intent;
They asked me to propose a health, said I, "Here's one that suits,
So fill your glasses up and drink to the tassels on the boots."

Spoken: I meant to drink the ladies' health, but I could think of nothing, but

Refrain: Those tassels on her boots, a style I'm sure that suits
    The Yankee girls with hair in curls, those tassels on her boots.

I asked this girl if I might call. She said, "You may,
But tell me why you gaze upon the ground in such a way?
You're sad, perhaps, for life is full of very bitter fruits."
"Oh no," I said, "I'm looking at the tassels on your boots."

Spoken: What is a more lovely sight when you walk down Broadway than to look at

Refrain: Those tassels on her boots, a style I'm sure that suits
    The Yankee girls with hair in curls, those tassels on her boots.

I called on her next day, and Cupid's cruel shoots
Soon made me throw myself before those tassels on her boots;
Now when we're married and we've got a lot of little toots,
I'll make them, whether boys or girls, wear tassels on their boots.

Spoken: If I were to have twenty children they should every one, wear
those pretty, pretty, pretty

Refrain: Those tassels on her boots, a style I'm sure that suits
    The Yankee girls with hair in curls, those tassels on her boots.

Tassels on Her Boots

'Twas at a fan-cy ball, I met my charm-er fair, 'Midst

waltz-ing swells and dash-ing belles, The pret-ti-est danc-er

there. I watched her while the mus-ic play'd the

lat-est waltz of Cootes, And fell in love, no not with

her, but the tas-sels on her boots. Oh yes Those

tas-sels on her boots, A style I'm sure that suits The

Yan-kee girls, with hair in curls, Those tas-sels on her

boots.

AWAKE, ARISE, YOU DROWSY SLEEPER

Sung by Lester A. Coffee, age seventy-five, Harvard, Illinois, in 1946. Mr. Coffee, the singer of many of these English ballads, was a resident of Pittsville, Wisconsin, until he moved to Illinois.

"Awake, arise, you drowsy sleeper,
Awake, arise, 'tis almost day,
And open wide your bedroom window,
Hear what your true-love has to say.

"Oh Mary dear, go ask your father,
Whether you my bride may be,
And if he says no, love, come and tell me,
It's the very last time I'll trouble thee."

"I dare not go to ask my father,
For he lies on his couch of rest,
And by his side he keeps a weapon,
To slay the one that I love best."

"Oh Mary dear, go ask your mother,
Whether you my bride may be,
And if she says no, love, come and tell me,
It's the very last time I'll trouble thee."

"I dare not go to ask my mother,
To let her know my love is near,
But dearest dear, go court some other,"
She gently whispered in my ear.

"Oh Mary dear, oh dearest Mary,
It is for you my heart will break.
From North to South to Pennsylvania,
I'll roam the ocean for your sake.

"And now I'll go down by some silent river,
And there I'll spend my days and years,
And there I'll plant a weeping willow;
Beneath its shade I'll shed my tears."

"Come back, come back, my wounded lover,
Come back, come back to me, I pray,
And I'll forsake both father, mother,
And with you I'll run away."

Awake, Arise, You Drowsy Sleeper

A-wake, a-rise, you drow-sy sleep-er, A-wake, a-rise, 'tis al-most day, And o-pen wide your bed-room win-dow Hear what your true love had to say.

EVERYBODY'S GOT A FINGER IN THE PIE

Sung by Lewis Winfield Moody, age seventy-six, Plainfield, Wisconsin, in 1941.

When a feller falls in love with his little turtle dove,
He will linger all around her until dawn.
He will kiss her for her mother, for her sister, for her brother,
'Til her daddy comes and kicks you out the door.
Pulls a pistol from his pocket, pulls the hammer for to cock it,
And he _____ that he brings.
But his daughter says he mustn't, 'tisn't loaded so he doesn't,
So they're kissing one another once again.
Chorus: For the old maids a'love it, and the widow's not above it,
   Everybody's got a finger in the pie.
   The girls they are so haughty and they say it's awful naughty
   But you bet your life they'll kiss you on the sly.

When a girl's sweet sixteen, Oh she thinks it's awful mean,
If she can't get out sometime for to mash.
She'll pucker up her mouth in a very pretty pout
As she fumbles underneath a big mustache.
She will make a feller shiver, she will make him pop a liver
She will tangle him all up with mucilage glue.
And then if you will tell her you're some other girl's feller
She will massacre your smeller if you do.

160

Everybody's Got a Finger in the Pie

When a fel-ler falls in love with his lit-tle tur-tle dove, he will lin-ger all a-round her un-til dawn. He will kiss her for her mo-ther, for her sis-ter, for her bro-ther 'til her dad-dy comes and kicks you out the door. Pulls a pis-tol from his pock-et, pulls the ham-mer for to cock it, and he that he brings. But his daugh-ter says he must'-nt, 'tis'-nt load-ed so he does'-nt, So they're kiss-ing one a-no-ther once a-gain. For the old maids a-love it, and the wid-ows' not a-bove it, ev-ery-bo-dy's got a fin-ger in the pie. The girls they are so haugh-ty and they say it's aw-ful naugh-ty, but you bet your life they'll kiss you on the sly.

FATHER SENT ME HERE A-COURTING

Sung by Miss M. E. Perley, Grand Forks, North Dakota, for Franz Rickaby in 1923.

Father sent me here a-courting,
Hi! Ho! Hum!
I'm in earnest, I'm not joking.
He! Ho! Hum!

You can stay and court the fire,
Teedle dinktum dinktum day!
I am ready to retire.
Teedle dinktum dinktum day!

I've a ring and forty shilling,
Hi! Ho! Hum!
You can have them if you're willing.
He! Ho! Hum!

I don't want your ring or money.
Teedle dinktum dinktum day!
I want a man that'll call me honey.
Teedle dinktum dinktum day!

Must I then change my religion?
Hi! Ho! Hum!
Must I turn a Presbyterian?
He! Ho! Hum!

You go home and tell your daddy,
Teedle dinktum dinktum day!
That you didn't find me ready.
Teedle dinktum dinktum day!

Father Sent Me Here A-Courting

Photo by Charles Van Schaick, Black River Falls.

PRETTY POLLY

Sung by Aunt Lily Richmond, age eighty-four, Lancaster, Wisconsin, in 1946.

If I were a fisherman down by the waterside
And Polly, a salmon, swimming close by my side,
I'd cast down my net, and I'd catch her in a snare.
I'd bring down pretty Polly, I vow and declare.

Pretty Polly

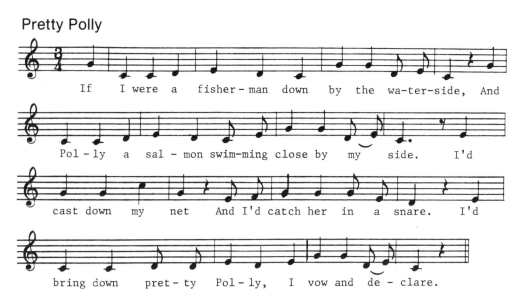

FORGET ME NOT

Sung by Chief White Eagle, Eau Claire, Wisconsin, for Franz Rickaby. "This is my only attempt, so far," Rickaby wrote, "to record a melody sung by an Indian. I heard a young fellow of the Winnebago sing at a Kiwanis Club luncheon when I was in Eau Claire, and detained him afterward to see what I could do with the melody. He sang so indistinctly and the rhythm and tune were so elusive that I didn't have much luck. . . The title given here is the nearest he could come to giving me a name for the song in English."

Forget Me Not

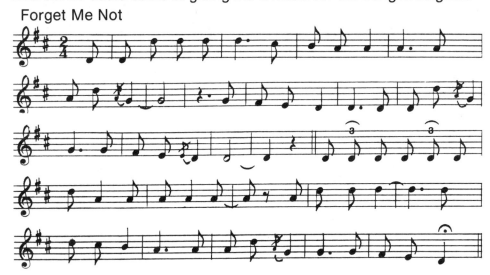

THE LANTERN'S GLEAM

Sung by Eryl Levers, age twenty-four, Madison, Wisconsin, in 1946.

The lanterns gleam while yellow flames leap and play,
And wild and vibrant music pours out.
And the rafters ring as supple dancers gay
Moving swiftly, circle about.

The Lantern's Gleam

THE BROKEN RING

Sung by Lester A. Coffee, age seventy-five, Harvard, Illinois, in 1946. To Mr. Coffee this was simply "another old song I learned as a boy."

A beautiful damsel stood at the gate one morning
Viewing the plain all around so gay,
When a gay young gentleman stepped up to her
Saying, "Madam, can you fancy me?"

"Can I fancy you? A man of honor,
A gentleman I take you to be.
How could you think of such a lady,
Who is not fit for your bride to be?"

"If you're not fit for to be my servant,
If you're not fit for my bride to be,
If you will only consent to marry me
You shall have servants to wait on thee."

"Kind sir, I've a lover on the ocean,
Seven long years he's been gone to sea
And seven more I'll still wait on him,
For if he's alive he'll return to me."

"Seven long years make an alteration.
Since your true love's been gone to sea,
Perhaps he's in the ocean drowned
Never to return to thee."

"If he's dead I hope he's happy
Or if he's in some battle slain,
Or if he's took some pretty girl married
I love that girl as well as him."

165

His fingers being both slim and slender,
HIs fingers being both slim and small
He showed her the ring they broke between them,
Down in the garden this maid did fall.

He picked her up from in the garden
And gave her kisses, one, two, by three
Saying, "Mary, oh Mary, don't you know me?
I'm your Willie returned from sea."

The Broken Ring

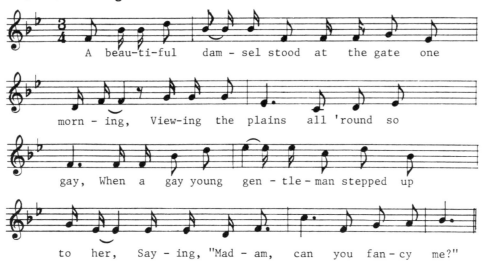

A beau-ti-ful dam - sel stood at the gate one

morn - ing, View-ing the plains all 'round so

gay, When a gay young gen - tle - man stepped up

to her, Say - ing, "Mad - am, can you fan-cy me?"

MARRIAGE

THE LASS OF GLENSHEE

Sung by Lester A. Coffee, age seventy-five, Harvard, Illinois, in 1946. Mr. Coffee learned this song from a visiting aunt when he was a young boy in Pittsville, Wisconsin.

One balmy bright morning as lilacs were blooming
I went for a walk on the velvety lea.
I met a fair maiden who also was roaming,
A-herding her flocks on the hills of Glenshee.

I kissed and caressed her, and said, "Bonny Lassie,
If you will but come to St. Johnson's with me,
Tonight in my arms I will kindly embrace you."
She blushed and consented, sweet lass of Glenshee.

Seven long years since we wedded together,
Seasons have changed but there's no change in me.
My bride she's as fair as the dew of the morning
Or the flowers that bloom on the hills of Glenshee.

The sun may forget to arise in the morning,
The lark may forget to revolve o'er the lea,
But never will I, while reason stays with me,
Forget to be kind to the lass of Glenshee.

The Lass of Glenshee

One balm-y bright morn-ing as li-lacs were bloom-ing I went for a walk on the vel-vet-y lee. I met a fair maid-en who al-so was roam-ing, a - herd - ing her flocks on the hills of Glen-shee.

THE OLD MAN CAME HOME AGAIN

Sung by Charles Dietz, age seventy-five, Monroe, Wisconsin, in 1946. The husband's queries and the wife's deceptive replies are similar in other versions of this song, notably *Our Goodman*. In some Southern versions, the milking maid has been changed into a cabbage head.

The old man came home again, as drunk as he could be,
"Dear wife, loving wife, 'tis curious to me,
Whose horse is in the place where mine ought to be?"
"You old fool, you blind fool, can't you hear nor see?
'Tis nothing but the sow pig my grandma sent to me."
"I've travelled, I've travelled some thousand miles or more
But the saddle on a sow pig I never saw before."

The old man came home again, as drunk as he could be.
"Dear wife, loving wife, 'tis curious to me,
Whose coat hangs in the place where mine ought to be?"
"You old fool, you blind fool, can't you hear nor see?
'Tis nothing but the bed-quilt my grandma sent to me."
"I've travelled, I've travelled some thousand miles or more,
But pockets on a bedquilt I never saw before."

The old man came home again, as drunk as he could be.
"Dear wife, loving wife, 'tis curious to me,
"Whose boots are in the place where mine ought to be?"
"You old fool, you blind fool, can't you hear nor see?
'Tis nothing but some pudding bags my grandma sent to me."
"I've travelled, I've travelled some thousand miles or more
But spurs on a pudding bag I never saw before."

The old man came home again, as drunk as he could be.
"Dear wife, loving wife, 'tis curious to me,
Whose head is in the bed where mine ought to be?"
"You old fool, you blind fool, can't you hear nor see?
'Tis nothing but the milking maid my gran'ma sent to me."
"I've travelled, I've travelled some thousand miles or more
But whiskers on a milking maid I never saw before."

The Old Man Came Home Again

Photo by Charles Van Schaick, Black River Falls.

DAN DOO

Sung by Charles Dietz, age seventy-five, Monroe, Wisconsin, in 1946. The ballad is more commonly known by its variant title *The Wife Wrapt in Wether's Skin,* which refers to the wether's (ram's) skin. Mr. Dietz learned the song from his mother, who came from New York State.

There was a good old man lived out west, Dan Doo, Dan Doo;
There was a good old man lived out west,
Tom Kling-klass Mc-Kling-gle.
He had an old wife that was none of your best,
And it's harum, barum, compario,
Hicky-u-ka-tack kleming-go, Tom Kling-klass Mc-Kling-gle.

This good old man came in from his plow, Dan Doo, Dan Doo;
This good old man came in from his plow,
Tom Kling-klass Mc-Kling-gle.
Said he, "Old wife, is breakfast ready now?"
It's harum, barum, compario.
Hicky-u-ka-tack kleming-go, Tom Kling-klass Mc-Kling-gle.

"There's some dry bread and meat in on the shelf, Dan Doo, Dan Doo;
There's some dry bread and meat in on the shelf,
Tom Kling-klass Mc-Kling-gle.
If you want more than that, you can git it yourself."
And it's harum, barum, compario.
Hicky-u-ka-tack kleming-go, Tom Kling-klass Mc-Kling-gle.

This good old man went down to the sheep-fold, Dan Doo, Dan Doo;
This good old man went down to the sheep-fold,
Tom Kling-klass Mc-Kling-gle.
He caught a sheep and did him hold,
And it's harum, barum, compario.
Hicky-u-ka-tack kleming-go, Tom Kling-klass Mc-Kling-gle.

He hung this sheep on a hickory pin, Dan Doo, Dan Doo;
He hung this sheep on a hickory pin,
Tom Kling-klass Mc-Kling-gle.
And away he jerked him out of his skin,
And it's harum, barum, compario.
Hicky-u-ka-tack kleming-go, Tom Kling-klass Mc-Kling-gle.

He put this sheepskin on his old wife's back, Dan Doo, Dan Doo;
He put this sheepskin on his old wife's back,
Tom Kling-klass Mc-Kling-gle.
The two little sticks, they went whickity whack,
And it's harum, barum, compario.
Hicky-u-ka-tack kleming-go, Tom Kling-klass Mc-Kling-gle.

"I'll go tell my father and mother and all my kin, Dan Doo, Dan Doo;
I'll go tell my father and mother and all my kin,
Tom Kling-klass Mc-Kling-gle.
You've whaled me once, and you won't do it again."
And it's harum, barum, compario.
Hicky-u-ka-tack kleming-go, Tom Kling-klass Mc-Kling-gle.

"You can go and tell your father and mother and all your kin,
Tom Kling-klass Mc-Kling-gle.
But I've whaled you once and I'll do it again."
And it's harum, barum, compario.
Hicky-u-ka-tack kleming-go, Tom Kling-klass Mc-Kling-gle.

This good old man travelled fourteen miles in fifteen days, Dan Doo, Dan Doo;
This good old man travelled fourteen miles in fifteen days,
Tom Kling-klass Mc-Kling-gle.
And if you don't cut a lap getting out of the way fast,
You can harum, barum, compario.
Hicky-u-ka-tack kleming-go, Tom Kling-klass Mc-Kling-gle.

Dan Doo

There was a good old man, lived out west, Dan
Doo, Dan doo, There was a good old man, lived out west
Tom Kling-glass Mc - Klin-gle. He had an old wife that was
none of your best, and it's har-um bar-um, com-par-i-o.
Hick - y - u - ka-tack Klem-ing - go, Tom Kling-glass Mc-Klin-gle.

THERE WAS AN OLD WOMAN IN LONDON

Sung by Noble B. Brown, age sixty-one, Millville, Wisconsin, in 1946. The old woman may change her place of residence, but the story remains essentially the same in the many variant versions of this song.

Oh, there was an old woman in London,
In London she did dwell.
She loved her husband dearly,
But another man twice as well.
A-turra-lurra, turra-lurra, turra lurra lay.

She went unto the doctor,
To see what she could find,
To see what she could find
That would make the old man blind.

"Go get six dozen marrow bones
And make him suck them all,
And he will be so stone blind
That he can't see you at all."

She got six dozen marrow bones
And made him suck them all,
And he was then so stone blind
That he couldn't see her at all

Said the old man, "I would drown myself
If I could see the way."
Said she, "My dearest husband,
I will show you the way."

She took him by the tender hand
And led him to the brim.
Said the old man, "I'll not drown myself
Unless you'll push me in."

The old woman, she stepped back a pace
To give a jump and a spring.
The old man stepped to one side,
'N' the old woman, she tumbled in.

And now my song is ended,
I won't sing any more,
But wasn't she a big fool;
And he was sixty-four?

There Was an Old Woman in London

Oh there was an old wo-man in Lon-don, in Lon-don she did dwell, She loved her hus-band dear-ly, but an-oth-er man twice as well, A-tur-ra lur-ra, tur-ra lur-ra, tur-ra lur-ra lay.

WHAT WILL I DO WITH THE BABY-O?

Sung by Pearl Jacobs Borusky, age thirty-nine, Antigo, Wisconsin,
for Helene Stratman-Thomas in 1940; and for Asher Treat in 1935.

What will I do with the baby-O?	Wrap him up in calico,
What will I do with the baby-O?	Wrap him up in calico,
What will I do with the baby-O?	Wrap him up in calico,
When I go down to Jellico?	And take him to his daddy-O.

What Will I Do With the Baby-o?

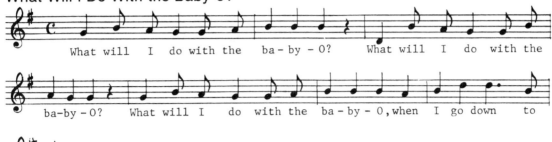

I NEVER WILL MARRY

Sung by Winifred Bundy, age seventy-five, Madison, Wisconsin, in
1941. Miss Bundy recalled her grandparents singing this song, for
which endless verses were invented to suit all occasions.

I never will marry a man who is poor.
He'd keep me a-beggin' from door to door.
Shiv-ah-roo, li-tee, di-di-dum-dum, di-di-dum-dum,
Di-di-dum-dum-dah-dee,
Shiv-ah-roo and a roo.

I never will marry a farmer's son,
For a farmer's work is never done.

I never will marry a man who gets drunk.
He sits in the corner and smells like a skunk.

I never will marry at all, at all,
But go to feast in Old Maids' Hall.
Shiv-ah-roo, li-tee, di-di-dum-dum, di-di-dum-dum,
Di-di-dum-dum-dah-dee,
Shiv-ah-roo and a roo.

I Never Will Marry

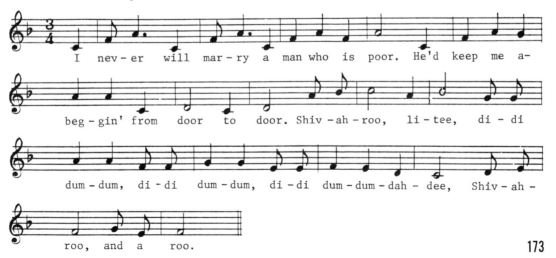

173

McCARTHY'S WIDOW

Sung by Gene Silsbe, age sixty-one, Colburn, Wisconsin, in 1941.

'Twas three years ago this very day, I took to me a wife.
And ever since she's proved to be a burden to me life.
She was the widdy of McCarthy and of course that was her name,
But for changing it to Kelly, sure she's not to blame.
She speaks about McCarthy and his virtues every day,
And she wishes I'd keep sober and be like him every way.
But she beat him with the broom stick every time the baby cried,
And made him rock the cradle 'til from cruelty he died.
Chorus: For she'd lick him, she'd kick him, she'd never let him be.
      She'd lash him, she'd slash him until he couldn't see.
      Oh, McCarthy wasn't hearty, now she has a different party.
      She might have licked McCarthy but she can't lick me.

For I'm going down to Pace's now, the purpose to get tight.
And when I do get home again, there's bound to be a fight.
I will smash up all the furniture before I do get through.
Upset the stove and — the first dumb thing I do.
The difference then in the two men, she hastily will see,
And know which is the best man, McCarthy or me.
Then, maybe she'd behave herself and learn to shut her mouth,
For if she gets me into jail, she'll have to get me out.

She said that every evening he done all the work he could;
He used to wash the dishes and he split the kindling wood.
He'd carry in the coal himself, no labor would he shirk;
He'd rinse the clothes on wash days before he went to work.
He lit the fires every morn and got the breakfast, too;
In fact, there was not anything at home he didn't do.
And if he didn't stir himself, and wash and mend his clothes
She'd often send the frying pan to try and break his nose.

McCarthy's Widow

174

wid-dy of Mc-Car-thy and of course, that was her

name, But for chang-ing it to Kel-ly, sure she's not to

blame. She speaks a-bout Mc-Car-thy and his

vir-tues ev-ery day, and she wish-es I'd keep

so-ber and be like him ev-ery way. But she

beat him with the broom-stick ev-ery time the ba-by

cried, And made him rock the cra-dle 'til from

cruel-ty he died. For she'd lick him, she'd

kick him, she'd nev-er let him be. She'd lash him, she'd

slash him un-til he could'-nt see. Oh, Mc-

Car-thy was'-nt heart-y, now she has a differ-ent

par-ty. She might have licked Mc-Car-thy but she

can't lick me.

LIZA

Sung by Eryl Levers, age twenty-four, Madison, Wisconsin, in 1946.

Oh, Liza, dear Liza,
If you end up an old maid,
You've only got yourself to blyme.
Oh, Liza, dear Liza,
Mrs. Henry Hawkins is a first-class nyme.

Liza

Oh Li - za, dear Li - za, If you end up an old maid, You've on - ly got your-self to blyme, Oh Li - za, dear Li - za. Mis-sus Hen - ry Haw - kins is a first class nyme.

OF LATE I'VE BEEN DRIVEN NEAR CRAZY

Sung by Lester A. Coffee, age seventy-five, Harvard, Illinois, in 1946. Coffee heard this song as a small boy at the same circus where he heard *The Donkey*.

Of late I've been driven near crazy
All on account of my wife.
She ran away with a Chinee
And left me to mourn all my life.
I wrote her a million of letters
And asked her my faults to forget.
No matter how many I wrote her,
These are the answers I get.

Wait 'til the gang on the corner
Refuses to take a big bowl.
Wait 'til the bank robbers in Canada
Bring back all the money they stole.
When Jay Gould and the great Knights of Labor
And all the trade unions agree,
And the people don't back-bite their neighbors
Then, my darling, I'll come back to thee.

She stole all my clothes and my money.
She left me as poor as a mouse.
Her actions were awfully funny.
She stole all I had in the house.
But I wrote her and said I'd forgive her
If she would but come back again.
This morning I received a large letter
And this is what it did contain.

Wait 'til the actors and married men
Agree with all business men.
Wait 'til we find one who's hen-pecked
That's in love with his mother-in-law.
When the K.C.'s and Eagles and Masons
Unite in a grand jubilee.
When the Chinese rule this nation
Then, my darling, I'll come back to thee.

176

Of Late I've Been Driven Near Crazy

Of late I've been driv-en near cra-zy, All on ac-count of my

wife. She ran a-way with a Chi-nee, And left me to

mourn all my life. I wrote her a mil-lion of let-ters, And

asked her my faults to for-get. No mat-ter how ma-ny I

wrote her, These are some of the an-swers I get.

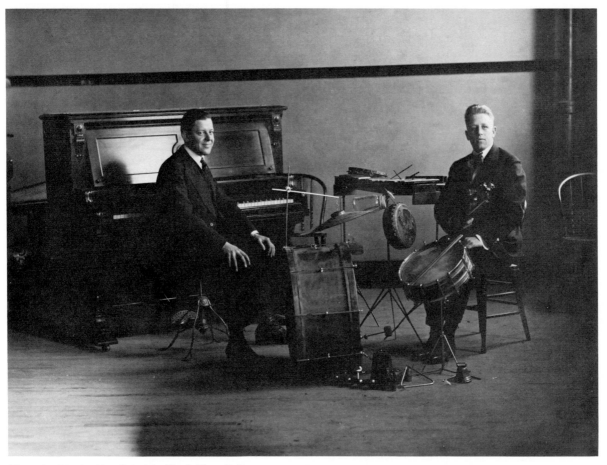

Photo by Charles Van Schaick, Black River Falls.

OLD AGE

LITTLE OLD LOG CABIN IN THE LANE

Sung by Aunt Lily Richmond, age eighty-four, Lancaster, Wisconsin, in 1946. The singer was the last surviving member of a group of slaves which fled Missouri near the end of the Civil War and settled near Lancaster in Grant County.

I am getting old and feeble now and cannot work no more.
Old Mister Sand and Massa are lying side by side,
And their spirits are roving with the blessed.
The things, they have changed, the darkies dead and gone.
I cannot hear them singing in the cane.
All the friends that they have left me is that little dog of mine,
In the little old log cabin in the lane.

Little Old Log Cabin in the Lane

178

Vicinity of Glenbeulah, Sheboygan County, ca. 1880.
Iconographic Collection, SHSW.

UNCLE JOE

Sung by Moses Morgan, age sixty-seven, Pickett, Wisconsin, in 1940. Morgan learned this song at the age of seven from his grandfather.

Young folks, come listen to my song.
I know you'll want to come along.
I've said before and I'll have you know
That the young folks call me Uncle Joe.
My hair was black, now all turned grey.
But what's the while, I feel gay.
I love to sing that song of glee
For it makes me young as I used to be.

When I was young, I knew life's joy.
But now I'm old, yet, I'm one of the boys.
I can take a snort, or sing a song
With any good friend that comes along.
I can tell a story or crack a joke
And never refuse to drink or smoke.
I'm a gay old sport and you'll all agree
That I feel as young as I used to be.

When I was young and in my prime
I was chasing the girls most of the time.
I'd take them out each day for a ride
I'd always have one by my side.
I'd hug and kiss them just for fun
And _____ done.
So if any girl here that's in love with me
She'll find me as young as I used to be.

I love to sing that song of glee
For it makes me young as I used to be.

179

Uncle Joe

Young folks, come lis-ten to my song. I know you'll want to come a-long. I've said be-fore and I'll have you know that the young folks call me Un-cle Joe. My hair was black, now all turned grey, but what's the care while I feel gay. I love to sing that song of glee, for it makes me young as I used to be.

JUST PLAIN FOLKS

Sung by Bessie Gordon, age forty, Schofield, Wisconsin, in 1941.

To a mansion in the city came a couple old and grey
To meet their son that left them long ago.
He had prospered and grown wealthy, since in youth he ran away,
But now his life was one of pomp and show.
But coldly did he greet them for his friends were by his side,
Who often heard him boast of home so grand.
But the old man sadly looked at him and said in modest pride,
As he gently took his dear wife by the hand;
"We are just plain folks, your mother and me.
Just plain folk, like our folks used to be.
As our presence seems to grieve you, we will roll away and leave you
For we're sadly out of place here, 'cause we're just plain folks."

Just Plain Folks

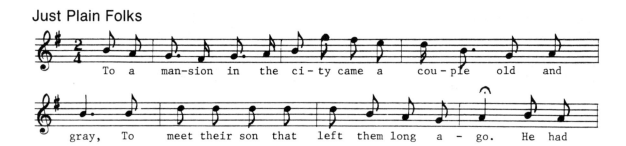

To a man-sion in the ci-ty came a cou-ple old and gray, To meet their son that left them long a-go. He had

180

pros - pered and grown weal - thy since in youth he ran a - way, but

now his life was one of pomp and show. But cold - ly did he

greet them for his friends were by his side, who'd of - ten heard him

boast of home so grand. But the old man sad - ly looked at him and

said in mod - est pride, as he gen - tly took his dear wife by the

hand. "we are just plain folks, your mo - ther and me. Just plain

folks like our own folks used to be. As our pres - ence seems to

grieve you we will roll a - way and leave you for we're

sad - ly out of place here, 'cause we're just plain folks.

ONCE I HAD TWO HANDS FULL OF GOLD

Sung by Pearl Jacobs Borusky, age thirty-nine, Antigo, Wisconsin, in 1940.

I once had two hands full of gold,
Beside a plentiful store,
But I didn't have a shoe to my foot,
Nor a hat upon my head,
Nor a hat upon my head.

181

Once I Had Two Hands Full of Gold

I once had two hands full of gold Be - side a plen - ti - ful store. But I did - n't have a shoe to my foot, Nor a hat up - on my head, nor a hat up-on my head.

XYZ Singers, Milwaukee, 1965.
Photo by *Milwaukee Sentinel.*

HARD TIMES

THE HOMESTEAD STRIKE

This song about the great Homestead Strike of 1892 in Pennsylvania was found among the papers of Helene Stratman-Thomas. The singer is unknown.

Oh, the trouble down at Homestead, it came about this way,
When a grasping corporation had the audacity to say:
"You must give up your income and forswear your liberty,
And we'll offer you a glorious chance to die in slavery."

The man who fights for honor, none can blame him.
May good luck attend him where he roams.
No son of his will ever live to shame him
When liberty and honor rule the homes.

The Homestead Strike

Oh, the trou-ble down at Home-stead it came a-bout this way, When a grasp-ing cor-po-ra-tion had the au-dac-i-ty to say: "You must give up your in-come and for-swear your lib-er-ty. And we'll of-fer you a glor-ious chance to die in slav-e-ry." The man who fights for hon-or, none can blame him. May good luck at-tend him where he roams. No son of his will ev-er live to shame him When lib-er-ty and hon-or rule the homes.

FOND DU LAC JAIL

Sung by Charles Robinson, age seventy-six, Marion, Wisconsin, in 1941. Helene Stratman-Thomas' notes indicate that this song had at least five more verses, and that she never encountered it again in her collecting.

In the morning you receive a dry loaf of bread
That's hard as a stone and heavy as lead.
It's thrown from the ceiling down into your cell,
Like coming from Heaven popped down into Hell.
Oh, there's hard times in Fond du Lac jail,
There's hard times, I say.

Your bed it is made of old rotten rugs,
Get up in the morning all covered with bugs.
And the bugs they will swear that unless you get bail
You're bound to go lousy in Fond du Lac jail.
Oh, there's hard times in Fond du Lac jail,
There's hard times, I say.

Fond Du Lac Jail

SAMUEL SMALL

Sung by Fanny Boulden, Larimore, North Dakota, for Franz Rickaby in 1923. Miss Boulden said that she learned this song from young people and students who sang it at her home. A manuscript version of the song, given to Rickaby by Dr. Harry Whitcomb of Grand Forks, North Dakota, was annotated thus: "The ballad of a deck-hand about to be hung for the killing of his work-mate, and sung from the scaffold. The blanks in the last stanza are left blank in the singing also."

Oh, my name is Samuel Small, Samuel Small.
Oh, my name is Samuel Small,
And I hate you one and all.
You're a gang of muckers all,
Damn yer eyes!

Oh, I killed a man they said, so they said.
Yes, I killed a man they said,
For I cracked him on the head,
And I left him there for dead,
Damn his eyes!

So they put me in the quad, in the quad.
Yes, they put me in the quad,
With a chain and iron rod,
And they left me there, by God!
Damn their eyes!

And the parson he did come, he did come.
And the parson he did come,
And he looked so — — glum
With his talk o' kingdom come,
Damn his eyes!

And the sheriff he came too, he came too.
And the sheriff he came too,
With his boys all dressed in blue—
They're a gang o' muckers too,
Damn their eyes!

So it's up the rope ye go, up ye go.
So it's up the rope ye go,
With yer friends all down below,
Saying, "Sam, I told ye so!"
Damn their eyes!

Saw my Nellie in the crowd, in the crowd.
Saw my Nellie in the crowd,
And I hollered right out loud,
"Needn't look so — — — proud,
Damn yer eyes!"

So this'll be my knell, be my knell.
So this'll be my knell,
Hope to — — — ye go to hell,
Hope to — — — ye sizzle well,
Damn yer eyes!

Samuel Small

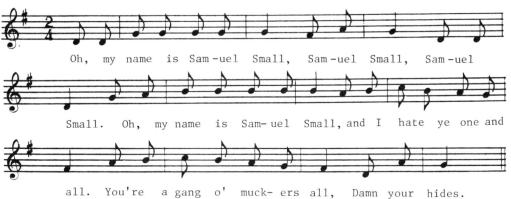

Oh, my name is Sam-uel Small, Sam-uel Small, Sam-uel Small. Oh, my name is Sam-uel Small, and I hate ye one and all. You're a gang o' muck-ers all, Damn your hides.

RAMSEY COUNTY JAIL

Sung by Lester A. Coffee, age seventy-five, Harvard, Illinois, in 1946. Coffee said that he considered this song an old one when he learned it as a boy.

Last night as I lay sleeping,
I had a pleasant dream.
I thought I was in Minnesota,
Down by a quiet stream
With a charming gal beside me.
The lights would never fail
And I awoke to find myself, be God
In the Ramsey County Jail.

Then combine, ye hump and biddy,
From Tepperty town I steer.
Like every honest fellow
I like my lager beer.

Like every jolly young fellow
I take my whiskey clear.
I've a rambling rake of a father
And the son of a gamboleer.

They took me to the prison.
They locked me twenty and four.
They gave me all that I could eat
But I always wanted more.
The beds were of the finest
And sleeping never failed
For the feathers they did tickle me so
In the Ramsey County Jail.

Ramsey County Jail

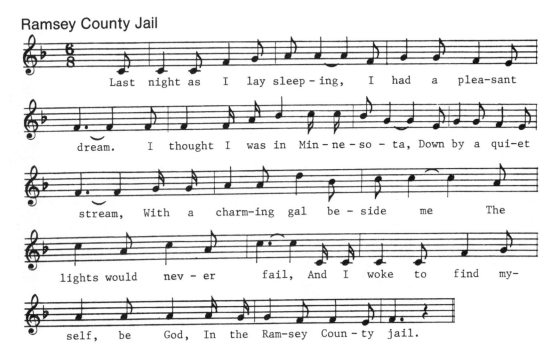

STOKES'S VERDICT

Sung by George Hankens, age seventy, Gordon, Wisconsin, for Franz Rickaby in 1923.

If you'll listen awhile I'll sing you a song
About this glorious land of the free,
And the difference I'll show twixt the rich and the poor
In a trial by jury, you see.

If you've plenty of "stamps" you can hold up your head
And walk out from your own prison door.
But they'll hang you up high if you've no friends or gold,
Let the "rich" go but hang up the poor.

In the trials for murder we've had now-a-days
The rich ones get off swift and sure.
While they've thousands to pay to the jury and judge,
You can bet they'll go back on the poor.

Let me speak of a man who's now dead in his grave,
A good man as ever was born.
Jim Fisk he was called and his money he gave
To the outcast, the poor and forlorn.

We all know he loved both women and wine,
But his heart it was right, I am sure.
Though he lived like a "prince" in a palace so fine,
Yet he never went back on the poor.

If a man was in trouble, Fisk helped him along
To drive the "grim wolf" from the door.
He strove to do right, though he may have done wrong,
But he never went back on the poor.

Jim Fisk was a man who wore "his heart on his sleeve."
No matter what people would say,
And he did all his deeds, (both the good and the bad)
In the broad open light of the day.

With his grand six-in-hand on the beach at Long Branch
He cut a "big dash," to be sure.
But "Chicago's great fire" showed the world that Jim Fisk
With his "wealth" still remembered the poor.

When the telegram came that the homeless that night
Were starving to death, slow but sure,
His "Lightning Express" manned by noble Jim Fisk
Flew to feed all her hungry and poor.

Now what do you think of this trial of Stokes,
Who murdered this friend of the poor?
When such men get free, is there anyone safe
If they step from outside their own door?

Is there one law for the poor and one for the rich?
It seems so—at least so I say—
If they hang up the poor, why—damn it—the rich
Ought to hang up the very same way.

Don't show any favor to friend or to foe,
The beggar or prince at his door.
The big millionaire you must hang up also
But never go back on the poor.

Oh! Shame on this "land of the free and the brave"
When such sights as this meet our eye!
The poor in their prisons are treated like slaves
While the rich in their cells they live high.

A poor devil "crazy with drink" they will hang
For a murder he didn't intend,
But a wealthy assassin with "political friends"
Gets off, for he's money to spend.

But if things go on this way we'll stand it no more.
The people will rise up in bands.
A vigilance committee we'll raise on our shores
And take the law in our own hands.

Stokes's Verdict

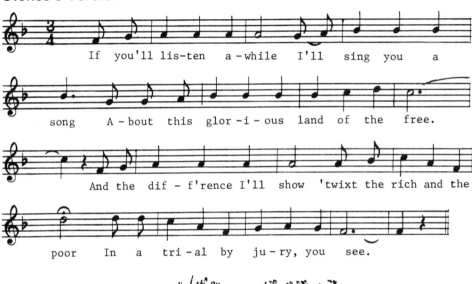

If you'll lis-ten a-while I'll sing you a
song A-bout this glor-i-ous land of the free.
And the dif-f'rence I'll show 'twixt the rich and the
poor In a tri-al by ju-ry, you see.

CRIME & OUTLAWRY

DICK TURPIN AND BLACK BESS

Sung by William Jacobs Morgan, age seventy-six, Berlin, Wisconsin, in 1946. Legends and songs abound about Dick Turpin, the English highwayman who was hanged in 1739.

When Fortune's blind goddess had shied my abode,
And friends proved unfaithful, I took to the road,
To plunder the wealthy, to relieve my distress,
And to aid me, I bought you, my bonny Black Bess.

How still you would stand when some carriage I'd stop,
While I picked up the jewels its inmates had dropped.
I ne'er robbed a poor man, nor did I distress
The widow or orphan, my bonny Black Bess.

When sable's black midnight her mantle had spread,
O'er the fair face of nature, how softly you tread.
Through fate or good fortune, though an unwelcome guest,
We took millions of fortune, my bonny Black Bess.

When Arden's famed justice did me hotly pursue,
From London to Yorktown, like lightning you flew.
No tollgate could stop you, broad rivers you crossed;
You took me in ten hours, my bonny Black Bess.

Ill fate now comes o'er me, and oppressed is my lot;
The law now pursues me for the man that I shot.
To save me, dear Bessie, you did do your best;
You are worn out and weary, my bonny Black Bess.

Hark, the bloodhounds approacheth, but they never can catch
A beast like you, Bessie, so gallant and brave.
You must die, my dear friend, oh, it does me oppress;
Lie there, I have shot you, my bonny Black Bess.

In future's bright ages, when I'm dead and gone,
My story be handed from father to son.
Though some may pity, yet they all must confess,
'Twas in kindness I shot you, my bonny Black Bess.

Now I'll climb yonder sapling, so stately and tall,
And there I'll await the swift fatal ball.
I'll die like a man, and I'll soon be at rest;
Fare thee well now forever, my bonny Black Bess.

Dick Turpin and Black Bess

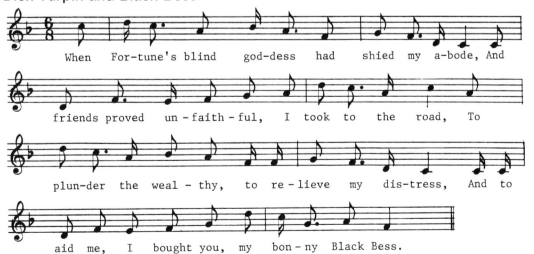

When For-tune's blind god-dess had shied my a-bode, And
friends proved un-faith-ful, I took to the road, To
plun-der the weal-thy, to re-lieve my dis-tress, And to
aid me, I bought you, my bon-ny Black Bess.

THE CHARMING YOUNG WIDOW I MET ON THE TRAIN

Sung by Lewis Winfield Moody, age seventy-six, Plainfield, Wisconsin, in 1941.

I live in Vermont and one morning last summer,
A letter informed me my uncle was dead.
And also requested I'd come down to Boston
As he's left me a large sum of money it said.
Of course I determined on making the journey,
And to book myself by the first class I was fain.
Though had I gone second, I'd have never encountered
The charming young widow I met on the train.

The widow and I, side by side, sat together
The seat it contained us two and no more.
The silence was broken by my fair companion
Who inquired the time by the watch that I wore.

I, of course, satisfied her, and then conversation
Fell _____ both to addle my brain.
Better _____ with excitement I fell so
Enchanted with the charming young widow I met on the train.

The train she rolled on 'til she stopped at the station.
A station _____ a few miles from Boston town.
My companion exclaimed as she looked out the window,
"Great heavens alive, there goes Minister Brown."

"He's my late husband's brother, oh would you so kindly
Detain him a moment, my child to maintain?"
Of course, I accepted the offer. To the platform
Tripped the charming young widow I met on the train.

But in my _____ I sought for
Oh, where was my watch, and where was my chain?
My ticket, purse and gold pencil were gone, sir.
And so was the widow I met on the train.

I warn all young men, who ride on the railway
To never get caught a similar way.
Beware of one who wiggle their right arm,
Who dress in deep mourning and their tears fall like rain.
Beware of your pocketbook, should they resemble
That charming young widow I met on the train.

190

The Charming Young Widow I Met on the Train

I live in Ver -mont and one morn-ing last sum-mer, a let-ter in - formed me my un - cle was dead. And al-so re- quest-ed I'd come down to Bos - ton as he'd left me a large sum of mon-ey, it said. Of course I de - ter-mined on mak - ing the jour - ney, And to book my-self by the first class I was fain. Though had I gone se-cond I'd have nev-er en - count-ered the charm - ing young wid - ow I met on the train.

BRENNEN ON THE MOOR

Sung by William J. Morgan, age seventy-six, Berlin, Wisconsin, in 1946. The song is also found in the notebooks of Franz Rickaby, who collected it from William N. Allen of Wausau. Allen told him that he patterned his ballad, *S. D. Knowles,* after *Brennen on the Moor.*

'Tis of a famous highwayman a long story I will tell.
His name was Willie Brennen and in Ireland he did dwell.
'Twas on the Calvert mountains he began his wild career.
And many a wealthy gentleman before him shook with fear.
Chorus: Brennen on the moor, Brennen on the moor,
      So bold, gay, and undaunted stood young Brennen on the moor.

A brace of loaded pistols he carried night and day.
He never robbed a poor man upon the king's highway.
But he'd taken from the rich, like Turpin and Black Bess,
He did divide it with a widow in distress.

One day he met a packman by the name of Cooler Bawn.
They traveled on together till the day began to dawn.
When Cooler found his money gone, likewise his watch and chain,
He then encountered Brennen and he robbed him back again.

Now Willie seeing the packman was as good a man as he,
He took him on the highway his comrade for to be.
The packman threw away his pack without any more delay
And he formed a faithful comrade until his dying day.

One day upon the highway as Willie he sat down
He saw the Mayor of Casuel a mile outside the town.
The Mayor he knew his features. "I think, you man," said he,
"Your name is Willie Brennen. You must come along with me."

Now Willie's wife she being in town, provisions for to buy,
When she saw her Willie she began to weep and cry.
I wish I had the temperers, as soon as Willie spoke.
She handed him a blunderbuss from underneath her cloak.

Now with his loaded blunderbuss the truth he did unfold.
He made the Mayor to tremble and robbed him of his gold.
Five thousand pounds were offered for his apprehension there,
And with his horse and saddle to the mountains did repair.

Now Willie being an outlaw upon the mountain high,
With cavalry and infantry to take him they did try.
He lay upon the briars that grew thick upon the field
Till he received a dozen wounds before that he would yield.

Brennen on the Moor

'Tis of a fam-ous high-way-man a story I will tell. His name was Wil-lie Bren-nen and in Ire-land he did dwell. 'Twas on the Cal-vert moun-tains he began his wild ca-reer, and ma-ny a wealth-y gen-tle-man be-fore him shook with fear. Bold and un-daunt-ed stood bold Bren-nen on the moor; Bren-nen on the moor, Bren-nen on the moor. Bold and un-daunt-ed stood bold Bren-nen on the moor.

192

Street musicians, Madison, ca. 1900.
Iconographic Collection, SHSW.

MURDER

MY FATHER KEEPS A PUBLIC HOUSE

Sung by Pearl Jacobs Borusky, age thirty-nine, Antigo, Wisconsin, in 1940.

My father keeps a public house
Down by the seaside shore,
And when you come to stay all night
He'll meet you at the door.

"I'll meet you in the morning—
Don't let your parents know.
My name it is young Edward Bolds,
Who plows the lowlands low."

Young Mary she lay sleeping.
She dreamed a frightful dream.
She dreamed she saw her true-love's blood
Come flowing in a stream.

Then she arose, put on her clothes
Just at the break of day,
Saying, "Father, where is that young man
Came here last night to stay?"

"His body sleeps within the deep—
Just where I do not know,
I sent his body bleeding
Into the lowlands low."

"Oh, father, cruel father,
You shall die a public show
For the murder of young Edward Bolds,
Who plowed the lowlands low."

My Father Keeps a Public House

194

DIRANDEL

Sung by Winifred Bundy, age fifty-seven, Madison, Wisconsin, in 1941. Miss Bundy conceded that "Dirandel" might have been a corruption of "Lord Randall" incurred as the song was passed from singer to singer; but this is the way she learned it.

Oh, where have ye been Dirandel, my son?
Oh, where have ye been my loving sweet one?
I've been to true love. Mother, make my bed soon
For I'm poisoned to the heart and I fain would lie down.

What had ye for dinner Dirandel, my son?
What had ye for dinner my loving sweet one?
Eels fried in butter. Mother, make my bed soon
For I'm poisoned to the heart and I fain would lie down.

And who had your leavings Dirandel, my son?
Oh who had your leavings my loving sweet one?
My hawks and my hounds. Mother, make my bed soon
For I'm poisoned to the heart and I fain would lie down.

Then where are your hounds Dirandel, my son?
Then where are your hounds my loving sweet one?
They swelled and they died. Mother, make my bed soon
For I'm poisoned to the heart and I fain would lie down.

I fear ye are poisoned Dirandel, my son.
I fear ye are poisoned my loving sweet one.
Oh yes, I am poisoned. Mother, make my bed soon
For my low love she is false and I fain would lie down.

What will you leave to your brother, Dirandel, my son?
What will you leave to your brother my loving sweet one?
My house and my lands. Mother, make my bed soon
For I'm poisoned to the heart and I fain would lie down.

What will you leave to your sister, Dirandel, my son?
What will you lave to your sister my loving sweet one?
My gold and my silvers. Mother, make my bed soon
For I'm poisoned to the heart and I fain would lie down.

What will you leave to your true love, Dirandel, my son?
What will you leave to your true love my loving sweet one?
Hellfire and brimstone. Mother, make my bed soon
For I'm poisoned to the heart and I fain would lie down.

Dirandel

Oh, where have you been, Di - ran - del, my son? Oh, where ha' ye been, my lov - ing sweet one? I've been to my true love, mo - ther make my bed soon, for I'm poi - soned to the heart and I fain would lie down.

ROWAN COUNTY TROUBLE

Sung by Grant Faulkner, age seventy-one, Crandon, Wisconsin, in 1941.

Come all ye young men and ladies, fathers and mothers too,
I cite to you the history of the Rowan County crew
Concerning bloody clan war and the many that are dead.
My friends, please give attention, remember how it read.

It was in the month of August and on election day,
John Martin he was wounded, they say by Willie Day.
Martin could not believe it, he could not think it so
He thought that Floyd Tolerud struck the fatal blow.

Martin did recover, some months then came to pass,
That in the town of Morehead those men both met at last.
Culver with a — too, about the street did walk
They seemed to be uneasy, no one wished to talk.

He stepped up to the grocery, he stepped up to the bar
But little did he think, dear friends, it was the fatal hour.
The sting of death was near him, Martin shot him at the door
If you were placed between them, guns sounding loud before.

The people they were frightened, they rushed out of the room.
A ball from Martin's pistol laid Culver in the tomb.
His friends soon gathered round him, his wife to weep and wail.
Martin was arrested and then confined in jail.

Placed in the jail of Rowan, there to remain awhile
In the hands of law and justice to bravely stand his trial.
The people talked of lynching him, at present, though they failed.
The prisoner's friends then moved him to the Winchester jail.

Some persons forged an order, their names I do not know.
The plan was soon agreed upon, for Martin they did go.
Martin seemed disturbed, he seemed to be in dread.
"They've got a plan to kill me," to the jailer Martin said.

They placed the handcuffs on him, his heart was in distress.
They hurried to the station, stepped on the Line Express.
Along the line she lumbered, all at her usual speed.
There were but two in number to commit this dreadful deed.

Martin was in the smoking car, accompanied by his wife
They did not want her present while taking her husband's life.
When they arrived at Barnard they had no time to lose
A man approached the engineer and bid him not to move.

They stepped up to the prisoner with pistols in their hands.
In death he soon was sinking, he died a wretched man.
His wife had heard the horrid sound, she was in another car.
She cried, "Oh Lord, they've killed him," when she heard the pistol fired.

I composed this as a warning, oh beware young man!
Your pistol will cause trouble, on this you may depend.
In the bottom of the whiskey glass, the scheming devil dwells
Burns the breast of those who drink it, and sends their souls to Hell.

Rowan County Trouble

Come all ye young men and la-dies, Fa-thers and mo-thers too. I cite to you the his-tory of the Round Coun-ty crew, Con-cern-ing blood-y clan war, and the ma-ny that are dead. My friends please give at-ten-tion, re-mem-ber how it read.

SHOTS ECHOING 'ROUND THE MOUNTAIN

Sung by Luther Royce, age twenty-eight, White Lake, Wisconsin, in 1941. According to Mr. Royce, this song about a Tennessee feud originated in Kentucky. He learned it from his grandmother's "collection on old pieces of paper in handwritin'."

Down in the Tennessee mountains,
Away from the sins of the world,
Dan Kelly's son, there he leaned on his gun,
A-thinking of Seth Terney's girl.
Dan was a hot-blooded youngster,
His dad raised him sturdy and right.
He had him sworn from the day he was born,
To shoot ev'ry Terney on sight.

Vowed he had shot from the Terney,
"Don't leave a hair on their head,"
Old Danny cried, as he laid down and died,
With young Danny there by his bed.
Dan took the vow from his pappy;
He swore he would kill ev'ryone,
His heart and the world, and his love for the girl,
He loaded his double-barrelled gun.

Moon shinin' down on the mountain,
Moon shinin' down on the hill,
Dan took a sip, swung his gun to his hip,
He set out to slaughter and kill.
Over the mountains he wandered,
This son of a Tennessee man,
With fire in his eye, and his gun at his side,
Looking for Seth Terney's clan.

Shots ringin' out from the mountain,
Shots ringin' out from the trees,
Dan Kelly's son, with the smoke in his gun,
The Terneys all down on their knees.
The story of Dan Kelly's vict'ry
Has spread far and wide o'er the world,
How Dan killed the clan, shot 'em down, to a man,
And brought back old Seth Terney's girl.

197

Shots Echoing 'Round the Mountain

Down in the Ten-nes-see moun-tains, A-way from the sins of the world. Dan Kel-ley's son, and he leaned on his gun, A-think-ing of Zeb Ter-ney's girl. Dan was a hot-blood-ed young-ster; His dad raised him stur-dy and right. He had him sworn from the day he was born to shoot ev-ery Ter-ney on sight.

'TWAS ON A COLD AND WINTER'S DAY

Sung by Pearl Jacobs Borusky, age forty, Pearson, Wisconsin, for Helene Stratman-Thomas in 1941; and for Asher Treat in 1935. Jean Richey, the popular contemporary folk singer, confirms the English origins of this song, which sometimes bears the title *The Jew's Garden.* She adds that Ben Mandell of New York City used to sing the song in a Brooklyn setting under the title *Johnnie and Willie.*

'Twas on a cold and winter's day.
The children had all gone to school
And they were all a-playing ball
And dancing all around.

They knocked it high and they knocked it dry
And they knocked 'gainst the Jew's castle wall.
Go in, go in, my little boy, Hugh,
Go in and get your ball!

I mustn't go in, I durst not go in
My school bell doth me call.
And if my master knew of this
He would surely make my blood boil!

Out stepped the Jew's daughter
With apples in her hand.
Come in, come in my little boy, Hugh,
And I'll give you one or two.

She took him by his little white hand
And led him through the hall.
She laid him into a stone wall
Where no one could hear him call.

She pierced him with a little pen knife
Which was both sharp and keen.
She wrapped him in a sheet of lead
And made a fold or two.

And threw him into a draw well,
Which was both cool and deep.

The day had fled, the night came on
The children had all gone home.

And every mother had her son,
But little Hugh's mother had none.

She broke her switch all off of the birch
And through the streets she ran.

She ran till she came to the Jew's gate,
And the Jews were all asleep.

She ran 'til she came to the draw well,
Which was both cold and deep.
Saying, "If you are here my little boy, Hugh,
Speak a word to your mother dear."

"Oh, here I am, dear Mother," he cried,
"And here I lain so long.
With a little pen knife pierced through my heart
And my blood still running strong."

"Oh, take me out of this draw well
And make me a coffin of birch.
Oh, take me out of this draw well
And lay me in yonder church."

'Twas on a Cold and Winter's Day

'Twas on a cold and win-ters day, the chil-dren had all gone to

school, and they were all a-play-ing ball and danc-ing all a-

round.

SIX KINGS' DAUGHTERS

Sung by Charles Dietz, age seventy-five, Monroe, Wisconsin, in 1946. This is one of the most widely circulated ballads in the world. Versions of it occur in southern as well as northern Europe; it is sung in Germany and Scandinavia, and it enjoys an extraordinary currency in Poland. Mr. Dietz learned the song from his English mother, who brought it to Wisconsin from New York State. He said that this ballad, like many others that he sang, were not sung in southern Wisconsin: "I cannot recall ever hearing them except in our own family. They most certainly did not come to me from anywhere in the South, either directly or indirectly. They are purely, as I have said, either English or Scotch."

Now mount you on the milk white steed
And I will mount the gray.
And we will ride to London town
And married we will be, be, be.
And married we will be.

She mounted on the milk white steed
And he the dapple gray.
He meant not to ride to London town
But he rode 'til they came to the sea, sea, sea.
He rode 'til they came to the sea.

Mount off, mount off, my pretty Polly
And tie your horse to a tree.
Mount off, mount off, my pretty Polly
For I've something to say to thee, thee, thee.
I've something to say to thee.

For six kings' daughters have I drowned here
And you the seventh shall be, shall be.
And you the seventh shall be.

Pull off, pull off, those costly robes
And lay them down by me.
They are too fine, those costly robes
To lay mouldering in the sea, sea, sea.
To lay mouldering in the sea.

She bade him turn himself about
And face the green willow tree.

Then jumped she up, so nimble and quick
And plunged him in the sea, sea, sea.
And plunged him in the sea.

Lie there, lie there you false-hearted knight.
Lie there instead of me.
For six kings' daughters you've drowned here
But the seventh has now drowned thee, thee, thee.
But the seventh has now drowned thee.

She mounted again the milk-white steed
And she led the dapple gray.
They rode 'til she came to her father's house
Three long hours before it was day, day, day.
Three long hours before it was day.

Six Kings' Daughters

Now mount you on the milk-white steed, and
I will mount the grey, And we will ride to
Lon-don town, and mar-ried we will be, be, be, and
mar-ried we will be.

THE FARMER HAD A DAUGHTER

Sung by Pearl Jacobs Borusky, age forty, Pearson, Wisconsin, in 1941. Mrs. Treat sang this song for Asher Treat in 1938 and again for Helene Stratman-Thomas in 1941. The origin of the song is English. Mrs. Borusky, who was born in Kentucky, brought it to Wisconsin as a little girl.

A farmer had a daughter
Whose beauty ne'er was told.
Her parents died and left her
Five hundred pounds in gold.
She lived with her uncle
Who caused her all her woe
And if you'll but list' to this pretty fair miss,
I'll prove it all to you.

Her uncle had a plow-boy
That Mary loved so well.
The way she loved that plow-boy
No human tongue could tell.
There was a wealthy squire
Came Mary for to see,
But she loved her uncle's plow-boy
On the banks of the Sweet and Dee.

A press-gang came to Willie
When he was all alone
He bravely fought for liberty,
But they were six to one.
His blood it flowed in torrents.
"Pray kill me now!" said he,
"For I'd rather die for Mary
On the banks of the Sweet and Dee."

One day while she was walking,
Lamenting for her love,
She spied this wealthy squire
Down in her uncle's grove.
He took a step toward her.
"Stand back, young man!" said she,
"For you've banished the only one I love
On the banks of the Sweet and Dee."

He threw his arms around her
And strove to set her down.
She spied a sword and pistol
Beneath his morning gown.
She drew the pistol from its belt,
The sword she used so free.
The pistol fired and the squire fell
On the banks of the Sweet and Dee.

Her uncle heard the noise
And hastened to the ground,
Saying, "Now you've killed my squire,
I'll give you your death wound."
"Stand back! Stand back!" said Mary,
"Stand back! Stand back!" said she.
The sword she drew and her uncle slew
On the banks of the Sweet and Dee.

A doctor was sent for,
A man of note and skill,
And also a lawyer,
That he might write his will.
He willed his gold to Mary
Who fought so manfully.
Then he closed his eyes no more to rise
On the banks of the Sweet and Dee.

The Farmer Had a Daughter

A farm-er had a daugh-ter Whose beau-ty ne'er was told. Her par-ents died and left her five hund-red pounds in gold. She lived with her un-cle who caused her all her woe, And if you'll but list to this pret-ty fair miss, I'll prove it all to you.

DEATH

LORD LOVELL

Sung by Winifred Bundy, age fifty-seven, Madison, Wisconsin, in 1941. This song demonstrates the necessity of considering ballads as songs, rather than merely as poems; for while the text is sad and mournful, the tune is lilting and rollicking, turning the tear into a smile.

Lord Lovell he stood at his castle gate,
A-combing his milk-white steed,
When along came Lady Nancy Belle,
A-wishing her lover good speed, speed, speed,
A-wishing her lover good speed.

"O where are you going, Lord Lovell?" she cried,
"O where are you going?" cried she.
"I'm going, my dear Lady Nancy Belle,
Strange countries for to see, see, see,
Strange countries for to see."

"When will you be back, Lord Lovell?" she cried,
"When will you be back?" cried she.
"In a year or two, or three, or more,
I'll return to you, Lady Nancy, cy, cy,
I'll return to you, Lady Nancy."

He had not been gone but a year and a day,
Strange countries for to see,
When languishing thoughts came into his mind,
Lady Nancy Belle he would see, see, see,
Lady Nancy Belle he would see.

He rode and he rode on his milk-white steed,
'Till he came to London town,
And there he heard the church bells ring,
And the people all mourning around, round, round,
And the people all mourning around.

"O who is dead?" Lord Lovell he said,
"O who is dead?" said he.
"A lady is dead," the people all said,
"And they call her the Lady Nancy, cy, cy,
And they call her the Lady Nancy."

He ordered the grave to be opened forthwith,
The shroud to be folded down,
And there he kissed her clay-cold lips,
Till the tears came trickling down, down, down,
Till the tears came trickling down.

Lady Nancy she died as it might be today;
Lord Lovell he died tomorrow.
Lady Nancy she died out of pure, pure grief;
Lord Lovell he died out of sorrow, sorrow, sorrow,
Lord Lovell he died out of sorrow.

Lady Nancy was laid in the cold church-yard;
Lord Lovell was laid in the choir,
And out of her bosom there grew a red rose,
And out of his backbone, a briar, briar, briar,
And out of his backbone a briar.

They grew and they grew till they reached the church top,
And they couldn't grow up any higher,
And there they entwined in a true lovers' knot,
Such as true lovers ever admire, mire, mire,
Such as true lovers ever admire.

202

Lord Lovell

Lord Lov - ell, he stood at his cas - tle gate, a-
comb - ing his milk-white steed. When a-long came la - dy
Nan - cy Belle, a - wish - ing her lov - er good
speed, speed, speed, a - wish - ing her lov - er good-
speed.

GHOST SONG

Given to Helene Stratman-Thomas by Mrs. Moody Price, age seventy-one, Dodgeville, Wisconsin, in 1946. Mrs. Price said that her mother had sung it in the 1880's. "This tune is a mournful dirge," she added, "and Moody [her husband] utterly despises it, so I did not dare sing it for you, but Mother could sing it and scream so really dreadful that people would jump most off their chairs."

There was an old woman, all skin and bone,
She lived in a churchyard all alone.
An' she looked up and she looked down
She spied an old man on the ground.
An' from his toes unto his chin
The worms crawled out and the worms crawled in.
She looked up to the clock and cried,
"Will I be so when I have died?"
"Oh, yes! Oh, yes!" the clock replied;
She gave a [real screech here] and then she died.

203

THE BUTCHER BOY

Sung by Mabel Hankins, Gordon, Wisconsin, for Franz Rickaby in 1923.

In Jersey City where I did dwell
A butcher boy I loved so well.
He courted me my heart away
And now with me he will not stay.

There is an inn in the same town
Where my love goes and sits him down.
He takes a strange girl on his knee
And tells to her what he don't tell me.

It's a grief for me, I'll tell you why;
Because she has more gold than I.
But her gold will melt and her silver fly.
In time of need she'll be poor as I.

I go upstairs to make my bed,
But nothing to my mother said.
My mother comes upstairs to me
Saying, "What's the matter, my daughter dear?"

"O Mother dear, you do not know
What grief and pain and sorrow, woe
Go get a chair to sit me down
And a pen and ink to write it down."

On every line she dropped a tear
While calling home her Willie dear;
And when her father he came home
He said, "Where is my daughter gone?"

He went upstairs, the door he broke
He found her hanging upon a rope.
He took his knife and cut her down
And in her breast those lines were found:
"Oh, what a silly maid am I
To hang myself for a butcher boy!

"Go dig my grave both long and deep,
Place a marble stone at my head and feet.
And on my breast a turtle-dove
To show the world I died for love."

The Butcher Boy

Alma Center Band in concert at Black River Falls.
Photo by Charles Van Schaick.

THE FATAL OAK

This song was clipped from the *La Farge Enterprise* and sent to Franz Rickaby by Lee Todd of Cornell, Wisconsin. It was apparently based on an incident that occurred on the Kickapoo River near its confluence with the Wisconsin River east of Prairie du Chien.

'Tis a mournful story I relate
Of three young men who met their fate.
While folded in the arms of sleep
They sank beneath the billows deep.

In blooming health they left the shore,
Ne'er thought they'd see their friends no more.
Down the Kickapoo on a raft
With De Jean, the Captain of the craft.

Down they floated down the Kickapoo
Laughing and joking as raftmen do,
Ne'er thought their fate would come so soon
When death would rob them of their bloom.

When night came on they made for shore
Where they had often stayed before;
'Neath the same oak tree which had been their stake
They went to sleep, no more to wake.

The Captain viewed the tree once more
And spoke as he had oftentimes before,
Saying, "I fear, my boys, when it is too late,
This very oak will seal our fate."

Early the next morning the Captain arose
And left his men in sweet repose.
For some wood he stepped out on the shore
For to prepare their breakfast o'er.

Scarcely had he stepped on shore
When looking at the tree once more,
He saw it start and then did cry,
"Awake, my boys, or you must die."

There was none but Wilson that awoke,
When, with a crash, down came the oak.
The Captain stood out on the shore
And saw them sink to rise no more.

For three long hours they searched in vain,
Till at last two bodies they obtained.
'Twas Hatfield and Totten, two boys so brave,
But Robert still slept beneath the grave.

By land the Captain started home,
Both night and day he journeyed on,
Taking those brave boys home to their friends
That they might see their last remains.

When the sun was setting in the west
Those two brave boys were laid to rest.
Their friends stood weeping round their tomb,
No more to see them in their bloom.

'Twas but a glance and all was o'er,
Their friends could see their faces no more.
Poor Juliet, the Captain's wife,
It seemed 'twould almost take her life.

The Captain strove to hide his grief,
But now he wrung his hands and cried,
Saying, "Oh, this is a bitter cup!
Aaron, how can I give up?"

Young Hatfield was the Captain's pride,
Long in his family did reside.
To him he seemed more like a son
Than like a child that was not their own.

Poor Robert's friends in deep despair,
They longed some tidings for to hear.
They searched the river for miles along
Till at Wyalusing his body was found.

And near the place where it was found
There may be seen a little mound.
'Twas strangers' hands that laid him there,
No friends to shed a farewell tear.

But since that time he was brought home.
Friends laid him in his earthly tomb.
Come, weeping mourners, dry your eyes,
Prepare to meet them in the skies.

Now think of those young and blooming youths
And travel no more on but what is truth.
For like a raft tied to a tree,
Every day there is a snare for thee.

YOUNG JOHNNY

Sung by Winifred Bundy, age fifty-seven, Madison, Wisconsin, in 1941. Miss Bundy said that she learned this song from a neighbor lady, Harriet Hunt Winslow, who was born in the 1830's.

One day young Johnny he did go
Down in the meadow for to mow.
A-too-dah-nick-ah, too-dah-nick-ah di-do day.

He scarce had mowed twice round the field
Before a serpent bit his heel.
A-too-dah-nick-ah, too-dah-nick-ah di-do day.

He threw his scythe upon the ground,
And with his eyes, then looked around.
A-too-dah-nick-ah, too-dah-nick-ah di-do day.

He took that serpent in his hand,
And went back home to sell it then.
A-too-dah-nick-ah, too-dah-nick-ah di-do day.

Oh, Sally dear, and do you see,
This pesky serpent has bitten me.
A-too-dah-nick-ah, too-dah-nick-ah di-do day.

Oh, Johnny dear, why did you go,
Down in that meadow, far and low?
A-too-dah-nick-ah, too-dah-nick-ah di-do day.

Oh, Sally dear, you know, you know,
'Twas father's hay I had to mow.
A-too-dah-nick-ah, too-dah-nick-ah di-do day.

Now, all young men a warning tend
And don't get bit by a rattlesnake.
A-too-dah-nick-ah, too-dah-nick-ah di-do day.

Young Johnny

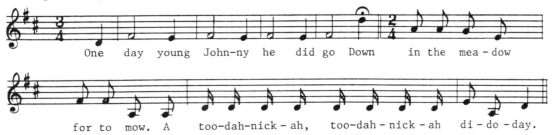

One day young John-ny he did go Down in the mea-dow for to mow. A too-dah-nick-ah, too-dah-nick-ah di-do-day.

ONCE I COURTED A CHARMING BEAUTY BRIGHT

Sung by Mrs. Ollie Jacobs, age seventy-nine, Pearson, Wisconsin, in 1941. Asher Treat took down the melody and words as Mrs. Jacobs sang it for him in 1933; when Helene Stratman-Thomas heard it eight years later, the melody varied ever so slightly from the earlier performance. Mrs. Jacobs learned the song in Kentucky in about 1880.

Once I courted a charming beauty bright,
I courted her by day and I courted her by night.
I courted her for love, and love I did obtain,
And I'm sure that she had no right to complain.

She had cruel parents I came for to know
To gather their daughter and 'way we would go.
But they put her in confinement and locked her up secure
And I never, no, never, got sight of my dear.

First to the window I thought I would go
To see if she had forgotten me or no.
But when she saw me coming she wrung her hands and cried,
"I never would forget you until the day I died."

Then to the war I thought I would go
To see if I could forget her or no.
But when I got there, the army shining bright,
I bore all my troubles to my own heart's delight.

Then seven long years I spent in Mexico.
Then back home I thought I would go.
But her mother saw me coming and ran to me and cried,
"My daughter loved you dearly, and for your sake she died."

Then I was struck like a man that was slain.
The tears from my eyes fell like showers of rain.
Saying, "Oh, Oh, this grief I cannot bear.
My darling's in her silent grave, and soon shall I be there."

Once I Courted a Charming Beauty Bright

Once I court-ed a charm-ing beau-ty bright, I

court-ed her by day and I court-ed her by night. I

court-ed her for love, and love I did ob-tain, And I'm

sure that she had no right to com-plain.

JIM BLAKE

Sung by Gladys Talbott for Franz Rickaby in 1920.

"Jim Blake, your wife is dying,"
Came over the wires tonight.
This message was brought to our city
By a boy nigh dead with fright.
He came to the office crying,
His face was pale and white.
"Take this to dad on his engine;
Mother is dying tonight."

Jim Blake, our oldest driver,
Who runs on the midnight express,
Has pulled both throttle and lever
Most all of his life, I guess.
And when I found this message
Was for old comrade Jim,
You bet I sent in a hurry
That there dispatch to him.

In less than half an hour
The train will be along.
"Tell wife I'll meet her at midnight;
Tell her that I'm praying for her."
I left the boy in the office,
Took the message to his wife,
Where I found her a dying woman
With scarcely a breath of life.

And when I entered the chamber
She took me first for Jim,
And fell back nigh exhausted
When she found it was not him,

She raised her eyes to heaven,
Her face was wan and white
As she said, in a dying whisper,
"God speed the express tonight."

O'er the hill and dale and valley
Thunders the midnight train,
Like lightning screeching and flashing
Amid that awful strain.
But Jim holds onto the lever
Guiding that crazy flight,
As a voice cries out of the darkness,
"God speed the express tonight."

And still another message
From the engineer, I guess:
"Tell wife I will meet her in Heaven;
Don't wait for the midnight express."
Ah, yes, there has been a disaster,
The train is in the ditch;
The engineer is dying,
Derailed by an open switch.

And still another message
From the engineer, I guess:
"Tell wife I will meet her in Heaven;
Don't wait for the midnight express."
And now they both lie dying,
Their trials in life are o'er.
God grant they will meet up in Heaven
Where trials are no more.

Jim Blake

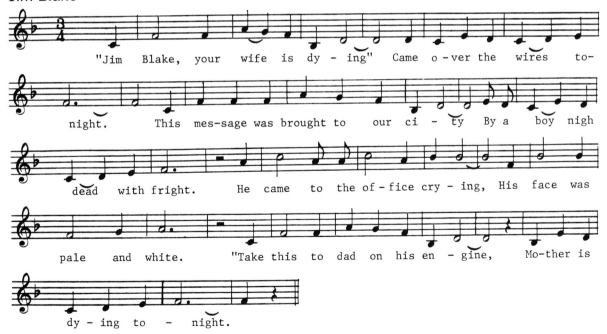

BILLY VANERO

Sung by Luther Royce, age twenty-eight, White Lake, Wisconsin, in 1941.

Billy Vanero heard them say,
In an Arizona town one day
That a band of Apache Indians
Was on the trail of death.

Heard them tell the murd'ring done;
Three men killed at Rocky Run.
"They're in danger at the cow ranch,"
He whispered under his breath.

Cow ranch forty miles away
In a little old spot that lay
In a deep and shady valley
In the mighty wilderness.

Sharp and clear a rifle shot
'Woke the echoes of the spot.
"I am wounded," cried Vanero
As he swayed from side to side.

And then he never spoke
As he dipped his pen of oak
From the warm blood
That was flowing from his side.

"Take this message," then said he,
"Straight to little Bessie Lee."
And he tied himself to the saddle
And gave his horse the rein.

Then at dusk the horse daw brown,
Wet with sweat came padding down
To the little lane at the cow ranch
And stopped at Bessie's door.

But the cowboy was asleep
And his slumbers were so deep
That old Bess could never wake him
Though she tried forevermore.

Billy Vanero

Bil-ly Van - er - o heard them say, in an Ar - i -
zo - na town one day, that a band of A - pach - e
In - dians was on the trail of death; Heard them
tell the mur- d'ring done, three men killed at Rock - y
Run. "They're in dan- ger at the cow ranch," he
Whis- per'd un- der his breath.

IN THE BAGGAGE COACH AHEAD

Sung by Bessie Gordon, age forty, Schofield, Wisconsin, in 1941.

'Twas a long dreary night and the train rattled on
All the passengers had gone to bed.
Except a poor man with a babe in his arms
And he fondled it close to his breast.

The innocent one began crying in vain,
As tho' its poor heart would break.
"Throw him out," said a man, "don't let him stay here
He's keeping us all awake."

"Throw him out," said another, "don't keep him in here
We paid for our berths and won't rest."
But never a word from the man with the child
As he fondled it close to his breast.

"Oh, where is its mother, go take it to her,"
A kind woman softly said.
"I wish that I could," was the sad man's reply,
"But she's dead in the coach ahead."

As the train rolled onward, the husband sat in tears
Thinking of the happy times of just those few short years.
Baby's face brings pictures of one who now lay dead.
Baby's tears can't waken her in the baggage coach ahead.

In the Baggage Coach Ahead

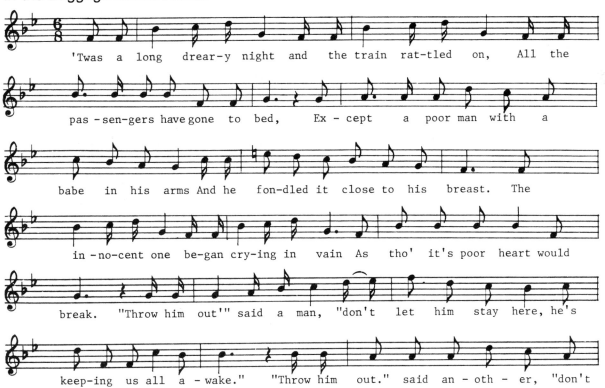

keep him in here. We paid for our berths and won't rest." But

nev - er a word from the man with the child as he fon-dled it close to his

breast. "Oh, where is it's mo-ther? Go take it to her." A

kind wo-man soft - ly said. "I wish that I could," was the

sad man's re - ply, "But she's dead in the coach a - head."

As the train rolled on - ward the hus-band sat in tears,

Think-ing of the hap - py times of just those few short

years. Ba - by's face brings pic-tures of one who now lay

dead. Ba - by's tears can't wa-ken her in the bag-gage coach a-

head.

Photo by Charles Van Schaick, Black River Falls.

WHO IS THAT UNDER MY BEDROOM WINDOW?

Sung by Dan Tanner, age seventy-five, Boyne City, Michigan, in 1941, and transcribed by Mr. Tanner's grand-nephew from a recording. This version came to Dan Tanner from his mother. He was born in Bangor, Maine, and spent his early boyhood in Michigan. At age twelve, he began working in the Kelly Mills near Wausau; later he returned to Michigan, where he worked in various lumber camps for seventeen years.

"Who is that under my bedroom window
A-weeping there so bitterly?"
"Arouse, arouse, you drowsy sleeper,"
He softly whispered unto me.

"Oh, Mary, dear, go ask your mother,
If you my wedded bride may be,
And if she says no, then come and tell me
And I no longer will trouble thee."

"Oh no, oh no, I cannot ask her,
For she is bound to set us free,
So, Willy dear, go court some other,"
She softly whispered unto me.

"Oh, I can climb the highest mountain
Or I can rob the richest nest,
Or I can court the fairest lady,
But not the one that I love best.

"O, Mary dear, go ask your father
If you my wedded bride may be,
And if he says no, then come and tell me,
And I no longer will trouble thee."

"Oh no, oh no, I dare not ask him,
For he lies on his bed of rest,
And beside him lies the silver dagger
To pierce the heart that I love best."

Then Willy seized the silver dagger
And pierced it through his aching heart,
Saying, "Here's farewell to my own dear Mary,
Farewell, farewell, now we must part."

Then Mary seized the bloody dagger
And pierced it through her snow white breast,
Saying, "Here's adieu to my cruel parents;
Willy and I have gone to rest."

Who Is That Under My Bedroom Window?

214

THE SONG OF MRS. SHATTUCK

Franz Rickaby copied this song from a manuscript in the possession of W. W. Bartlett, a historian and folklorist of Eau Claire, Wisconsin. A notation on the manuscript reads: "The words of the beautiful and touching ballad, author unknown, were found in the earliest copy in existence of the *Eau Claire Times,* May 23, 1857. No music was given with the words, but at a Local History and Folk-Lore Day Program of the Eau Claire Women's Club in 1923, the song was sung to the tune of 'Auld Lang Syne.' "

Farewell, my dear husband and children, farewell.
How I feel to leave you, there is no one can tell.
We've enjoyed all the pleasure this life can afford,
And now I must leave you and dwell with my Lord.

In my richest attire on the Fourth of July,
How little we knew that death was so nigh!
My whole family circle, my husband and me,
Came nigh getting killed by a limb from a tree.

While passing through the green woods and down a long hill,
A storm was fast approaching, my blood seemed to chill.
My soul was filled with horror, but all did no good.
It was bound to overtake us while passing through the wood.

The storm came on quickly, the wind it did blow.
The lightning did flash and the thunder did roll.
The trees were fast a-falling, the limbs all around.
One fell on our wagon and swept us to the ground.

We were picked up insensible, all of our sad fate,
And carried to the neighbor's, our destiny to wait.
But when I survived from the wounds I received
The state of my family my spirit did grieve.

But I have no time to murmur, for soon I must go
To leave my dear family and friends here below.
But your Master has told you that you can come to me,
For I must go forever and cannot come to thee.

My thanks to the Grangers for this kindness to me.
There's a lodge up in heaven for thee and for me.
The Savior is our President, our password is prayer.
We will gain the lost victory when we get up there.

Farewell, Christian friends this whole world around.
I shall sleep in the grave till the trumpet shall sound.
Then my Master will call me and bid me arise
To meet you in glory in yonder bright skies.

Farewell, my dear husband, for you I do love.
Prepare for to meet me in heaven above.
We will celebrate a day far better than this
Where the storm and the tempest of this life is past.

Farewell, my dear children, I bid you adieu.
The time is fast approaching when I must leave you.
But your father will love you as he has done before.
Prepare for to meet me on Canaan's bright shore.

My family is surviving and free from all pain.
They all have got better and gone home again.
But oh, how lonesome and lonely it will be,
For that bright and happy home is no longer for me.

YOUNG MARY

Sung by Charles Dietz, age seventy-five, Monroe, Wisconsin, in 1946. Franz Rickaby also collected this song from C. A. Yoder of Bloomington, Indiana, and a Mrs. Gordon of Charlevoix, Michigan, in 1919. The latter told Rickaby that her parents had brought the song directly from Scotland.

On a cold winter's night,
When the winds blew across the wild moor,
Young Mary came wand'ring with her child in her arms
Till she came to her own father's door.

"Oh father, dear father," she cried,
"Come down and open the door,
Or the child in my arms it will perish and die
By the winds that blow across the wild moor."

But the old man was deaf to her cries,
Not a sound of her voice reached his ear.
The watch-dog did howl and the village bells tolled
And the winds blew across the wild moor.

Oh, how must the old man have felt
When he came to the door in the morn?
Young Mary was dead, but the child was alive,
Close pressed in its dead mother's arms.

Ah, frenzied he tore his grey hairs
While the tears down his cheeks they did pour,
Saying, this cold winter's night she has perished and died
By the winds that blew across the wild moor.

The old man grieved, pined away,
And the child to its mother went soon.
No one, they say, has lived there to this day,
And the cottage has gone to ruin.

And the villagers point out the spot
Where the willows weep o'er the door,
Saying, There Mary died, once a gay village bride,
By the winds that blew across the wild moor.

Young Mary

On a cold win-ter's night, When the winds blew a-cross the wild moor, Young Ma-ry came wan-d'ring with her child in her arms, 'Til she came to her own fa-ther's door.

GRANDFATHER'S STORY

Sung by Fred Bainter, Ladysmith, Wisconsin, for Franz Rickaby in 1923.

A story, cried the children, grandfather dear.
Come tell us such a story as we would like to hear.
The old man he answered, with Mary on his knee,
I will tell to you a story. Come listen unto me.

It was up beyond the mountains where the Indians then
Wandered unmolested, two adventurous men
With their guns and their axes they boldly made their way,
They built their humble cabin and chased the mountain prey.

But ere the years were many, each one took a wife,
And here they lived contented, a rude but happy life.
And each one in the summer their little homestead tills,
And each one in the winter would hunt upon the hills.

But soon from infant faces each home grew brighter long,
The dim old forest echoed with children's shout and song.
The forest paths were treaden by merry dancing feet,
The paths between the cabins where the children loved to meet.

But time flew quickly onward; they were not children long.
James Tenny grew to manhood, a hunter bold and strong.
And Nancy Foes, the maiden, her mother's only child,
As fair a flower as ever in such a desert smiled.

A love had grown between them while in the wild woods bower.
James led the little Nancy to seek the early flower.
A love that streamed unnoted had grown so deep and wide
Their hearts like freighted vessels would float upon the tide.

The autumn days were ended, the snow was on the hills;
The frost had chained the river and hushed its dazzling rill.
The log fire in the cabin was blazing strong and bright
When James and little Nancy bid farewell in its light.

With his rifle on his shoulder and his stag-hound by his side
He plunged into the forest, the forest long and wide.
In tents for weeks together, from love and home afar,
To trap the mink and otter and hunt the wolf and bear.

Sun rose and set as ever, day glided after day;
Amid the storm and sunshine the winter passed away.
While Nancy at her spinning in the twilight dim
Turned ever toward the forest watching in vain for him.

The north wind shook the cabin and heaped the snow-drifts 'round.
It creaked upon the tree-tops; she shuddered at the sound.
And in her dreams she saw him all on an icy bed
Stretching his arms for succor, or lying cold and dead.

At length from anxious watching her brain grew wild at last.
She heard a strain of anguish in every mountain blast.
Her lover seemed to call her; his voice was in her ear,
And she resolved to seek him amid the mountain drear.

So when the silvery moonbeams shone o'er hill and moor
She wrapped her cloak about her and left her father's door.
The crusty snow-drift bore her, leaving no track behind,
So no one on the morrow her devious paths could find.

James Tenny started homeward, a hunter strong and bold;
A traveller bought his pelfry and paid him yellow gold.
With his rifle on his shoulder and a heart of joy and pride,
He trod the snowy valleys and clumb the mountain side.

With footsteps pressing onward as love and home drew nigh,
He turned to see the reason that his stag-hound stood and cried.
Beneath the leafless maple close beside his way,
All pale and cold and lifeless beheld a maiden lay.

With a cheek as pale as ashes and a heart that beat with fear,
"Oh heavens," he cried in anguish, "who could have wandered here?"
And when he stooped to raise her and gaze upon the dead
You might have thought his spirit as well as hers had fled.

For a while he knelt beside her, bewildered by his woe;
And then he gently raised her and bore her through the snow.
Pressed close upon his bosom mile after mile he bore
This precious lifeless burden unto her father's door.

Oh, I need not try to tell you what anguish had been there,
What wild and anxious watching, or unavailing prayers.
Nor need I paint the anguish to none but unto God
When we laid the little Nancy to sleep beneath the sod.

No more the hunter shoots the moose or the deer,
But pauses 'neath the shadelands to wipe away a tear.
The youths and the maidens in the country around
Heave a sigh of sorrow as they pass that hollow ground.

Beneath the sigh of sorrow and a silent prayer,
Thinking of the fond hopes that have perished there,
A-thinking of the loved one that perished mournfully
How a gentle maiden perished beneath that maple tree.

Grandfather's Story

A sto-ry, Cried the chil-dren, Grand-fath-er dear. Come
tell us such a sto-ry as we would like to hear. The
old man, he an-swer'd, with Ma-ry on his knee, I will
tell to you a sto-ry. Come lis-ten un-to me.
If you go out a-bout the town Up-on a win-ter's day, You
see the lads and las-sies dressed out in fash-ions gay.

YOUNG CHARLOTTE

Sung by Winifred Bundy, age sixty-two, Madison, Wisconsin, in 1946. Miss Bundy learned this song from her mother, Olive Morgan Bundy, who emigrated from Canada to the United States when she was fourteen. Although it is often considered to be an English ballad, there is evidence that it is based upon an incident reported in the *New York Observer* of February 8, 1840, in which a girl was said to have frozen to death while riding to a ball.

Young Charlotte lived by the mountain side, in a lone and dreary spot.
No other dwelling for miles around, except her father's cot.
And yet, on many a winter's eve, young swains would gather there,
For her father kept a social board, and she was very fair.

Her father loved to see her dressed prim as a city belle.
She was the only child he had and he loved his daughter well.
In a village some fifteen miles off there's a merry ball tonight.
Though the driving wind is cold as death, their hearts are free and light.

And yet how beams those sparkling eyes as the well-known sound she hears,
And dashing up to her father's door young Charles and his sleigh appears.
"O daughter dear," her mother said, "those blankets round you fold,
For it is a dreadful night to ride and you'll catch your death of cold."

"Oh nay, oh nay," fair Charlotte said, and she laughed like a gypsy queen;
"To ride with blankets muffled up one never would be seen."
Her gloves and bonnet being on, she stepped into the sleigh.
And away they ride by the mountain side, and it's o'er the hills and away.

There's music in those merry bells as o'er the hills we go.
What a creaking noise those runners make as they strike the frozen snow!
And muffled faces silent are as the first five miles are passed,
When Charles with few and shivering words the silence broke at last.

"What a dreadful night it is to ride! My lines I scarce can hold."
When she replied in a feeble voice, "I am extremely cold."
Charles cracked his whip and urged his team far faster than before,
Until at length five other miles in silence were passed o'er.

"Charlotte, how fast the freezing ice is gathering on my brow!"
When she replied in a feeble voice, "I'm getting warmer now."
And away they ride by the mountain side beneath the cold starlight,
Until at length the village inn and the ball-room are in sight.

When they drove up, Charles he got out and offered her his hand.
"Why sit you there like a monument that hath no power to stand?"
He asked her once, he asked her twice, but she answered not a word.
He offered her his hand again, but still she never stirred.

He took her hand into his own. 'Twas cold as any stone.
He tore the veil from off her face and the cold stars on her shone,
And quick into the lighted hall her lifeless form be bore.
Fair Charlotte was a frozen corpse, and a word she ne'er spoke more.

He took her back into the sleigh and quickly hurried home;
And when he came to her father's door, oh, how her parents moaned.
They mourned the loss of their daughter dear, while Charles wept o'er their gloom,
Until at length Charles died of grief and they both lay in one tomb.

Young Charlotte

Young Char-lotte lived by the moun-tain side, in a lone and drear-y spot. No oth-er dwell-ing for miles a-round, ex-cept for her fa-ther's cot. And yet, on man-y a win-ter's eve, young swains would gath-er there, For her fa-ther kept a so-cial board, and she was ver-y fair.

Photo by Ray Weinkauf, Wausau.

HARRY BALE

Sung by Henry Humphries, age seventy-five, Hancock, Wisconsin, in 1940.

Come all, kind friends and parents, my brothers one and all.
I have a tale to tell you which will make your blood run cold.
'Twas of a poor unfortunate boy, a humble young farmer,
Whose parents reared him tenderly, not many miles from here.

In the county of Arkrego, in the township of Lake Bear,
There stands a little shingle mill, it was run about one year.
'Twas there this horrible deed was done, caused many to weep and wail.
'Twas there this young man lost his life. His name was Harry Bale.

His occupation seemed to be head sawyer in the mill.
He followed it successfully two years, two months, until
The time had come for him to go and leave the world of care.
We know not when our doom may come, all our bad deeds to share.

On the twenty-second of April, in the year of seventy-nine,
He went to the mill as usual, no harm did he design.
In lowering of the feed bar that set the carriage in gear,
He got too near the funnel saw and it wounded him severe.

It ripped him through the shoulder blade and halfway down the back.
He then fell on the funnel floor and the carriage it came back.
He started for the shanty, his strength was failing fast.
He said, "Oh, boys I'm wounded and I fear it is my last."

His brother, Ben, was sent for, likewise his sister too.
The doctor came and dressed the wound, alas it was too true.
For when his cruel wound was dressed, he unto them did say,
"'Twas all in vain, there is no hope, I soon must pass away."

No father did young Harry have to weep beside his bed.
No kind and loving mother is soothe his aching head.
He lingered on a day and night, 'till death relieved his pain,
Though I hear his voice forevermore, he'll never speak again.

Harry Bale

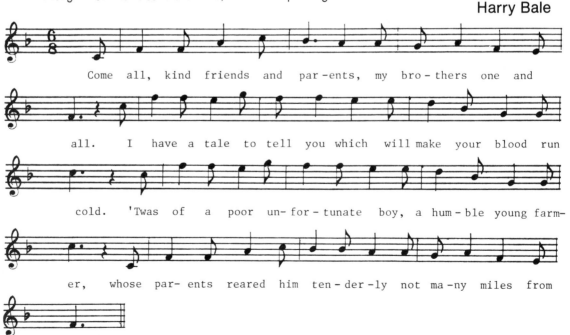

222

THE MISTLETOE BOUGH

Sung by Winifred Bundy, age fifty-seven, Madison, Wisconsin, in 1941.

The mistletoe hung on the castle hall,
The holly branch shone on the old oak wall.
The baron's retainers were blythe and gay
Keeping their Christmas holiday.
The Baron beheld with a father's pride
His beautiful daughter, young Lovell's bride.
And she with her bright eyes seemed to be
The star of that goodly company.
Oh, the mistletoe bough, oh, the mistletoe bough.

"I'm tired of dancing now," she cried.
"Here tarry a moment, I'll hide, I'll hide.
And Lovell be sure thou art first to trace
The clue to my secret hiding place."
Away she ran, and her friend began
Each tower to search, each nook to scan.
And Lovell, he cried, "Where dost thou hide?
I'm lonely without thee, my own dear bride."
Oh, the mistletoe bough, oh, the mistletoe bough.

They sought her that night, they sought her next day,
They sought her in vain as the years passed away.
In the highest, the lowest, the loneliest spot
Young Lovell sought wildly, but found her not.
The years passed away and his grief, at last,
Was told as a sorrowful tale long passed.
And when Lovell appeared, the children cried,
"See the old man weep for his fairy bride."
Oh, the mistletoe bough, oh the mistletoe bough.

At length an old chest that had long lain hid
Was found in the castle and they raised the lid.
A skeleton form lay moldering there
With a bridal wreath of the lady fair.
Oh, sad was his face in sport or jest.
She hid from her lord in the old oak chest.
It closed with a spring and her bridal bloom
Lay withering there in a living tomb.
Oh, the mistletoe bough, oh, the mistletoe bough.

The Mistletoe Bough

The mis - tle - toe hung on the cas - tle hall. The

hol - ly branch shone on the old oak wall. The

bar - on's re - tain - ers were blythe and gay,

keep - ing their Christ - mas hol - i - day. The

bar - on be - held with a fa - ther's pride, his

beau - ti - ful daugh - ter, young Lo - vell's bride. And

she with her bright eyes seemed to be The

star of that good - ly com - pan - y. Oh, the

mis - tle - toe bough, Oh, the mis - tle - toe bough.

THE DYING WISCONSIN SOLDIER

Sung by George M. Hankins, Gordon, Wisconsin, for Franz Rickaby; and by William J. Morgan, Berlin, and Noble B. Brown, Millsville, for Helene Stratman-Thomas in 1946. Brown's mother learned one version of this song from her father, a Union Army veteran who had been in both Libby and Andersonville prisons.

The sun was sinking in the west
And filled with glittering rays
O'er the branches of a forest where
A dying soldier lays.
'Neath the shade of the palmetto,
'Neath a sultry southern sky,
Far away from his dear Wisconsin home
They've laid him down to die.

A crowd was gathered near him,
His comrades in the fight,
And a tear rolled down each manly cheek
As he breathed his last good-night.
One dear friend and companion too,
Was kneeling by his side
Trying for to stay the life-flow blood,
But alas, in vain he tried.

His heart filled with deep anguish
When he saw it was in vain,
And down his loved companion's cheeks
The tears fell down like rain.
Out spoke the dying soldier,
"Charlie, weep no more for me;
I am crossing a dark river
Where all beyond is free."

"Now, comrades, gather closer,
Listen to what I have to say.
I've a story I would tell you
Ere my spirit pass away.
'Way up in loved Wisconsin,
In that big old pine tree state,
There is one who for my coming
With a saddened heart will wait."

"A dear young girl, my sister,
My beauty and my pride,
She has been my care through childhood—
I have no other one beside.
I have been to her a brother,
Shield her with a father's care;
I have tried from grief and anguish
Her gentle heart to spare."

"When our country was in danger
And called for volunteers,
She threw her arms around my neck
And bursting into tears,
Saying, "Oh my dearest brother,
Drive those traitors from our shores;
Though my heart it needs your presence,
Your country needs you more.""

225

"'Tis true I love my country;
I will give to it my all,
If it were not for my sister
I would be content to fall.
But, comrades, I am dying,
I ne'er shall see her more.
She will vainly watch my coming
At her little cabin door."

"My mother she lies sleeping
Beneath the churchyard sod,
And many and many's the day since
Her spirit went to God.
My father he lies sleeping
Beneath the dark blue sea.
I've no brothers and no sisters;
There is only Nell and me."

"Now, comrades, gather closer,
Listen to my dying prayer.
Who will be to her a brother,
Shield her with a father's care?"
Thus spoke the dying soldier,
And in one voice it seemed to fall,
"We'll be to her all brothers;
"We'll protect her one and all."

One bright smile of gladness
Over the soldier's face had spread;
One quick convulsive shudder
And the soldier boy was dead.
On the banks of the Potomac
They have laid him down to rest,
With his knapsack for a pillow
And his gun across his breast.

The Dying Wisconsin Soldier

The sun was sink-ing in the west, And fell its ling'-ring ray, Through the branch-es of the for-est, Where a wound-ed sold-ier lay 'Neath the shade of a pal-met-to, 'Neath the sun-ny south-ern sky, Far from his loved Wis-con-sin home, They laid him down to die.

Dead on Antietam battlefield, 1862.
Photo from Library of Congress.

JAMES BIRD

Sung by George M. Hankins, Gordon, Wisconsin, for Franz Rickaby. Rickaby reported that Hankins felt strongly that James Bird, who was executed for allegedly deserting under fire at the Battle of Lake Erie in 1813, had been done a terrible injustice. A similar version of the ballad was given Rickaby by Mrs. M. A. Olin of Eau Claire in 1923.

Sons of freedom, listen to me,
And ye daughters too give ear,
You a sad and mournful story
As was ever told shall hear.

'Mongst the troops that marched to Erie
Were the Kingston volunteers,
Captain Thomas them commanded
To protect our west frontiers.

Soon they come where noble Perry
Had assembled all his fleet
Here the gallant Bird enlisted
Hoping soon the foe to meet.

Where is Bird? The battle rages.
Is he in the strife or no?
Though the cannons roar tremendous,
Dare he meet the hostile foe?

Yes, behold him! See him and Perry!
In the self-same ship they fight.
Though his mess-mates fall around him,
Nothing can his soul affright.

But behold, a ball has struck him!
See the crimson current flow.
"Leave the deck," exclaimed brave Perry.
"No," cries brave Bird, "I will not go."

"Here on deck I took my station
Ne'er will Bird his colors fly.
I'll stand by you, gallant Captain,
Till we conquer or we die."

Through he fought though faint and bleeding,
Till our stars and stripes arose,
Vict'ry having crowned our efforts
All triumphant o'er our foes.

Now did Bird receive a pension?
Was he to his friends restored?
No; nor never to his bosom
Clasped the maid his heart adored.

"Dearest parents" said the letter,
"This will bring sad news to you.
Do not mourn your first beloved,
Though this brings his last adieu."

"I must suffer for deserting
From the big *Niagaree*.
Read this letter, brother, sisters,
'Tis the last you'll have from me."

Sad and gloomy was the morning
Bird was ordered out to die.
Where's the breast not dead to pity
But for him would heave a sigh?

Lo, he fought so brave at Erie,
Freely bled and nobly dared.
Let his courage plead for mercy,
Let his precious life be spared.

See him march and bear his fetters.
Harsh they clank upon the ear.
But his step is firm and manly,
For his heart ne'er harbored fear.

See him kneel upon his coffin.
Sure, his death can do no good!
Spare him—Hark! O God, they've shot him!
See his bosom stream with blood!

Farewell, Bird, farewell forever,
Friends and home he'll see no more,
But his mangled corpse lies buried
On Lake Erie's distant shore.

228

James Bird

Sons of free-dom, lis-ten to me, And ye daugh-ters too, give ear, You a sad and mourn-ful sto-ry As was ev-er told shall hear.

RICHMOND ON THE JAMES

Sung by William N. Allen, Wausau, Wisconsin, for Franz Rickaby in 1923.

A soldier boy from Boston lay gasping on the field.
When the battle fray was over, the foe was forced to yield.
He fell, a youthful hero, before the foeman's aim
On the blood-red fields at Richmond, near Richmond on the James.

But one still stood beside him, a comrade in the fray.
They had been friends together from boyhood's early day,
And side by side had struggled through fields of blood and flame,
To part that eve near Richmond, near Richmond on the James.

Said he, "I charge you, comrade and friend in days of yore,
And those far distant dear ones that I shall see no more,
Though scarce my lips can whisper those dear and well known names,
Yet bear to them my blessing from Richmond on the James."

"Give my good sword to my brother, and this badge that's on my breast
To that young gentle sister, the one whom I love best.
Give one lock from my forehead to a mother who still loves dreams
Of her soldier boy returning from Richmond on the James."

"I wish the arms of mother were folded 'round me now,
Or that her hand could linger one moment on my brow.
I know that she is praying where her blessed hearth-light gleams,
For her soldier boy's returning from the Richmond on the James.

"Near to my heart, dear comrade, you'll find some dark brown braids
Of one who was the fairest of all our village maids.
We were to join in wedlock, but death the bridegroom claims,
And she's far away who loves me, from Richmond on the James."

"Does this pale face now haunt her, dear friend that looks on me?
Or is she laughing, singing, in careless girlish glee?
Perhaps that she is joyous and loves but joyous things,
Now dreams her love lies bleeding at Richmond on the James."

And though I know, dear comrade, you'll miss me for a while,
When those who once did love thee again on thee shall smile,
Again you will be foremost in all their youthful games
While I shall lie near Richmond, near Richmond on the James."

And far from those who loved him this youthful hero sleeps
Unknown among the thousands for whom his country weeps;
But no truer heart, no braver than his at sunset beams
Was laid that eve near Richmond, near Richmond on the James.

The land was filled with mourning, from cot to hall left lone.
We miss the youthful faces that used to meet our own.
And lonely wives and mothers will weep with titled dames
For those who fell at Richmond, at Richmond on the James.

Richmond on the James

A sol-dier boy from Bos-ton lay gasp-ing on the field. When the bat-tle fray was o-ver the foe was forced to yield. He fell a youth-ful he-ro be-fore the foe-man's aim, On the blood-red fields at Rich-mond, near Rich-mond on the James.

THE HUNTERS OF KAINTUCKY

Sung by George M. Hankins, Gordon, Wisconsin, for Franz Rickaby in 1923. In *The American Songbag,* Carl Sandburg credits Samuel Woodworth as the author of this song about Andrew Jackson's victory over the British at the Battle of New Orleans in 1815. He also mentions that Franz Rickaby heard it in Midwestern lumber camps, ca. 1920.

Ye gentlemen and ladies fair, who grace this famous city,
Just listen, if you've time to spare, while I rehearse a ditty.
And for the opportunity conceive yourselves quite lucky.
For it's hardly ever that you see a hunter from Kaintucky.
Chorus: Oh, Kaintucky, the hunters of Kaintucky.
          Oh, Kaintucky, the hunters of Kaintucky.

But Jackson he was wide awake and was not scared at trifles,
For well he knew what aim we'd take with our Kaintucky rifles.
So he led us down by a cypress swamp, the ground was low and mucky.
There stood John Bull in martial pomp, but here was old Kaintucky.

A bank was raised to hide our breasts, not that we thought of dying,
But then we always liked a rest unless the game was flying.
Behind it stood our little band, not wishing to be greater,
The flower of old Kaintucky's land, half horse, half alligator.

They did not let our patience tire before they showed their faces.
We did not choose to waste our fire, so snugly kept our places.
But when so nigh we saw them wink, we thought it time to stop them,
And it would have done you good, I think, to've seen Kaintuckians.

So Pakenham he told his boys, if he in fight was lucky,
He'd have our girls and cotton bags in spite of old Kaintucky.
But when they found 'twas vain to fight where lead was all their booty,
You can bet they swiftly took their flight and left us all the beauty.

And now if a daring foe annoys, whate'er his strength and forces,
We'll show them that Kaintucky's boys are alligator's horses.
And now if a daring foe annoys, remember what our trade is;
Just send for us Kaintucky boys, and we'll protect you, ladies.

The Hunters of Kaintucky

Ye gen-tle-men and la-dies fair who grace this fa - mous ci-ty, Just list - en, if you've time to spare, while I re-hearse a dit - ty. And for the op-por - tun - i - ty con-ceive your - selves quite luck - y, For it's hard-ly ev - er that you see a hunt - er from Kain-tuck - y. Oh, Kain - tuck - y the hunt-ers of Kain-tuck - y. Oh, Kain-tuck - y, the hunt - ers of Kain - tuck-y.

TWO SOLDIERS LYING AS THEY FELL

Sung by Winifred Bundy, age fifty-seven, Madison, Wisconsin, in 1941.

Two soldiers lying as they fell
Upon the reddened clay,
As daylight falls on night in peace,
Breathes their lives away.
Brave hearts that stirred each lonely breast,
Fate only made them pause,
As they lie dying side by side
A softened feeling glows.
They will go no more to their loved homes dear,
But together both will wait
For the sunny-haired and bright-eyed one
Beyond the golden gate.

Among New Hampshire's snowy hills
They pray for me tonight.
A mother and a little girl
With hair like morning light
And as the thought broke forth,
Alas, a cry of anguish wild,
That could no longer be repressed,
"Oh God, my heart, my child."

Then spoke the other dying man,
"Across that Georgian plain
There wait and look for the loved ones
I never shall see again.
A little girl with dark bright eyes,
Each day is at the door.
A father's kiss, a father's smile
Will greet her there no more."

The parting look, the fleeting breath,
The dying hands entwined.
The last dark fades, and over all
The stars of heaven shine.
And now the girl with golden hair
And she with dark eyes bright,
On Hampshire's hills and Georgia's plain
Are fatherless tonight.
They will go no more to their loved homes dear,
But together both will wait
For the sunny-haired and bright-eyed one
Beyond the golden gate.

Two Soldiers Lying as They Fell

Two sol-diers ly-ing as they fell Up-on the red-den'd clay, as day-light falls on night in peace, breathes there their lives a-way. Brave hearts that stirred each lone-ly breast, fate on-ly made them pause. As they lie dy-ing side by side, a sof-tened feel-ing glows. They will go no more to their sun-ny-haired and bright-eyed ones Be-yond the gold-en gate.

HOW ARE YOU, CONSCRIPT?

This song and next were sent to Helene Stratman-Thomas by Arthur C. Gower (born 1852) of Lake Hallie, Chippewa County, Wisconsin. Both allude bitterly to the Civil War draft, which could be evaded by making a cash payment to the government or by hiring another man to serve.

How are you, conscript? Oh, how are you today?
The provost marshal's got you
In a very tight spot, they say,
Unless you've got three hundred greenbacks
To pony up and pay.

I'M IN WANT OF A SUBSTITUTE

I'm in want of a substitute. Oh, show me the man who will
Buckle on his armor and fight for Uncle Sam.
I'm in want of a hero, with a heart so brave and true,
Who will fight for his country and the red, white, and blue.

How Are You, Conscript?

How are you, Con-script? Oh, how are you to-day? The
pro-vost mar-shal's got you in a ve-ry tight spot they
say, Un-less you've got three hun-dred green-backs to
po-ny up and pay.

I'm in Want of a Substitute

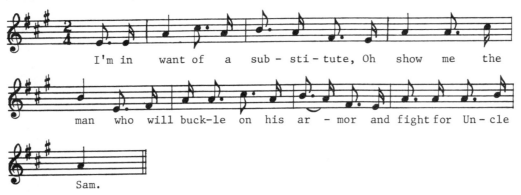

I'm in want of a sub-sti-tute, Oh show me the
man who will buck-le on his ar - mor and fight for Un-cle
Sam.

'TWAS AUTUMN AND THE LEAVES

Sung by Mrs. Ollie Jacobs, age seventy-nine, Pearson, Wisconsin, in 1940.

'Twas autumn, the leaves were around me descending.
The din of their arms sounded dismal to hear.
I thought it had broken my heart strings asunder.
I thought I would see my dear Sandy no more.
For Sandy, my love, was engaged in the action.
Without him I'd value this world not a fraction.
My shepherd was saved and my country defended
By freedom's brave sons on the banks of Champlain.

234

Henry A. Cooper, Wisconsin drummer boy, 1861.
Iconographic Collection, SHSW.

WHEN SHERMAN MARCHED DOWN TO THE SEA
Sung by William N. Allen, Wausau, Wisconsin, for Franz Rickaby.

Our camp-fires shone bright on the mountain
That frowned on the river below,
As we stood by our guns in the morning
And eagerly watched for the foe.
When a rider came out from the darkness
That hung over mountain and tree,
And shouted, "Boys, up and be ready,
For Sherman will march to the sea."

Then cheer after cheer for bold Sherman
Went up from each valley and glen,
Till the bugles re-echoed the music
That came from the lips of our men.
For we knew that the stars in our banner
More bright in their splendor would be
And that blessings from Northland would greet us
When Sherman marched down to the sea.

Then forward, boys, forward to battle,
We marched on our wearisome way,
Till we stormed the wild heights of Resaca—
God Bless those who fell on that day.
And Kennesaw high in its glory
Frowned down on the flag of the free,
And the east and the west bore our standards
When Sherman marched down to the sea.

Still onward we pressed till our banners
Shone out from Atlanta's grim walls,
And the blood of the patriots dampened
The soil where the traitor's flag falls.
But we paused not to weep for the fallen
Who slept by each river and tree,
But we twined them a wreath of the laurel
When Sherman marched down to the sea.

Oh, proud was our army that morning
That stood by the cypress and pine,
When Sherman says, "Boys, you are weary,
But today fair Savannah is mine."
Then sang we a song for our chieftain
That echoed o'er river and lea,
And the stars in our banner shone brighter
When Sherman marched down to the sea.

When Sherman Marched Down to the Sea

Our camp - fires shone bright on the moun - tain That frowned on the riv - er be - low, As we stood by our guns in the morn - ing And eag-er - ly watch'd for the foe. When a rid - er came out from the dark - ness That hung o - ver moun-tain and tree, And shout - ed "Boys, up and be read - y, For Sher - man will march to the sea."

MANY BRAVE BOYS MUST FALL

Sung by Winifred Bundy, age fifty-seven, Madison, Wisconsin, in 1941.

Heavily falls the rain, wild are the breezes tonight,
While 'round our hearts the hours as they passed, are happy and warm and bright.
Gathered around the fireside, though it be summertime,
We sit and talk of brothers abroad, forgetting our evening chime.
Chorus: Brave boys are they, gone to their country's call.
       And yet, and yet, we must not forget
       That many brave boys must fall.

Thinking no less of them, but loving our country the more,
We send them forth to die if they must, the treaty is at our door.
On the dread scene of carnage, soon to be strewn with graves,
It brothers must fall then bury them where
Our banner shall over them wave.

Many Brave Boys Must Fall

Heav-i-ly falls the rain, Wild are the bree-zes to-night. While round our hearts the hours as they pass'd are hap-py and warm and bright. Gath-er'd a-round our fire-side, Though it be sum-mer-time, We sit and talk of bro-thers a-broad, For-get-ting our e-vening chime. Brave boys are they, Gone to their coun-try's call. And yet, and yet, we must not for-get That ma-ny brave boys must fall.

DISASTER

LOST ON THE LADY ELGIN

Sung by Hamilton Lobdell, age eighty-seven, Mukwonago, Wisconsin, for Helene Stratman-Thomas in 1941; and by I. B. Keeler, Bemidji, Minnesota, for Franz Rickaby in 1923. On September 8, 1860, the *Lady Elgin,* a crack Lake Michigan passenger steamship, carried a large charter group of Milwaukee's Third Ward Irish to Chicago to hear Stephen A. Douglas speak. That night, on the return voyage, the *Lady Elgin* was rammed by a lumber freighter, and half its 600 passengers perished off Winnetka, Illinois.

Up from the poor man's cottage, forth from the mansion door,
Sweeping across the waters and echoing along the shore;
Caught by the morning breezes, borne on the evening gale,
Cometh the voice of mourning, a sad and solemn wail.
Lost on the *Lady Elgin,* sleeping to wake no more,
Numbered with those three hundred who failed to reach the shore.

Staunch was the noble steamer, precious the freight she bore;
Gayly she loosed her cables a few short hours before.
Grandly she swept our harbor, joyfully rang her bell.
Little thought we ere morning 'twould toll so sad a knell.
Lost on the *Lady Elgin,* sleeping to wake no more,
Numbered with those three hundred who failed to reach the shore.

Oh, 'tis the cry of children weeping for parents gone;
Children who slept at evening, but orphans woke at dawn.
Sisters for brothers weeping, husbands for missing wives,
Such were the ties dissevered by those three hundred lives.
Lost on the *Lady Elgin,* sleeping to wake no more,
Numbered with those three hundred who failed to reach the shore.

Lost on the Lady Elgin

Up from the poor man's cottage, forth from the mansion door, Sweeping across the waters, and echoing 'long the shore. Caught by the morning breezes, borne on the ev'ning gale, Cometh the voice of mourning, a sad and solemn wail. Lost on the Lady Elgin, sleeping to wake no more, Numbered with those three hundred who fail'd to reach the shore.

JIM BLUDSOE

Franz Rickaby recorded this as a poem written by John Hay, Wausau, Wisconsin. It was recited to Helene Stratman-Thomas around 1941 by Harry Dyer, age seventy-seven, Madison.

No, I cannot tell where he lives
Because he don't live you see.
Leastways he's got out of the habit
Of living like you and me.

Where have you been these last three years
What you haven't heard folks tell
About Jim Bludsoe cashing in his checks
That night on the *Prairie Belle.*

He weren't no saint;
Then engineers are pretty much all alike.
One lives at Natchez, under the hill,
Another one here in Pike.

A peerless chap and his talk was Jim,
But an awkward man in a row.
But he never flunked nor he never lied;
I reckon he never knowed how.

And this was all the religion he had
Was to treat his engines well.
Never was he passed on the river
In the mind of the pilots' bell.

And if ever the *Prairie Belle* took fire,
A thousand times he swore
That he'd hold her nose again' the bank
'Til the last soul got ashore.

All boats have their day on the Mississip'
And her day came at last.
Moon Star was a better boat
And she vowed that she'd never be passed.

And she came a-tearing along that night,
The oldest craft in the line,
With a nigger squat on the safety valve
And her furnace crammed, resin and pine.

240

A fire broke out as she cleared the bar
And burnt a hole in the night.
And quick as a flash, she turned and made
For that willer bank on the right.

There was shriekin' and cursin' as the bell rolled out
Over all the infernal roar.
"I'll hold her nose agin' the bank
'Til the last galoot's ashore."

Through the hot, black breath of the burning boat
Jim Bludsoe's voice was heard.
And they all had faith in his cussedness
'Cause they knowed he would keep his word.

And true enough, they all got off
Before the smokestack fell.
And Bludsoe's ghost went up alone
In the smoke of the *Prairie Belle*.

You are no saint, but on judgment day
I'd take my chance with Jim,
While along side of some pious gentlemen
Who wouldn't have shook hands with him.

He seen his duty, a dead sure thing;
And he went for it thar and then.
And Christ ain't goin' to be too hard
On the man that died for men.

Iconographic Collection, SHSW.

THE CHATSWORTH WRECK

Sung by F. A. Fair, Grand Forks, North Dakota, for Franz Rickaby in 1923. Fair explained that the wreck occurred in 1881 at Chatsworth, Illinois. The train had been bound for Niagara Falls; two excursioners from Fair's home town of Berwick, Illinois, were aboard it. (Helene Stratman-Thomas later commented, in a handwritten note on Rickaby's manuscript, that her aunt had nearly taken the fatal journey.) The final verse was sometimes used as a chorus.

From city, town and hamlet there came a merry throng
To view the great Niagara, with joy they sped along.

The maiden and her lover, the husband and the wife,
The merry prattling children so full of joyous life.

With hand upon the lever and eye upon the track
The engineer is standing while the shades of night grow black.

To see the smouldering timbers that lay along the ridge,
Oh God, in pity save them! It is the railway bridge.

A mighty crash of timbers, a sound of hissing steam;
The groans and cries of anguish, a woman's stifled scream.

The dead and dying mingled with the broken beams and bars;
An awful human carnage, a dreadful wreck of cars.

All honor to the brave ones who flame and fire fought
All through that night of horror, a glory dearly bought.

Over land and o'er the water this thrilling message crossed,
The bridge was burned at Chatsworth, a hundred lives were lost.

But oh, how much of sorrow, and oh, how much of pain
Awaited those who journeyed on that fatal railway train.

The Chatsworth Wreck

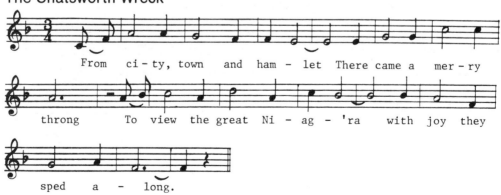

From ci-ty, town and ham-let There came a mer-ry throng To view the great Ni-ag-'ra with joy they sped a-long.

THE BROOKLYN THEATER FIRE

Sung by Lester A. Coffee, age seventy-five, Harvard, Illinois, in 1946. Coffee referred to an old scrapbook for the lyrics, but said that he well remembered the tune of this song, which commemorates a terrible fire of December 5, 1876, in which 295 New York theatergoers died. Sometimes a chorus—"Never forget those two orphans"—is repeated after each verse.

In the evening bright stars they were shining,
And the moon it shone clear on the land.
Our city in peace and in quiet;
The hour of midnight at hand.

Hark, do you hear the cry, "Fire"?
How dismal the bells they do sound.
The Brooklyn Theater is burning,
It's fast burning down to the ground.

We never can forget those two orphans.
Bad luck seemed to stand in their way.
It seems they were brought to our city,
The lives of our dear friends to take.

The doors they were open at seven.
The curtains were rolled up at eight.
And those that had seats, they were happy.
Outsiders were mad they were late.

The play it went on very smoothly
'Til sparks from the curtain did fly.
It was then the women and children,
"Oh God, save our lives," they did cry.

Next morning among the black ruins,
Oh God, what a sight met our eyes!
The dead they were lying in heaps
And some could not be recognized.

Mothers were weeping and crying
For sons who were out on that night.
Oh God, may their souls rest in heaven,
All those who were innocent and bright.

What means this large gathering of people
Upon such a cold winter day?
What means this long line of hearses
That gather in their mournful array?

It's away to the cemetery of Greenwood
Where the winds of the cold winter blow.
It's there where the funeral is going
The dead and unknown for to lie.

The Brooklyn Theater Fire

In the even - ing bright stars they were shin - ing, And the moon it shone clear on the land. Our ci - ty in peace and in qui - et, The hour of mid-night at hand. Hark, do you hear the cry "Fire"? How dis - mal the bells they do sound. The Brook - lyn Thea - ter is burn - ing, It's fast burn - ing down to the ground.

243

THE PERSIA'S CREW

Sung by M. C. Dean, Virginia, Minnesota, for Franz Rickaby. The *Persia* was a Great Lakes freighter that went down with all hands during a terrible storm on Lake Huron on November 18, 1869. The ballad celebrating her loss became a great favorite among sailors of the inland seas.

Sad and dismal is the story that I will tell to you,
About the schooner *Persia,* her officers and crew.
They sank beneath the waters deep in life to rise no more,
Where wind and desolation sweep Lake Huron's rock-bound shore.

They left Chicago on their lee, their songs they did resound;
Their hearts were filled with joy and glee for they were homeward bound.
They little thought the sword of death would meet them on their way,
And they, so full of joy and life, would in Lake Huron lay.

In mystery o'er their fate was sealed; they did collide, some say.
And that is all that will be revealed until the Judgment Day.
But when the angels take their stand to sweep these waters blue
They will summon forth at Heaven's command the *Persia's* luckless crew.

Her captain, he is no more; he lost his precious life.
He sank down among Lake Huron's waves, free from all mortal strife.
A barren coast now hides from view his manly, lifeless form.
And still in death is the heart so true that weathered many a storm.

There was Daniel Sullivan, her mate, with a heart as true and brave
As ever was compelled by fate to fill a sailor's grave.
Alas, be lost his noble life; poor Daniel is no more.
He met a sad untimely end upon Lake Huron's shore.

Oh Daniel, Dan, your many friends mourn the fate that has on you frowned.
They look in vain for your return back to Oswego town.
They miss the love-glance of your eye, your hand they'll clasp no more
For still in death you now do lie upon Lake Huron's shore.

Now around Presque Isle the sea birds scream their mournful notes along.
In chanting to the sad requiem, the mournful funeral song,
They skim along the waters blue and then aloft they soar
O'er the bodies of the *Persia's* crew that lie along the shore.

The Persia's Crew

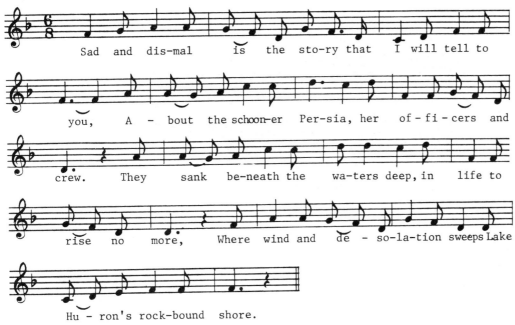

Sad and dis-mal is the sto-ry that I will tell to you, A - bout the schoon-er Per-sia, her of-fi-cers and crew. They sank be-neath the wa-ters deep, in life to rise no more, Where wind and de - so-la-tion sweeps Lake Hu - ron's rock-bound shore.

THE NEWHALL HOUSE FIRE

Sung by Ella Mittelstaedt Fischer, age seventy-five, Mayville, Wisconsin, in 1946. Until 1946, the burning of the Newhall House in Milwaukee stood as America's worst hotel fire; seventy persons died in the early-morning hours of January 10, 1883. As a girl of twelve Mrs. Fischer witnessed the fire, and fifty years later she could not sing the song without being overcome with emotion.

'Twas a grey and early morning when the dreadful cry of "Fire"
Rang out upon the cold and piercing air.
A little word alone was all it did require
For to send dismay and panic everywhere.

When the dreadful alarm a-sounded through that oft-condemned hotel
They rushed in mad confusion every way.
The smoke was suffocating and blinding them as well.
The fire keen could not be held at bay.

The firemen worked like demons as to all within their power
To save a life or try to soothe the pain.
It made the strongest hearts sick, for within a half an hour
All the hushed and further efforts were in vain.

From every window men and women wildly would beseech
For help in tones of anguish and despair.
What could have been their feelings when the ladder could not reach
And death leaped 'round them everywhere?

Up in the highest window stood a servant girl alone,
And the crowd all stood with bated breath.
They turned away their faces with many a stifled groan
When she jumped to meet perhaps as hard a death.

In one window you could see him, and his wife stood by his side,
They say he was a millionaire.
To save him from the dreadful fire they left no means untried.
Gold nor treasure had no value there.

A boy stood in a window, and his mother down below.
And when she saw the flames approaching wild,
With upraised hands to pray for him, she knelt down in the snow.
And the stoutest heart could not restrain a tear.

She madly rushed toward the fire and she madly tore her hair,
Saying, "Take me, God, but spare my pride and joy."
She saw the flames surround him, and then in dark despair,
Said, "Oh God, have mercy on my only boy."

They tell us now this old hotel had been on fire before,
And not considered safe for several years.
But still the men that own it, let it run on as before,
Yet they are not to blame, it now appears.

Incendiarism this time has been the cause, they say;
But who the culprit is they cannot tell.
But Milwaukee will not rest neither by night nor day
'Til the matter is investigated well.

But that will be no benefit to those who passed away
In this, Milwaukee's greatest burning pyre.
And "Peace be to the ashes," is the best that we can say
For the victims of this great and dreadful fire.

The Newhall House Fire

'Twas a grey and ear-ly morn-ing when the dread-ful
cry of fire Rang out up-on the cold and pier-cing
air. A lit-tle word a-lone was all it did require for to send dis-may and pan-ic ev-ery-where.

Mill fire, Alma, Buffalo County, ca. 1895.
Photo by Gerhard Gesell.

CONTESTS

THE LITTLE BROWN BULLS

To judge from the number of times this song was recorded, it must easily have been one of the most popular of its time. The story of the song is of a log-skidding contest between two yokes of oxen which took place in the Wisconsin pinery in the 1870's. No two singers sang the same verson of either melody or lyrics. Helene Stratman-Thomas heard the song from Harry Dyer of Madison, Adolph Williams of Hayward, Arthur Moseley and Charles Bowlen of Black River Falls, Robert Walker of Crandon, and Emery De Noyer of Rhinelander, Wisconsin, all during the 1940's.

Not a thing on the river McClusky did fear
As he skidded the logs with his big spotted steers.
Says Bull Gordon, the Yankee, "You'll have your hands full
If you skid one more log than my Little Brown Bulls."

The day was appointed and soon it drew nigh
For twenty-five dollars their fortune to try.
'Twas up to the logs and then fasten them on.
Hurry up, time's a-wastin', and it's no longer dawn.

Then shouted McClusky as they started to pull,
"I'll skid two to one of the little brown bulls."
To his little brown bulls Gordon said, "Never fear
For we'll easily beat them, those big spotted steers."

Now the sun had gone down when the foreman did say,
"Turn out, boys, turn out. You've enough for the day."
As they scaled them and counted McClusky did smile
'Til the foreman says, "Mac, you're behind by a mile."

The boys then all laughed and McClusky did swear
As he tore out by handfuls his long yellow hair.
So it's fill up your glasses and fill them up full,
And we'll drink to Bull Gordon and his Little Brown Bulls.

The Little Brown Bulls

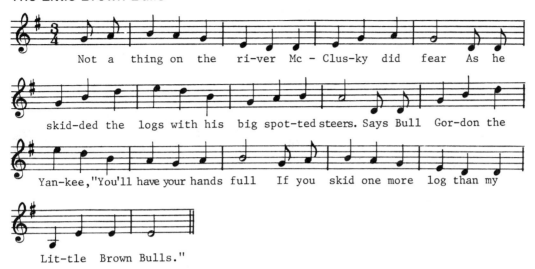

Not a thing on the ri-ver Mc-Clus-ky did fear As he

skid-ded the logs with his big spot-ted steers. Says Bull Gor-don the

Yan-kee, "You'll have your hands full If you skid one more log than my

Lit-tle Brown Bulls."

THE O'KELLY BROTHERS

Sung by C. C. Talbott, Forbes, North Dakota, for Franz Rickaby in 1922. The melody was Talbott's; the words were later supplied by his daughter, Gladys Talbott Edwards, who noted: "You will see that many of these stanzas are defective. Papa makes the tune to fit them."

Says Brady to Patrick O'Kelly one day, "O'Kelly, you owe me a V."
"Now I know that I do, but you bet I'll not pay, for I haven't the money you see."
"Now I know that you have, for I know you're the man that got twenty-five for his vote."
"You lie," says O'Kelly, "and you I can whip," he said as he pulled off his coat
"Now I don't like that last remark, Pat. Shut up, or I'll give you a thump."
But Pat being drunk so he didn't mind that. He said it again like a chump.
Chorus: And the doctor thinks O'Kelly will recover,
Though he may be laid up for a month or more,
For when Dan stuck out his paw, sure he broke O'Kelly's jaw
And so many stars ye niver saw before.

The other day at a game of baseball the umpire was O'Kelly's son, James.
He was makin' mestakes and the boys all alike was callin' him indacent names.
'Twas in the eighth innin' the trouble begin. Sure Jimmie was spoilin' for a fight.
"For kickin' I fine ye tin dollars, McKnight." At this the boys set up a howl.
Sure O'Cool he batted a home run to right. Jimmie Kelly pronounced it a foul.
Chorus: And the doctor thinks O'Kelly will recover,
Though he may be laid up for a month or more,
For when the boys went in for blood, Jimmie Kelly's name was mud,
And so many stars ye niver saw before.

There was Michael O'Kelly, a brother to Pat, who went out to have a big time.
He was playin' draw poker in Brien's resort and no one expected a fight.
The trouble began when the deal came to Mike. He dealt out big hands all around.
Sure Michael was raisin' 'em all out of line when somebody called him at that.
He shouted, "You suckers, the money is mine, for I have got five aces pat."

Chorus: And the doctor thinks O'Kelly will recover,
Though he may be laid up a month or more.
For he broke O'Kelly's face and kicked his teeth all out of place,
And so miny stars ye niver saw before.

There was Daniel O'Kelly, a brother to Mike, who wint out to have a big time.
He drank day and night, and bad whiskey at that, and for it he spent his last dime.
While mopin' around he spied Casey's mule tied up in the yard to a rail.
And Danny he thought what fine fun it would be just to burn off the poor esle's tail
So Dan lit the tail. It became very hot, and he laughed at the joke like a fool.
But in the excitement poor Danny forgot to git out of the way of the mule.
Chorus: And the doctor thinks O'Kelly will recover,
Though he may be laid up for a month or more.
For when the mule reached out for Dan there was one sore Irishman,
And so miny stars ye niver saw before.

The O'Kelly Brothers

Says Bra-dy to Pat-rick O'-Kel-ly one day, "O'-
Kel-ly, you owe me a five." "Now I know that I do, but you
bet I'll not pay, for I have-n't the mon-ey you see." Now I
know that you have, for I know you're the man that
twen-ty five for his vote, "You lie," says O'-Kel-ly, and
you I can whip," he said as he pulled off his coat. "Now
I don't like that last re-mark, Pat. Shut up, or I'll give you a
thump." But Pat be-ing drunk so he did-n't mind that, He
said it a-gain like a chump.

Chorus:

And the doc-tor thinks O' - Kel-ly will re-cov-er Though he may be laid up for a month or more. For when Dan stuck out his paw, sure he broke O'-Kel-ly's jaw, And so mi - ny stars ye ni-ver saw be - fore.

Bessie Gordon of Schofield, Marathon County,
seated at her small reed organ behind the bar.
Photo by Helene Stratman-Thomas.

THE TWENTY POUND DOG

Sung by Robert Walker, age fifty-eight, Crandon, Wisconsin, in 1941.

Me name is Tim McCarthy.
I live in a town of renown.
Had a bet with one Tim O'Flattery
That me bull dog could wallop the town.

He said, "He knows one Pat Murphy
Who lived way below, down on the bog,
That had a big black and tan terrier
That could wallop me twenty pound dog."

I fetched out me bull twenty pounder
He acted as proud as a king.
And he eyed Murphy's black and tan terrier
As they both sashayed 'round in the ring.

They fought for an hour and a quarter
They mixed it up down on the bog,
'Til the terrier walked away with the laurels
From the corpse of my twenty pound dog.

Oh, gentlemen he was a dandy
Pat Murphy, that dirty old hog,
Walked around with that terrier called Andy,
That walloped me twenty pound dog.

I swore I would have satisfaction.
I pulled off me coat and me hat.
And I made at that _____
From the _____ right down to small fat.

I then took a slice at the terrier,
And I knocked him 'way out on the bog,
And then all the way home I swore vengeance—
Sweet vengeance for me twenty pound dog.

The Twenty Pound Dog

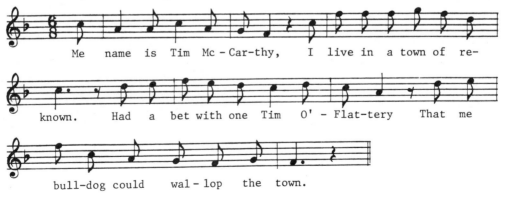

252

THE NOBLE SKEW BALD

Sung by Fred Bainter, Ladysmith, Wisconsin, for Franz Rickaby in 1923. Bainter learned this song in 1883 on the Menomonie (Red Cedar) River. It is about a famous Irish horse race which included the "witch horse," Skew Bald.

Come gentlemen, come sportsmen, come listen you all,
I'll sing you the praise of the noble Skew Bald.
It's how he came over you may understand.
It was by one Melvin, the marrow of our land.

You've heard of his values and wonders before,
But now he is challenged by young Silas Score
To run with Miss Grissel, that famous gray mare,
For ten thousand guineas on the plains of Kildare.

Skew Bald in the barn to his master did say,
"O master, dear master, don't you be afraid;
If you will on my side some thousands to hold
I will bring to your castle large pilons of gold."

Sir Arthur he wrote to Sir Wright the next day,
Make ready, make ready, tomorrow's the day.
Your horse and your saddle and all things prepare,
For we must hurray to the plains of Kildare.

The day being appointed, those horses walked out.
There was many a nobleman from east, west and south
Stood a-viewing the horses just as they stood there.
They bet all their money on the famous gray mare.

The horses being ready, were brought to the post.
The riders got orders that moment to mount,
When the voice from the spectators, saying, "Now clear the way,
For the moment's approaching. No longer delay."

The signal being given, like lightning did fly,
Skew Bald like an arrow the gray mare went by.
Oh, had you been there for to see them come around,
You'd have thought to your heart that they ne'er touched the ground.

When they came to the center of the course
Skew Bald to his rider began a discourse,
Saying, "Rider, dear rider, I pray you tell me
How far is Miss Grissel this moment from me?"

"Skew Bald, you do run at a beautiful style.
The gray mare's behind you one half English mile.
If you'll mend in your running, I'll warrant you there
That this very heat you will distance the mare."

Skew Bald hearing this, he sprung off at a speed,
And at every leap covered forty-odd feet.
"Stick fast to your saddle, my boy, never fear,
For you ne'er shall be jostled on the plains of Kildare."

When they came to the last winning post,
Skew Bald to the nobles, "You can now drink a toast.
Drink a health to Miss Grissel, that famous gray mare
That's now lying dead on the plains of Kildare."

The Noble Skew Bald

Come gent-le-men, come sportsmen, come lis-ten you all, I'll
sing you the praise of the no-ble Skew Bald. It's now he came
o-ver you may un-der-stand It was by one Mel-vin, the
nar-row of our land.

THE BOLD BENICIA BOY

This song was included in a manuscript sent by Professor George Lyman Kittredge to Franz Rickaby. It celebrates an exhibition boxing match between Tom Sayers, the British champion, and John Heenan, an American challenger. It should be noted that despite Heenan's victory in the song, Sayers in fact defeated him in a title match in 1860.

It was down in merrie England
All in the bloom of spring.
And England filled her glasses,
She filled them to the brim;
She drank this toast to Englishmen,
"The bravest of the brave,
Who rule all men and whether it be
On land or on the wave."

Then Uncle Sam put on his specs
As he looked o'er the main.
"And is this your English bully
A-bellowin' again?
Oh, doesn't he remember
Ben Franklin good and strong
Who used to play with lightning
When his day's work was done?"

"Johnny Bull, don't you remember
Our Washington of old,
And likewise Lake E-ri-e
With Perry brave and bold?
It was there you got a lesson
Which caused you for to sigh;
So beware of Yankee muscle—
Johnny Bull, mind ye' eye."

It was down in merrie England
All in the bloom of spring,
And England's bold champion
Stood stripped within the ring
To fight the noble Heenan,
The valiant son of Son of Troy,
And to try his British muscles on
The brave Benicia Boy.

Oh the copper was now tossed in air;
The minutes did begin,
"It's two to one," said England:
They both went rushin' in.
They fought like noble heroes
Till one received a blow,
And the red crimson tide
From the Yankee's nose did flow.

"We have got first blood," cried Johnny Bull,
"Let England shout for joy,"
Which cheered the British bully
And the brave Benicia Boy.
The tiger rose within him,
The lightning seized his eye;
"You may smile away, Old England,
But, Johnny, mind yo' eye."

Then the grandest round of all
That the world has ever seen:
The son of Uncle Sam took up
The champion off his feet,
And with his grasping withers
He hurled him in the air,
And over the ropes he knocked him—
How the Englishmen did stare.

Then come all you Yankee heroes
Whose fame and fortune's made,
Look on that lofty eagle
And never be afraid!
May the Union last forever!
The flag is now unfurled
And the Star Spangled Banner
Proudly floats o'er the world!

HUNTERS' CHORUS

Sung by Mrs. James H. Fowler, age seventy-four, Lancaster, Wisconsin, in 1946.

The hunter winds his bugle horn
To horse, to horse, hello, hello.
The fiery coursers snuff the morn
And thronging serfs the mark pursue.

The eager pack with couple freed
Dash through the break, the briar, the brae.
While answering horn, and hound, and steed
The mountain echoes, startling quick.

Up jumps from yonder tangled thorn
A deer more white than mountain snow.
And louder vang the hunters' horn
Hark, forward, forward, hello, hello.

Hunters' Chorus

The hunt - er winds his bu - gle horn, "To horse, to horse, hello, hel - lo." The fi - ery cours -ers sniff the morn and
throng-ing serfs the mark pur -sue.

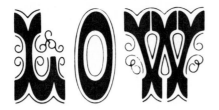

LOW LIFE

PLEASE, MISTER BARKEEPER

Sung by Gene Silsbe, age sixty-one, Hancock, Wisconsin, in 1941.

"Please, Mr. Barkeeper, has father been here? He's not been at home today.
'Tis almost midnight and mother's in fear some accident keeps him away."
"No, no, little stranger. Oh yes he's been here. Some officers took him away.
He's gone to the lock-up, I'm sorry, my dear. He's done something wicked they say."
Chorus: "Oh, it was not my father who did the bad deed; 'twas drinking that maddened
his brain.
Oh, let him go home to dear mother, I plead. I'm sure he'll not touch it again."

"Please, Mr. Policeman, my father is lost; a man said you took him away.
Oh, can't he go home, sir, and what will it cost, if mother will send you the pay?"
"No, no, little pleader, your father can't go. We put him in prison today.
Go home to your mother and quick let her know what's keeping your father away."

"Please, Mr. Jailer, please let me go in, they say that my father's inside.
I scarcely can tell how unhappy we've been, we couldn't have felt worse has he died.
Please, Sir, it was drinking that made him do wrong. I'm sure he'll not drink anymore.
Oh, just a few minutes, a minute's not long." But no one would open the door.

All day the young watcher stood fast by the door, in vain with his father to speak.
It creaked its great hinges twice ten times or more, as prison doors only can creak.
Then stealing in darkness, to home sad as death, a promise most solemn he swore,
"Dear mother, I'll shun it as long as I live. I'll taste it and touch it no more."

Please, Mister Barkeeper

sor-ry my dear. He's done some-thing wick -ed they say.

Oh, it was not my fa- ther who did the bad deed, "Twas

drink- ing that mad- dened his brain. Oh, let him go

home to dear mo- ther I plead. I'm sure he'll not

touch it a - gain.

GAMBLER'S BLUES

Sung by Bessie Gordon, age forty, Schofield, Wisconsin, in 1941.

I was down in old Joe's barroom at the corner of the square,
And the drinks were served as usual, and a goodly crowd was there.

At my right stood Joe McKinny, his eyes bloodshot and red,
And he looked at the crowd all 'round him, and these were the words he said:

As I passed by the old infirmary, I saw my baby there,
All stretched out on a table, so cold and still and fair.

Sixteen coal-black horses all hitched to a rubber-tired hack
Took seven pretty girls to the graveyard, only six of them coming back.

Now when I die just bury me in a box, with a coat and hat,
With a twenty-dollar gold piece on my watch chain to let the Lord know I'm standing pat.

Six crapshooters as pall bearers, let a chorus girl sing me a song;
Put a dance band on the hearse, to raise heck as we go along.

Now that you've heard my story, I'll take another shot of booze.
And if anybody happens to ask you, well, I've got those gambler's blues.

Gambler's Blues

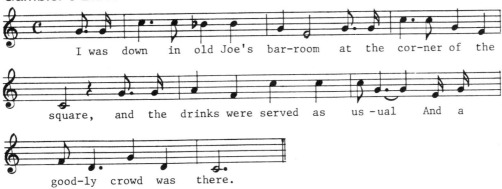

I was down in old Joe's bar-room at the cor-ner of the

square, and the drinks were served as us -ual And a

good-ly crowd was there.

MOTHER, QUEEN OF MY HEART
Sung by Alfred Whitt, age fifteen, Crandon, Wisconsin, in 1941.

I had a home down in Texas, down where the bluebonnets grew.
I had the kindest old mother; we were happy there, just we two.
But one night the angels called her, a debt that we all have to pay.
She called me close to her bedside, these last words to say,

"Son, don't go drinking and gambling. Promise mother you'll always go straight."
Many years have passed since that parting, the promise I broke all the same.
I first started gambling for pastime, but soon got the best of me all.
I found that I'd spent all my money, never thinking that I'd ever fall.

One night I had bet all my money; nothing was left to be seen.
I needed one card to beat them and that card was a queen.
The cards were dealt 'round the table. Each man took his turn at the draw.
I drew the card that would beat them; I turned it and this is what I saw.

I saw my dear mother's picture; somehow it did seem to say,
"Son, you have broken your promise." I threw the cards all away.
I gave my winnings to a newsboy, for gambling and me had to part.
And now I shall always remember Mother, the queen of my heart.

Mother, Queen of My Heart

Photo by *Milwaukee Journal*.

FATHER, DEAR FATHER, COME HOME WITH ME NOW

Sung by Laura Avanell, age eighty, Linden, Wisconsin, in 1946. A similar version was given to Franz Rickaby in 1923 by a young man in one of his classes at the University of North Dakota.

Father, dear father, come home with me now,
The clock in the steeple strikes one.
You said you were coming right home from the shop
As soon as your day's work was done.
Our fire's gone out, our house is all dark,
And mother's been watching since tea,
With poor brother Benny so sick in her arm,
And no one to help her but me.
Chorus: Come home, come home, come home,
     Please father, dear father, come home.
     Hear the sweet voice of the child
     Which night winds repeat as they roam.
     Oh, who could resist the most plentiful prayer,
     "Please father, dear father, come home."

Father, dear father, come home with me now,
The clock in the steeple strikes two.
The night has grown colder, and Benny is worse,
But he has been calling for you.
Indeed he is worse; Ma says he will die,
Perhaps before morning shall dawn.
And this is the message she sent me to bring:
Come quickly or he will be gone.

Father, dear father, come home with me now,
The clock in the steeple strikes three.
The house is so lonely, the hours are so long
For poor weeping mother and me.
Yes, we are alone. Poor Benny is dead,
And gone with the angels of light:
And these are the very last words that he said,
"I want to kiss papa tonight."

Father, Dear Father, Come Home With Me Now

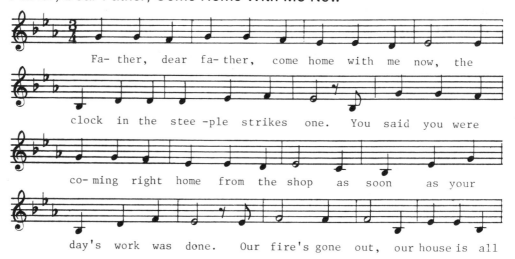

Fa- ther, dear fa- ther, come home with me now, the
clock in the stee -ple strikes one. You said you were
co- ming right home from the shop as soon as your
day's work was done. Our fire's gone out, our house is all

dark, and mo-ther's been wat-ching since tea, With

poor bro-ther Ben-ny so sick in her arm, and no one to

help her but me. Come home, come home, come home, please

fa-ther, dear fa-ther come home. Hear the sweet

voice of the child which night winds re-peat as they

roam. Oh, who could re-sist the most plen-ti-ful

prayer, "Please fa-ther, dear fa-ther, come home."

THE GAMBLING MAN

Sung by Myrth Whitt, age thirty-nine, Crandon, Wisconsin, in 1941. Although this version came to Wisconsin by way of Kentucky, it has acquired local color with the insertion of Crandon—instead of Georgia—in the last line.

I gambled down in Washington
Not many more weeks than three,
When I fell in love with a pretty little girl
And she fell in love with me.

She took me in her parlor;
She cooled me with her fan;
She whispered low in her mother's ear,
"I love that gambling man."

"Daughter, dear daughter,
How can you treat me so
To leave your poor old mother
And with a gambler go?"

"Mother, dear mother,
I know I love you well
But the love I have for that gambling man
No human tongue can tell.

"Mother, oh mother,
I'll tell you if I can,
If you ever see me again
I'll be with the gambling man."

We've gambled down in Washington;
We've gambled down in Spain;
We're goin' back to Crandon
To gamble our last game.

The Gambling Man

Gam-bled down in Wash-ing-ton not man-y more weeks than three, When I fell in love with a pret-ty lit-tle girl and she fell in love with me. She took me in her par-lor, She cooled me with her fan; She whis-pered low in her moth-er's ear, "I love a gam-bling man."

PLAIN LUST

BORING FOR OIL

Sung by Lewis Winfield Moody, age seventy-five, Plainfield, Wisconsin, in 1940.

One morning in a ramble I met this fair maid.
Though handsome and lovely, to her I did say,
"For all of my fortune I'm willing to toil,
If you show me a place to go boring for oil."

The fair maid she stammered, "Young man, I declare,
I know where that place is and watch it with care.
And no one has seen it since I was a child;
And if you go there you shall surely strike oil."

"Fain," say I to myself, "My fortune is made.
If you show me that place now I'll see you're repaid."
She hoisted her garments for me to see all,
And she showed me the place to go boring for oil.

_____ a hundred times over,
And I bade her be seated on nature's green shore.
She screamed and she hollered, and tried to recoil,
When I pulled out old Satan, and went boring for oil.

We had not bored long _____
When the oil from her oiler then gently did flow.
She screamed and she hollered, my character to soil,
"You've broken my bladder a-boring for oil."

Boring for Oil

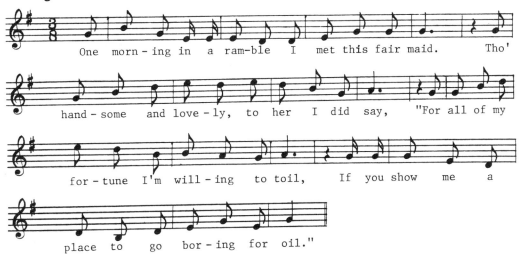

PADDY MILES, THE FISHERMAN

Sung by John Christian, Coloma, Wisconsin, in 1940.

Paddy Miles was a fisherman, young and light-hearted,
And a very respectable young man, you bet.
Except on the ocean where he was a —
I see all kind of fish that came into his net.
Paddy wanted but one thing and that was a wife, sir,
To keep his mansion in ordered array.
"I've catched many things in my life," said Paddy,
"The most difficult thing is in catching a wife."

One morning as Paddy was out on the ocean,
And catching red herring and sprats in galore,
A sight met his eyes which set him in commotion,
Such a sight in his lifetime he had ne'er seen before.
A pretty young mermaid, as naked as Venus,
Was washing her bubbies and combing her hair.
Said Pat, "There is but a few waves between us,
Come out and float up along side of me here."

Said she, "Mr. Pat, I can see you've a notion.
You want to be green 'cause you're reared on the land.
How could I be out of my bed in the ocean?
It's my only bed, it is made of the sand.
No, for shame, _____
_____
Put your pipe to mine, and a little free motion
And I'll be the soul that will tickle your ——."

And Pat he kept urging and then started begging.
Said she, "Mr. Pat, I can see you're afloat."
While her little green tail kept urging and wagging,
He kept still and slapped her right into the boat.
It hurt Paddy's feelings while squeezing her belly
And then he was balked by one scaly swish.
For she was but female down to the belly
And the rest of her body was nothing but fish.

"Holding you in my arms is a terrible bother.
How your daddy got you is a puzzle to me.
I know you're a maid, you're made like any other,
And a maid all your lifetime you're likely to be.
Go back to your cockscomb, your cockscomb, your daddy
_____ soft your fish bottom I find.
But give me a maid, made the right way," said Paddy,
"With a passage before her and a big arse behind."

Photo by Charles Van Schaick, Black River Falls.

Paddy Miles, the Fisherman

Pad - dy Miles was a fish - er - man, young and light-heart - ed,

And a ve - ry re - spect - a - ble young man, you bet. Ex-

cept on the o - cean where he was a I see all kind of

fish that came in - to his net. Pad - dy want - ed but one thing and

that was a wife, sir, To keep his man - sion in or - dered ar-

ray. "I've catched man - y things in my life, said Pad - dy

The most di - fi - cult thing is in catch - ing a wife.

265

THE LITTLE BALL OF YARN

Sung by blind, one-armed Emery De Noyer, age sixty-three, Rhinelander, Wisconsin, in 1941. On her transcription of this song, Helene Stratman-Thomas noted De Noyer's remark after singing it: "Gosh darn it! You know, I don't like to sing dirty songs."

It was in the month of May when the birds did skip and play,
And the blackbirds were singing like a charm.
It was here I met this Miss, said, "I'm glad of this.
Can't I wind up your little ball of yarn?"

"Kind sir," she said to me, "Oh a stranger I can see,
Perhaps you will do me a lot of harm.
Why don't you go to those who have money and fine clothes
And wind up their little ball of yarn?"

So he grabbed me 'round the waist, and he gently laid me down,
And the blackbirds were singing like a charm.
I pulled up my clothes and he pulled out his hose
And he wound up my little ball of yarn.

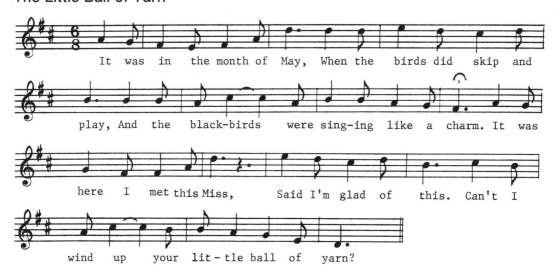

So quickly I arose, from my waist pulled down my clothes,
And the blackbirds were singing like a charm.
Feared that I'd been seen, I skipped across the green,
After winding up my little ball of yarn.

Now come all you pretty maids who dwell beneath the glades,
And rise up so early in the morn.
Be like the catbird and the thrush, keep your head beneath the brush
And both hands on your little ball of yarn.

For it was shortly after this that I went out to piss,
And found a pain that caused me quite alarm.
I found to my mishap, he gave me a dose of clap,
After winding up my little ball of yarn.

The Little Ball of Yarn

It was in the month of May, When the birds did skip and play, And the black-birds were sing-ing like a charm. It was here I met this Miss, Said I'm glad of this. Can't I wind up your lit-tle ball of yarn?

THE RED LIGHT SALOON

Sung for Helene Stratman-Thomas by Henry Humphries, age seventy-six, Hancock, Wisconsin; by John Christian, Coloma, Wisconsin; and by Bill Neupert, age fifty-three, Schofield, Wisconsin, in 1940-1941. This song exists in many versions throughout the United States, the principal difference between one version and another being the degree of unprintableness. What follows is a mild variant.

Come on, oh ye fellows, I'll sing you a song
If you pay me attention it won't take me long.
I'll sing you a song how my fortune befell
While taking a stroll to the city hotel.

It was in the last days of the month of July
And to make good connections with the train I did try.
The train left the station, I'm left there to doom,
So I paid a last visit to the Red Light Saloon.

I boldly walked in and stepped up to the bar,
And a pretty young damsel said, "Have a cigar."
I took her cigar and sat down on a chair —
Finally this maiden came tripping down there.

She boldly walked up and sat down on my knee,
Saying, "You are a fine lad and that I can see.
You are a shanty boy and that I well know
For your muscle is hard from your head to your toe."

Then she played with my mustache and the curl in my hair,
Which then was not ugly, I'm bound to declare.
And I jumped right up and put my cigar down,
Says I, "Pretty, fair maid, let's go have a round."

Then early next morning I bid her goodbye,
As she gave me a kiss with a tear in her eye.
And I didn't discover till early in June
That she'd slipped me a keepsake from the Red Light Saloon.

I'll curse that young lady till the forest turns blue;
And with whiskey and women, I swear I am through.
But I know as I swear I would give my fortune
Just to be back again in the Red Light Saloon.

The Red Light Saloon

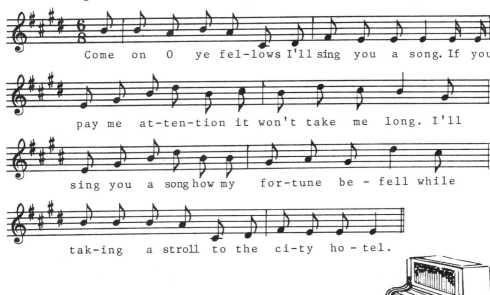

Come on O ye fel-lows I'll sing you a song. If you
pay me at-ten-tion it won't take me long. I'll
sing you a song how my for-tune be - fell while
tak-ing a stroll to the ci-ty ho - tel.

267

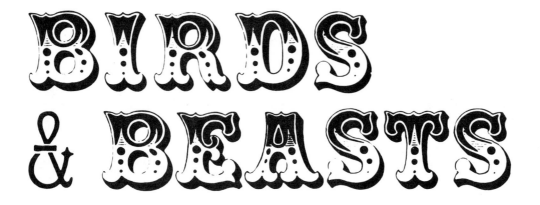

BIRDS & BEASTS

MY OLD HEN'S A GOOD OLD HEN

Sung by Pearl Jacobs Borusky, age thirty-nine, Antigo, Wisconsin, in 1940.

My old hen's a good old hen,
She lays eggs for the farmer men.
Sometimes one, sometimes two,
Sometimes enough for the whole darn crew.
Cluck, old hen, cluck, I tell you.
Cluck, old hen, or I'm a-gwine a sell you.
Cluck, old hen, cluck, I say,
Cluck, old hen, I'll give you away.

My Old Hen's a Good Old Hen

My old hen's a good old hen, she lays eggs for the farm-er men. Some-times one, some-times two, some-times enough for the whole darn crew. Cluck, old hen, cluck, I tell you. Cluck, old hen, or I'm a-gwine a sell you. Cluck, old hen, cluck, I say, Cluck, old hen, I'll give you a-way.

THE MAGPIE AND THE LARK

Sung by Eryl Levers, age twenty-four, Madison, Wisconsin, in 1946.
This is usually sung as a round.

In a snug little field in a neighboring park,
On a beautiful morning in spring,
A sly magpie jack saw a pert little lark
And he thought he could teach him to sing.
"Oh no," said the lark with a comical look
As he wobbled in front with his tail,
" 'Twould be so much trouble and far too much work,
And I know it would most likely fail.
For he who would be the opposite color,
And who has checks on, can never expect to be white."

The Magpie and the Lark

In a snug lit-tle field in a neigh-bor-ing park on a
beau-ti-ful morn-ing in spring, a sly mag-pie jack saw a
pert lit-tle lark and he thought he could teach him to
sing. "Oh no," said the lark, with a com-i-cal look as he
wab-bled in front with his tail,"'Twould be so much trou-ble and
far too much work, and I know it would most like-ly fail. For
he who would be the op-po-site fit to be tied, and who has
checks on can ne-ver ex-pect to be white."

District schoolhouse, Bloomfield, Walworth County.
Iconographic Collection, SHSW.

THE SHANGHAI ROOSTER

Sung by Adolph Williams, Hayward, Wisconsin, in 1946.

I had a farm out west, of farms it was the best.
Had a cross-eyed mule with freckles and red hair,
And one old Shanghai rooster with a wart on his left ear.
But now he's dead and climbed the golden stair.
Chorus: Oh, his fur was like a toothbrush, his comb was like an ax.
His head caved in like a sugar hogshead stave.
Now the hens are all on strike, haven't laid since Friday night.
They are weepin' o'er my Shanghai rooster's grave.

No more he'll come home late, at the hour of halfpast eight
Singin' cock-a-doodle-do and goodbye Nell.
For my poor old Shanghai rooster in battle nobly fell.
With the neighbor's bulldog he fought long and well.

He'll never crow again, wink his eye at some old hen.
Oh, I often said he should have been in jail.
Now the only thing that keeps me from goin' out and gettin' drunk
Is a feather from my Shanghai rooster's tail.

The Shanghai Rooster

I had a farm out west. Of farms it was the best. Had a

cross-eyed mule with freck-les and red hair. And

one old Shang-hai roost-er with a wart on his left ear. But

now he's dead and climbed the gold-en stair. Oh, his

fur was like a tooth-brush, his comb was like an axe. His

head caved in like a su-gar hogs-head stave. Now the

hens are all on strike, Have-n't laid since Fri-day

night. They are weep-in' o'er my Shang-hai roost-er's grave.

271

THE FROG SONG

For four hundred years the song about the marriage of the frog to the mouse has amused English-speaking children and grownups. The versions of this song in America are seemingly endless. The end-rhymes of the simple couplets intrigue the memory and challenge the singer to enlarge upon the incidents of the story and to create new verses. Two variants appear below.

FROGGIE WENT TO TAKE A RIDE

Sung by Winifred Bundy, age fifty-seven, Madison, Wisconsin, in 1941. Miss Bundy remarked, "I don't know how many generations of our family were sung to sleep on this one. We particularly loved that repetitious chorus."

Froggie went to take a ride,
Rigdom body mid-ah ki-mo,
Sword and pistol by his side,
Rigdom body mid-ah ki-mo,
Ki-mo ka-ro dout-oh shar-oh, ki-mo, ka-ro,
String strang come-a-diddle, anybody rig,
Rigdom body mid-ah ki-mo.

He rode up to Miss Mouse's door,
Rigdom, etc.
He jumped in the middle of Miss Mouse's floor,
Rigdom, etc.

He took Lady Mouse upon his knee,
Rigdom, etc.
Said, "Lady Mouse, will you marry me?"
Rigdom, etc.

Uncle Rat came riding down,
Rigdom, etc.
To get his niece a wedding gown,
Rigdom, etc.

He took her home where he did dwell,
Rigdom, etc.
That was in the bottom of a well,
Rigdom, etc.

The water took her up to the chin,
Rigdom, etc.
She wished she were a maid again,
Rigdom, etc.

Froggie Went to Take a Ride

Frog-gie went to take a ride, Rig-dom bo-dy mid-ah ki-mo. Sword and pis-tol by his side, Rig-dom bo-dy mid-ah ki-mo, Ki-mo ka-ro dout-oh shar-oh, ki-mo ka-ro, String strang come-a-did-dle an-y-bo-dy rig, Rig-dom bo-dy mid-ah - ki-mo.

272

FROGGIE WOULD A-WOOING GO

Sung by Charles Dietz, age seventy-five, Monroe, Wisconsin, in 1946. Since dancing was frowned upon in his family, Dietz felt that the song was incomplete and he made up the following final verse: "They learned to dance / And they did right well; / Then they died / And went to Hell."

A froggie would a-wooing go,
Uh-hum,
Froggie would a-wooing go,
Whether his mother would let him or no,
Uh-hum.

Said the frog, "Miss Mouse, will you marry me?"
Uh-hum,
Frog said, "Miss Mouse, will you marry me?"
"I'll have to ask Uncle Rat," said she,
Uh-hum.

"Who shall the wedders they all be?"
Uh-hum,
"Who shall the wedders they all be?"
"Bear, the bug, and the bumble bee."
Uh-hum.

"Where shall the wedding supper be?"
Uh-hum,
"Where shall the wedding supper be?"
"Down in the trunk of a hollow tree."
Uh-hum.

First to come was a little brown bug,
Uh-hum,
First to come was a little brown bug,
He had whiskey in a jug,
Uh-hum.

The last to come was a big tom cat,
Uh-hum,
The last to come was a big tom cat,
He ate the bride up, just like that,
Uh-hum.

Froggie jumped into the lake,
Uh-hum,
Froggie jumped into the lake,
He got eat by a big black snake,
Uh-hum.

Big black snake, he swum to land,
Uh-hum,
Big black snake, he swum to land,
He got killed by a nigger man,
Uh-hum.

Nigger man, he came from France,
Uh-hum,
Nigger man, he came from France,
T' teach the ladies how to dance,
Uh-hum.

Froggie Would A-Wooing Go

A frog-gie would a-woo-ing go, uh-hum. Frog-gie would a-woo-ing go, Wheth-er his mo-ther would let him or no, uh-hum.

THE BIRDIES' BALL

Sung by Mrs. James H. Fowler, age seventy-four, Lancaster, Wisconsin, in 1946. Mrs. Fowler's father sang this to her as a lullaby when she was a baby.

The spring dove said to the nightingale,
"I mean to give you birds a ball.
Pray, ma'am, ask the birdies all.
The birdies great and the birdies small."
Chorus: Tra-la la-la-la, Tra-la la-la-la,
    Tra-la la-la-la. Tra-la-la.
    Tra-la la-la-la, Tra-la la-la-la,
    Tra-la la-la-la. Tra-la-la.

Soon they came from bush and tree
Singing merry their songs of glee.
Each one dressed in his Sunday best.
Each one just from his cozy nest.

The wren and the cuckoo danced for life.
The raven waltzed with the yellow bird's wife.
The awkward owl and the bashful jay
Wished each other a very good day.

They danced all day 'till the sun was low
And the mother birds prepared to go.
And then the birds both great and small
Went home to their nests from the birdies' ball.

The Birdies' Ball

The spring dove said to the night-in gale, "I mean to give you

birds a ball." "Pray ma 'm," asked the bird-ies all, The

bird-ies great and the bird-ies small. Tra-la la-la-la

Tra-la la-la-la, Tra-la la-la-la, Tra-la-la. Tra-la la-la-la,

Tra-la la-la-la, Tra-la la-la-la, Tra-la-la.

274

Photo by Charles Van Schaick, Black River Falls.

THE CIRCUS

WHEN THE CIRCUS COMES TO TOWN

Lyrics by James O'Dea, music by Robert Adams. This song was provided by courtesy of the Circus World Museum, Baraboo.

Cy Perkins was the village scamp of Jayville-on-the-Pike;
Cy Perkins with his funny jokes you couldn't well dislike.
At the country general store, where he loafed from ten til four,
He'd keep the boys a'laughing til their very sides were sore.

When the circus bills in summer on the fences would appear,
Then Cy would say, "This is the grandest time of the year,
For there's nothing half so fine as the circus folks in line,
When they come trooping into town, oh, that's the fun for mine.
Chorus: For when the circus comes to town, I want to see
       The whole darn'd shooting match from A to Z.
       I want to see the clown when he drives about the town
       And I want to hear the steam piano play, by gee.
       I'll spend as much as sixty-seven cents
       To walk right up and see the show commence.
       With my gal, Samantha Brown, in her stunning new spring gown
       I'll be a regular cut-up when the circus comes to town.

I like to see the horses in the ring a'doing a jig;
There's nothing half so funny as the educated pig.
And the acrobats so great, who are always up to date
Are the only kind of actors I could ever tolerate.

When they pass around the crimson lemonade, I like to choke,
For that's the only drink on which I ever would go broke.
From the clown, so full of fun, to the girl who weighs a ton,
With the freaks and all included I'm in love with everyone.

When the Circus Comes to Town

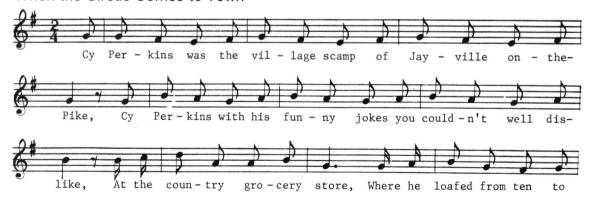

Cy Per - kins was the vil - lage scamp of Jay - ville on - the-
Pike, Cy Per - kins with his fun - ny jokes you could - n't well dislike, At the coun - try gro - cery store, Where he loafed from ten to

276

four, He'd keep the boys a-laugh-ing til their ve-ry sides were

sore. When the cir-cus bills in sum-mer on the fen-ces would ap-

pear, Then Cy would say, "This is the grand-est time of all the

year. For there's noth-ing half so fine As the cir-cus folks in

line, When they come troop-ing in-to town, Oh! that's the fun for

mine. For when the cir-cus comes to town I want to see the

whole darn'd shoot-ing match from A to Z, I want to see the

clown, When he drives a-bout the town. And I want to hear the

steam pi-an-o play, by Gee! I'll spend as much as six-ty sev-en

cents to walk right up and see the show com-mence, With my

gal, "Sa-man-tha Brown, In her stun-ning new spring gown. I'll

be a reg-'lar cut-up when the cir-cus comes to town.

JUMBO THE ELEPHANT

Lyrics by F. H. Evans, music by J. A. Snow. This song was provided through the courtesy of the Circus World Museum, Baraboo.

"O have you seen the elephant?" is all the people's cry;
The great and mighty elephant who stands so broad and high.
He daily eats a ton of hay, and drinks upon the sly
A tub of circus lemonade and several pints of rye.
Chorus: O have you seen the elephant, from England late he came.
　　　　He is the king of elephants and Jumbo is his name.

Old Jumbo likes a social glass, but he is never drunk
Though people say he always keeps a bottle in his trunk.
But then there's always snakes around, and Jumbo thinks it right
To keep some rye on hand to cure an accidental bite.

When people went to see him first they wondered at his size;
And then he looked so funny too, and winked his knowing eyes.
But they were very much surprised when soon the monster ran
And left the ring between the acts to go and see a man.

Jumbo the Elephant

278

Photo by Charles Van Schaick, Black River Falls.

279

HANNIBAL HOPE

Poem by John Lowitz and Frank French. This song was provided by courtesy of the Circus World Museum, Baraboo. The "Calve" referred to in the second verse was Emma Calve, a French operatic singer of the turn of the century.

There was once a moke named Hannibal Hope with a circus, understand,
Who used to play the steam Calliope and drum in the side-show band.
He left a gal named Mandy Green in Nashville, Tennessee,
And when the big show billed that town, she fairly howled with glee.
On circus day her friends so gay, of every style and shade
Were all on hand to hear the band and see the big parade.
And when she heard that Calliope a-coming down the line,
Miss Mandy cried with all her might, "My Golly, ain't that fine."
Chorus: "You may talk about your opera stars, but they don't shine for me.
     Angels playing on golden harps, well that ain't one, two, three.
     But I'm willing to bet that you will never forget
     Such music as is made when Hannibal Hope
     Plays the steam Calliope in the circus street parade."

As a Zulu Queen Miss Mandy Green had to join out with that show
Just to be near her Hannibal Hope she loved his music so.
While on the way to the lot one day, she passed a noisy group,
Who were discussing members of a famous opera troupe.
She heard them praise Caruso's voice, they called Calve sublime,
They boosted oratorio, but how they knocked ragtime.
Said one, "We've no musicians now, the masters are all dead."
Miss Mandy couldn't stand no more, she rushed right up and said:
Chorus: "You may talk about your opera stars, but they don't shine for me.
     Angels playing on golden harps, well that ain't one, two, three.
     But I'm willing to bet that you will never forget
     Such music as is made when Hannibal Hope
     Plays the steam Calliope in the circus street parade."

Hannibal Hope

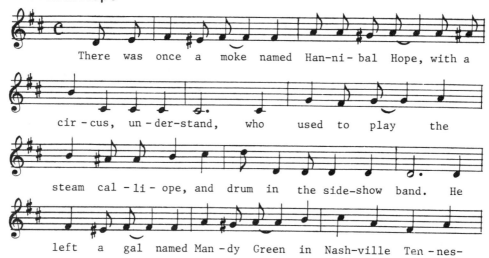

see, And when the big show billed that town, she

fair-ly howl-ed with glee, On Cir-cus day her

friends so gay, of ev-'ry style and shade, were

all on hand to hear the band and see the big pa-

rade! And when she heard that cal-li-ope, a'-

com-ing down the line, Miss Man-dy cried with

all her might, "My Gol-ly ain't that fine!

You may talk a-bout your op-e-ra stars, but

they don't shine for me. Ang-els play-ing on

gold-en harps, well they ain't one, two, three! But I'm

will-ing to bet that you will nev-er for-get, such

mu-sic as is made, When Han-ni-bal Hope plays the

steam cal-li-ope in the cir-cus street pa-rade."

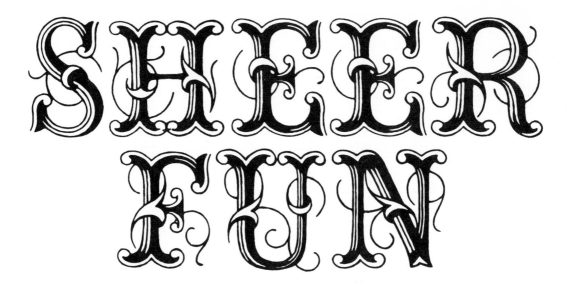

SHEER FUN

S. D. KNOWLES

This song was given to Franz Rickaby by its author, William N. Allen of Wausau, Wisconsin, who called it "Ballad of a Blowhard, By a Shanty Boy." The S. D. Knowles celebrated in Allen's song was a local farmer who threatened a lawsuit when he heard of the song.

This song is not a song of love, 'tis not a song of flowers,
'Tis not about the babbling brooks, nor of the shady bowers.
It is not about the ocean where the briny billow rolls.
But 'tis of a hump-backed blow-hard, his name is S. D. Knowles.
Chorus: Oh, humpy S. D. Knowles, old babbling S. D. Knowles.
        There never was a blow-hard that could blow like S. D. Knowles.

When he was a little baby in the good old state of Maine,
His father was a homely cuss, his mother somewhat plain.
But the sun in all its glory, as this planet round it rolls
Ne'er gazed upon a cherub half so fair as S. D. Knowles.

But as he grew to riper years his cherub looks decayed,
And bad looks with a vengeance came and, what is worse, they stayed.
Where smiles and dimples used to lurk around his mouth and chin
There's nothing left but wrinkles now, and hideous ghastly grins.

And if you meet him in the woods some sultry afternoon
You'll swear that some menagerie has lost its boss baboon.
And when he wanders through the fields when autumn days are near,
The potato bugs will tremble and the hoppers shake with fear.

His woolly pate looks something like a Tennessee brush fence,
And underneath those tangled locks there's neither wit nor sense.
And the feathers of a porcupine, when something frightens him,
Looks just exactly like the beard that grows on S. D.'s chin.

He wears a grin upon his face at evening, noon, and morn.
Just like the grin some coon will wear when in some neighbor's corn.
He wears a hump upon his back just like a log canoe,
When you see him you will know him, he's always dressed in blue.

His father was a blow-hard too, and when S. D. was young
The old man took him on his knee and thus he wagged his tongue:
"There is one thing, my darling son, that you must bear in mind,
To sail through life successfully you must have a fair wind.

Then listen to my sage advice, remember what I say.
When you are on the sea of life and many leagues away,
You'll meet with calm and adverse winds wherever you may go.
Now to have wind always ready you must early learn to blow."

S. D. took his old dad's advice and very soon became
The greatest blow-hard to be found in all the state of Maine.
Contention arose between them, and one cold wintry day
S. D. got mad, his back arose, he blowed his dad away.

And then he turned his grinning phiz towards the western states
Where he heard that pine was plenty and that men grew rich and great.
He left the good old state of Maine without much change to spare,
And now this champion blow-hard dwells upon the big Eau Claire.

He logs and threshes, farms and blows, and drives an old plug team.
Makes horse-shoes, crotches, sleds, and yokes, and runs a wood machine.
His neighbors very often wish, and will wish so again,
That he had always stayed down east, in the good old state of Maine.

Ye Wausau boys who love to hear a wild and frightful yarn
Go down and hire a livery at Jimmie Edee's barn,
And if you have a leisure day, a day or two to spare,
Drive over to where old Knowles resides upon the big Eau Claire.

This blow-hard's habitation you easily can find.
He dwells on Section thirty-three, town twenty-nine, range nine.
He'll broadly grin and blandly smile and explicitly explain
The crooks and turns of all the streams in all the state of Maine.

He'll tell you of the dangers, the hardships we went through,
How he can ride a Norway log and pole a bark canoe,
What havoc he has made among the spruces and the pines,
And how many miles on snow-shoes he walked on section lines.

The countless cords of wood he's sawed were gorgeous to see
Down in the Irish settlement out west of Mosinee;
What mammoth loads of wheat and oats and rye and buckwheat straw,
And sand and rocks and sapling logs his old plug team can draw.

How he could handle the goad-stick and whack a six-ox team,
The mammouth loads of logs he hauled when he was seventeen;
What a terror he was to the deer, the wolves, and bear
Before he came out west to dwell upon the big Eau Claire.

How he can play the Irishman and make the Dutchman squeal,
And wade through Scandinavians like a hungry ox through meal;
How he can pound the Polanders, and make the Frenchmen swear,
And wallop all the Chippewas upon the big Eau Claire.

His manifold adventures to you he will explain
When he was a shanty-boy in the good old state of Maine.
And you will wonder to yourselves as you meander home
Why so smart a man as S. D. Knowles is not more widely known.

S. D. Knowles

This song is not a song of love, 'tis not a song of

flowers, 'Tis not a-bout the bab-bling brooks, nor

of the sha-dy bowers. It is not a-bout the o-cean

where the brin-y bil-low rolls. But 'tis of a

hump-backed blow-hard, his name is S. D. Knowles.

Oh, hum-py S. D. Knowles; old bab-bling S. D.

Knowles. There nev-er was a blow-hard that could

blow like S. D. Knowles.

I'VE GOT A MOTTO

Sung by Eryl Levers, age twenty-four, Madison, Wisconsin, in 1946.

I've got a motto always merry and bright;
Look around you and you will find
Every cloud is silver-lined.
The sun shines bright,
Although the sky is a grey one.
I've often said to myself, I've said,
"Cheer up, Collee, you'll soon be dead.
It's short life but a gay one."

Fontana graded school, Walworth County.
Iconographic Collection, SHSW.

IRISH JUBILEE

Sung by F. S. Putz, age sixty-nine, Almond, Wisconsin, and by Emery De Noyer, age sixty-three, Rhinelander, Wisconsin, in 1941.

Chorus: Should old acquaintance be forgot,
           Wherever we may be?
           Think of the good old times we had
           At the Irish jubilee.

A short time ago, boys, an Irishmen named Orrity
Was elected to the Senate by a very large majority.
He felt so elated so he went to Dennis Cassidy,
Who owned a building of a very large capacity.

He says to Cassidy, "Go over to O'Leary
For a thousand pounds of chewing gum and give it to the poor.
Then go over to the butcher shop and order up a ton of meat.
Be sure that the boys and girls have all they want to drink and eat.

Send out invitations in twenty different languages.
Don't forget to tell them to bring their own sandwiches.
They made me their senator and so to show my gratitude
They'll have the finest supper ever given in this latitude.

Tell them the music will be furnished by O'Rafferty.
'Sisted on the pipes by Felix McCafferty.
Whatever the expenses are, remember I'll put up the tin.
And anyone who doesn't come be sure and do not let them in."

Cassidy at once sent out the invitations
And everyone that came was a credit to their nations.
Some came on bicycles because they had no fare to pay
And those who didn't come at all, made up their minds to stay away.

Two by three they marched into the dining hall
Young men, old men, girls who were not men at all.
Single men, double men, men who had their teeth in pawn
Blind men, deaf men, and men who had their glasses on.

Before many minutes every chair was taken
'Til the front rooms and mushrooms were packed to suffocation.
When everyone was seated they started to lay out the feast.
Cassidy say, "Rise up, and give us each a cake of yeast."

He then said, "As manager he would try and fill the chair."
And we all sat down and we looked at the bill of fare.
There was pigs head, goldfish, mockingbirds and ostriches,
Ice cream, cold cream, vaseline and sandwiches.

Bluefish, green fish, fish hooks and partridges.
Fish balls, snowballs, cannonballs and cartridges.
We ate oatmeal 'til we could hardly stir about.
Catsup, hurry up, sweet kraut and sauerkraut.

Dressed beef, naked beef, beef with all its dresses on
Sody crackers, firecrackers, limberg cheese with dressing on.
Beefsteak and mistakes were down on the bill of fare.
Roast ribs, spareribs, and ribs that we couldn't spare.

Reindeer, snowdeer, deer meat, and antelope.
The women ate some mushmelon, the men said they, canteloupe.
Red herring, smoked herring, herring from old Erin's Isle.
Bologna, fruit cake, and sausages a half-a-mile.

There was hot corn, cold corn, corn salve and honeycomb.
Reed birds, read books, sea bass and seafoam,
Fried liver, baked liver, Carter's little liver pills.
Everyone was wondering who was going to pay the bill.

For dessert we had toothpicks, ice picks, and skipping rope,
We washed them all down with a big piece of shaving soap.
We ate everything that was down on the bill of fare
And then looked on the back of it to see if any more was there.

The band played hornpipes, gas pipes and Irish reels.
We danced to the music of the wind that shakes the barley fields.
And the pipers played old tunes and spittoons so very fine
And then paid piper, Heisig, so very fine and handed him a glass of wine.

They welted the floor 'til they were heard for miles around
When Ganniger was in the air, his feet were never on the ground.
A finer lot of dancers you never set your eyes upon,
And those who couldn't dance at all were dancing with their slippers on.

Some danced jig steps, door steps and highland fling.
Murphy took his knife out and tried to cut the pigeon wing.
And when the dance was over, Cassidy, they told us
To join hands together and sing that good old chorus:

Chorus: Should old acquaintance be forgot
        Wherever we may be?
        Think of the good old times we had
        At the Irish jubilee.

Irish Jubilee

A short time a-go, boys, an I-rish-man named O'-Hir-ty was e-lect-ed to the sen-ate by a ve-ry large ma-jor-i-ty. He felt so e-lat-ed so he went to Den-nis Cas-si-dy, who owned a build-ing of a ve-ry large ca-pac-i-ty, He says to Cas-si-dy, "Go o-ver to O'-Lea-ry For a thou-sand pounds of chew-ing gum and give it to the poor.

Chorus:

Should old ac-quaint-ance be for-got, where-ev-er we may be. Think of the good old times we had at the I-rish Ju-bi-lee.

288

Madison, 1886.
Photo by Edwin R. Curtiss.

THE PICKLED JEW

Sung by Robert Walker, age fifty-eight, Crandon, Wisconsin, in 1941. Walker learned this song from an Irishman in a lumber camp, and believed that the logger had composed it.

Two middle-age brothers in New York once dwelt,
In all kinds of merchandise freely they dealt.
And those two brothers 'twixt me and you,
Those two brothers were rich, were as rich as a Jew.
Derry down, down, down, Derry down.

Now Moses and Isaac, I'll call them by name,
For making sharp bargains they were of just fame.
If people need money, it always was lent
And they never would charge over ninety percent.
Derry down, down, down, Derry down.

One day the lad Moses his days they were o'er,
For the Lord called on Moses to settle the score.
No mortal on earth can reserve his last call
For now Moses was taking his last leave of all.
Derry down, down, down, Derry down.

So then said old Isaac with a voice like an elk,
"All his money and riches I'll have for myself.
But here is his will and I'll read it right through
And find out what Moses would have me to do."
Derry down, down, down, Derry down.

He picked up the will and as sure as you live,
All my money and riches to my brother I'll give
For the money and riches, I'd have him to toil,
He must bury my body on good English soil.
Derry down, down, down, Derry down.

He went to the captains, but he could not prevail
For none with the body would agree to set sail.
So not to be beaten, he went right to work
And embarged him on board as a barrel of salt pork.
Derry down, down, down, Derry down.

One day as Isaac was walking the wharf
He met with the captain, a surly-faced dwarf.
Said he to the captain, looking steadfast and down.
"I hope you delivered my pork safe and sound."
Derry down, down, down, Derry down.

"Oh no," said the captain, "that I cannot say,
For in sight of land we were near cast away.
Drawing near to old England we had a revolt,
Then provisions got short and we had to break bolt."
Derry down, down, down, Derry down.

"Break bolt," said old Isaac, "you're worse than the Turk.
You didn't disturb my barrel of salt pork?"
"Oh yes," said the captain, speaking up very gruff,
"We ate up your pork, it was damnably tough."
Derry down, down, down, Derry down.

"Oh God," said old Isaac, "You're worse than a sinner.
You would eat up my poor brother, Moses, for dinner."
"Oh God," said the captain, "has me and my crew
Been living three weeks on a barrel of tough Jew?"
Derry down, down, down, Derry down.

"But now," said the captain, "to finish the joke
I will pay you for Moses as though he were pork."
"Oh no," said old Isaac, "we will cheat one another
For the Lord won't allow us to sell our own brother."
Derry down, down, down, Derry down.

But Isaac 'served the captain putting back his own gold.
Then he said to the captain, "Dear captain, please hold.
Now seeing you can't pay for that brother of mine,
You might at least pay for the barrel and brine."
Derry down, down, down, Derry down.

290

The Pickled Jew

Two mid-dle-aged bro-thers in New York once dwelt. In
all kinds of mer-chan-dise free-ly they dealt. And those two
bro-thers, 'twixt me and you, those two bro-thers were
rich, were as rich as a jew. Der-ry down, down,
down, Der-ry down.

THE IRISH BARBER

Sung by C.C. Talbott, Forbes, North Dakota, for Franz Rickaby.

It was in the city not far from this spot
Where a barber he set up a snug little shop.
'Twas silent and sad, but his smile was so swate
That he pulled iv'rybody right in from the strate.
Chorus: To me fal-dee-dee di-do di-do-dee.

One horrid bad custom he thought he would stop.
Nobody for credit should come to his shop.
So he bought him a razor full of notches and rust
To shave the poor divils who came there for trust.

One day a poor Irishman passed by the way
Whose beard had been growing for many a day.
He looked at the barber, hung down his head:
"Will ye trust me a shave fer the true love of God?"

"Walk in," says the barber. "Sit down in that chair
And I'll soon mow yer beard off right down to a hair."
With lather he splattered the paddy's big chin
And with his trusty razor to shave he begin.

"Ach, murther!" says the paddy, "Now what are ye doin'?
Lave off wid yer tricks or me jaws ye will ruin.
Be the powers, ye will pull ivery tooth in me jaw.
Be jabers, I'd rather be shaved with a saw."

"Kape still," says the barber, "don't make such a din.
Quit workin' yer jaw or I'll be cuttin' yer chin."
"It's not cut, but it's *saw* wid the razor yez got.
Sure 'twouldn't cut butter without 'twas red hot."

"Let up," says the paddy. "Don't shave any more."
The Irishman bolted right straight for the door.
"Ye kin lather and shave all yer friends till ye'r sick,
But, be jabers, I'd rather be shaved wid a brick."

Not many days later as Pat passed the door,
The ninny he set up a terrible roar.
"Now look at the barber! Ye may know he's a knave.
He's givin' some divil a 'love o' God' shave."

291

The Irish Barber

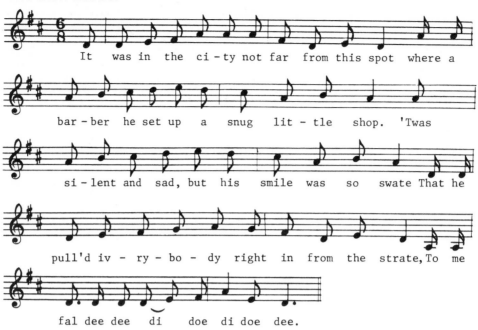

It was in the ci-ty not far from this spot where a
bar-ber he set up a snug lit-tle shop. 'Twas
si-lent and sad, but his smile was so swate That he
pull'd iv-ry-bo-dy right in from the strate, To me
fal dee dee di doe di doe dee.

OLD WILLIS IS DEAD

Sung by Charles Dietz, age seventy-five, Monroe, Wisconsin, in 1946.

Old Willis is dead and in his grave laid.
Him, ham, and in his grave laid.
The apple tree limbs go over his grave.
Him, ham, go over his grave.

The apples began to get ripe and fall off.
Him, ham, to get ripe and fall off.
Out came an old woman to gather them up,
Him, ham, to gather them up.

Old Willis arose and hit her a knock.
Him, ham, he hit her a knock.
Which made the old woman go hippity-hop.
Him, ham, she went hippity-hop.

Old Willis is Dead

Old Wil-lis is dead and in his grave laid, Him, Ham, and
in his grave laid. The ap-ple tree limbs go o-ver his grave,
Him, Ham, go o-ver his grave.

PADDY DOYLE AND BIDDY O'TOOLE

Sung by Charley Bowlen, Black River Falls, Wisconsin, in 1940.

One Paddy Doyle lived in Killarney,
He courted a girl named Biddy O'Toole.
Her tongue was tipped with a bit of the blarney,
The same as with Pat, with the golden rule.

Each day and night he'd meet his colleen
And often to himself he'd say,
"What need care I when she's me darlin'
Comin' for to meet me on the way?"

One heavenly night in last September
Paddy went out for to met his love.
Which night it was, I don't remember,
But the moon shone brightly from above.

That day the boy had had some liquor,
Which made his spirits light and gay.
Says he, "What's the use of me walking the quicker
When I know she'll meet me on the way?"

Pat filled his pipe and fell to humming
As merrily on his way he jogged.
But the kig and whiskey overcome him
And Patty lay down upon the sod.

He'd not lay long without a comrade,
One that could kick up the hay.
A big jackass came, smelled of Patty,
And lay down beside him on the way.

Pat hugged and smugged the hairy "divil"
And threw his hat to worldly cares.
She's mine to — as the heavens' blushes
But — must so she's like a bear.

He streched his hand to the donkey's nose
At that the ass began to bray
Pat let the —
Who served his knee and — away.

He then ran home as fast as he could
At a railroad speed or faster I'm sure.
He never stopped a leg or a foot
'Til he came to his charming Biddy's door.

By now, the time was growing morning
Upon his knees he fell to pray
Oh, let me in my Biddy darlin'
I've been a-killed and a-murdered upon the way.

He told his story mighty civil
While she prepared the whiskey glass.
How he hugged and smugged with a hairy "divil"
_____ Dorian's ass.

I knew it was me Biddy darlin'
And they were wed the very next day.
But he never got back the old straw hat
The jackass ate upon the way.

Paddy Doyle and Biddy O'Toole

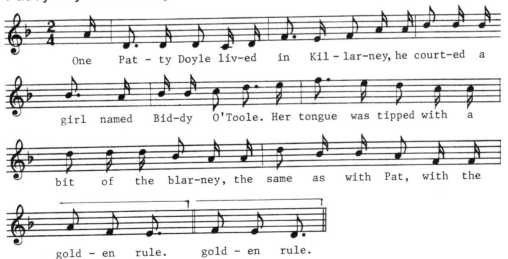

One Pat-ty Doyle liv-ed in Kil-lar-ney, he court-ed a

girl named Bid-dy O'Toole. Her tongue was tipped with a

bit of the blar-ney, the same as with Pat, with the

gold-en rule. gold-en rule.

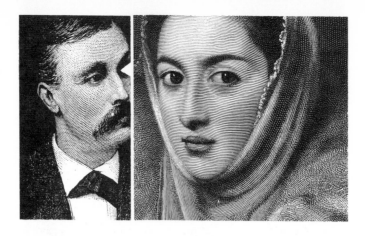

THE KEYHOLE IN THE DOOR

Sung by Lewis Winfield Moody, age seventy-six, Plainfield, Wisconsin, in 1941.

We left the parlor early and of course, 'twas scarcely nine,
And by some great good fortune her door was next to mine.
And I, like bold Columbus, strange regions to explore,
I took my position by the keyhole in the door.

I waited there in silence upon my bended knee.
I waited there in silence and I waited patiently.
She first took off her collar and she dropped it on the floor,
And then I watched her pick it up, through the keyhole in the door.

Then up before the fire, her pretty feet to warm,
With nothing but a chemise on to hide her graceful form.
Then she took off the chemise and I'll ask for nothing more.
It's a fact I saw her do it through the keyhole in the door.

Then down upon the pillow she laid her little head;
The angels they watched over her 'til darkness round her spread.
I knew the show was o'er for I could see no more.
A telescope is nothing, boys, to a keyhole in the door.

The Keyhole in the Door

We left the par-lor ear-ly and of course 'twas scarce-ly

nine, and by some great good for-tune her door was next to mine. And

I like bold Co-lum-bus strange re-gions to ex-plore, I

took my po-si-tion by the key-hole in the door.

294

Photo by Charles Van Schaick, Black River Falls.

I'LL SELL MY HAT, I'LL SELL MY COAT

Sung by Pearl Jacobs Borusky, age thirty-nine, Antigo, Wisconsin, in 1940.

I'll sell my hat, I'll sell my coat,
To buy my wife a little flat boat.
Down the river we shall float
And bibble in the lusheye lorry.
Schule, schule, schule I-rue.
Schule I rack-a-shack, schule I barbeque.
When I sell my salla babba eel
Come bibble in the lusheye lorry.

I'll sell my pants, I'll sell my vest,
To get enough money to go out west.
And there I think I can do my best.
Come bibble in the lusheye lorry.
Schule, schule, schule I-rue.
Schule, I rack-a-shack, schule I barbeque.
When I sell my salla babba eel,
Come bibble in the lusheye lorry.

I'll Sell My Hat, I'll Sell My Coat

I'll sell my hat, I'll sell my coat, to buy my wife a
lit-tle flat boat. Down the ri-ver we shall float and
bib-ble in the lush-eye lor-ry. Schule, schule,
schule I-rue. Schule I rack-a-sack, schule I bar-be-que.
When I sell my sal-la bab-ba eel, come bib-ble in the
lush-eye lor-ry.

REUBEN WRIGHT AND PHOEBE BROWN

Sung by Hamilton Lobdell, age eighty-seven, Mukwonago, Wisconsin, in 1941. Lobdell said that he learned this song from his brother, who sang it in his singing and spelling lessons.

My sister a maiden dwelt,
Her name was Phoebe Brown,
   (Spoken): Her cheeks were red and her hair was black. She was considered by all good
            judges, by all odds to be the
Best-looking girl in town.

Now Reuben was a nice young man
As any in the town,

   (Spoken): And Phoebe loved him dearly, but on account of his being obliged to work
            elsewhere for a living, he couldn't make himself agreeable
To old Mr. and Mrs. Brown.

But Phoebe's heart was brave and strong,
She feared no parents' frown.
   (Spoken): And as for Reuben Wright, I heard him say more than a dozen times that with the
            exception of Phoebe, he didn't give a cent
For the whole race of Brown.

So Reuben Wright and Phoebe Brown
Determined they would marry.
   (Spoken): Three weeks ago last Tuesday night they started for old Parson Brown's of
            Webster, determined to take the plunge in matrimony, although it was
            tremendous dark
And it rained like old Harry.

Old Captain Brown was wide awake.
He loaded his old gun.
   (Spoken): He then pursued the loving pair, and he overtook them when they got halfway to
            the parson's, when Phoebe and Reuben started
Off on the run.

Old Brown he took a deadly aim
Right at young Reuben's head,
   (Spoken): But then it was, a burning shame, he saw his own daughter, Phoebe,
Drop right down, stone dead.

Then anguish filled young Reuben's heart,
And vegeance crazed his brain.
   (Spoken): He drew a tremendous jackknife out—two and a half feet long—and he plunged
            it fifty or sixty times right into old Brown, and it is doubtful
If he ever came to again.

Then Reuben Wright with frenzy tore
The hair from off his scalp.
And when that scalp the pain was such,
   (Spoken): That he woke, found himself sitting up in bed, bootjack on his chest. For, having
            been out to a tea party the night before, he so regaled himself with buckwheat
            cakes, all piping hot, that he
Had a nightmare while in bed.

Reuben Wright and Phoebe Brown

In Man-ches-ter a mai-den dwelt, Her name was Phoe-be

Brown. Her cheeks were red and her

The best look-ing girl in town.

NOW HE'S SORRY THAT HE SPOKE

Sung by Noble Brown, age sixty-one, Millville, Wisconsin, in 1946.

A dude into the country went to meet his cousin Pat
And there he saw an animal that he supposed a cat.
It nestled in the wagon track; it had two white stripes down its back.
He thought it was the cutest cat that he did ever see.
He stepped up close and softly said, "Here Kitty, come to me."
But now he's sorry that he spoke.
Yes, now he's sorry that he spoke.
They had to bury all his clothes
And then put clothes-pins on their nose.
They threw him in the lake to soak,
And now he's sorry that he spoke.

A man named Patrick Hoolihan once worked around the docks.
He went down to the quarry where men were blasting rocks.
They had some brand new dynamite; they said it didn't work just right.
Pat grabbed a piece and lit a match. With many a smile and smirk
He said, "I'll show you the reason why it's wet and will not work."
But now he's sorry that he spoke.
Yes, now he's sorry that he spoke.
He shot up to the milky way;
He hasn't come back to this day.
A loud report, a little smoke,
And now he's sorry that he spoke.

Now He's Sorry That He Spoke

A dude in-to the coun-try went to meet his cou-sin Pat. And there he saw an a-ni-mal that he sup-posed a cat. It nes-tled in the wa-gon track, It had two white stripes down its back. He thought it was the cut-est cat that he did ev-er see. He stepped up close and soft-ly said, "Here kit-ty come to me." But now he's sor-ry that he spoke. Yes now he's sor-ry that he spoke. They had to bur-y all his clothes And then put clothes-pins on their nose. They threw him in the lake to soak, and now he's sor-ry that he spoke.

PAT MALONE FORGOT THAT HE WAS DEAD

Sung by Robert Walker, age fifty-eight, Crandon, Wisconsin, in 1941.

Times were hard in Irish town; everything was going down.
Pat Malone was pushed for ready cash.
He'd the life insurance spent; all his money, too, had went,
And all of his affairs had gone to smash.
His wife spoke up and said, "Now, dear Pat, if you were dead
This twenty thousand dollars we could take."
And so Pat laid down and tried to make out that he had died
Until he smelled the whiskey at the wake.
Then Pat Malone forgot that he was dead.
He raised himself in the bed and what he said,
"If this wake goes on a minute, to be sure the corpse is in it,
You'll have to keep me drunk to keep me dead,"

So they gave the corpse a cup, and afterward they filled it up,
And laid him down again upon the bed.
And before the morning grey, everybody felt so gay
They forgot that Pat was only playing dead.
So they loaded him from the bunk, still alive but awful drunk,
And put him in the coffin with a prayer.
And the driver of the cart said, "Be God, I'll never start
Until I see that someone pays the fare."
Then Pat Malone forgot that he was dead.
He raised himself in the coffin, while he said,
"If you fairly doubt my credit, you'll be sorry that you said it.
You drive on or else the corpse will break your head."

So the funeral started out on the cemetery route,
And the neighbors tried the widow to console.
'Til they got beside the base of Malone's last resting place.
And gently lowered Patrick in the hole.
Then Pat began to see, just as plain as one could see,
That he'd forgot to reckon on the end.
And as clods began to drop he broke loose the coffin top,
And quickly to the earth he did ascend.
Then Pat Malone forgot that he was dead,
And from the cemetery quickly fled.
He came nearly going under, it's a lucky thing, by thunder,
That Pat Malone forgot that he's not dead.

Pat Malone Forgot That He Was Dead

Times were hard in I-rish town, Ev-ery-thing was

go-ing down, Pat Ma-lone was pushed for read-y cash.

He'd the life in-sur-ance spent, all his mon-ey,

too, had went, and all of his af-fairs had gone to

smash. His wife spoke up and said, "Now, dear

Pat, if you were dead This twen-ty thou-sand

dol-lars we could take. And so Pat laid down and

tried To make out that he had died Un-til he smelled the

whis-key at the wake. Then Pat Ma-lone for-got that he was

dead. He raised him-self in the bed and what he

said, "If this wake goes on a min-ute, to be

sure the corpse is in it, You'll have to keep me

drunk to keep me dead."

O, PRETTY GIRLS, WON'T YOU LIST AND COME

Sung by Pearl Jacobs Borusky, age thirty-nine, Antigo, Wisconsin, in 1940. Asher Treat also collected this song from Mrs. Borusky and her mother in 1933.

O, pretty girls, won't you list and come?
O, pretty girls, won't you list and come?
O, pretty girls, won't you list and come
And follow the music of the fife and drum?

The drum shall beat and the fife shall play,
The drum shall beat and the fife shall play,
The drum shall beat and the fife shall play
And merrily on we'll march away.

Over the hill and a great way off,
Over the hill and a great way off,
Over the hill and a great way off
O, don't you hear that Indian cough?

THERE WAS AN OLD LADY LIVED OVER THE SEA

This satire on Britannia and headstrong young America was sung by James Merrick Drew, St. Paul, Minnesota, for Helene Stratman-Thomas in the 1940's.

There was an old lady lived over the sea,
And she was an island queen.
Her daughter lived out in a far countree
With an ocean of water between.
The old lady's pockets were full of gold,
But never content was she;
So she called on her daughter to pay her a tax
Of three pence a pound on her tea.

"Oh, mother, dear mother," the daughter replied,
"I'll ne'er do the thing you ax.
I'm willing to pay a fair price for the tea
But never a three penny tax."
"You shall," quoth the mother and reddened with rage,
"For you're my own daughter, you see,
And sure 'tis quite proper a daughter should pay
Her mother a tax on her tea."

And so the old lady her servants called up
And packed off a budget of tea.
And eager for three pence a pound, she put in
Enough for a large family.
She ordered her servants to bring home the tax,
Declaring her child should obey
Or, old as she was and almost woman grown,
She'd half whip her life away.

The tea was conveyed to the daughter's door,
All down by the ocean's side,
But the bouncing girl poured out every pound
In the dark and boiling tide.
And then she called out to the island queen,
"Oh, mother, dear mother," cried she,
"The tea you may have when 'tis steeped enough,
But never a tax from me."

There Was an Old Lady Lived Over the Sea

There was an old la-dy lived o - ver the sea, and
she was an is - land queen. Her daugh-ter lived out in a
far coun - try, With an o - cean of wa-ter be - tween. The
old la - dy's pock-ets were full of gold, But nev-er con-
tent-ed was she. So she called on her daugh-ter to
pay her a tax Of three pence a pound on her
tea, Of three pence a pound on her tea.

303

WHISKEY JOHNNY

Sung by Noble B. Brown, age sixty-one, Millsville, Wisconsin, in 1946. Brown said that this was a typical sea chantey, and made up some lines to replace those he could not remember.

Whiskey is the life of man,
Whiskey, Johnny.
Oh, I'll drink whiskey while I can.
Whiskey for my Johnny.

Oh, Whiskey straight and whiskey strong.
Whiskey, Johnny.
Give me some whiskey and I'll sing you a song.
Whiskey for my Johnny.

Oh, Whiskey makes me wear old clothes,
Whiskey gave me a broken nose.

Whiskey killed my poor old dad,
Whiskey drove my mother mad.

If whiskey comes too near my nose,
I tip it up and down she goes.

I had a girl, her name was Lize,
She puts whiskey in her pies.

My wife and I can not agree;
She puts whiskey in her tea.

Here comes the cook with the whiskey can,
A glass of grog for every man.

A glass of grog for every man,
And a bottle full for the chanteyman.

Whiskey Johnny

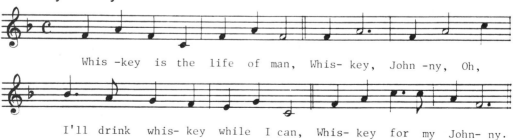

Whis-key is the life of man, Whis-key, John-ny, Oh,

I'll drink whis-key while I can, Whis-key for my John-ny.

THE GIRL WITH THE WATERFALL

Sung by Hamilton Lobdell, age eighty-seven, Mukwonago, Wisconsin, in 1941.

If you go out about the town
Upon a winter's day.
You see the lads and lassies
Dressed out in fashions gay.

Some are short and some are stout,
Others lean and tall.
But the only one that takes my eye
Is the girl with the waterfall.

She goes about dressed out in silk
Suspended by a hoop.
She wears a comely jockey hat
Shaped like —.

And on its side it's fastened
To things like billard balls.
It's the only sign for you to follow
The girl with the waterfall.

One day I strolled into the park
To chance upon a lark,
My feelings were beyond control,
I thought it but a dream.

This angel she came strolling in,
To me did loudly call.
I thought it was a vulgar sign
For the girl with the waterfall.

The way she shoveled down the fruit,
I tell you, it wasn't slow,
And when she thought she had enough
She 'rose and turned to go.

But something dropped right from her hand,
'Twas neither light nor small.
Pepper had caused this girl to sneeze
And she dropped her waterfall.

I very politely picked it up,
"It skidded here," I said.
She took it with an angry frown
And slapped it on her head.

She turned around, gave me a look
Which caused my flesh to crawl,
"Beware, young man, sir, how you play
With a lady's waterfall."

The Girl With the Waterfall

If you go out a - bout the town u -pon a win -ter's day, You'll see the lads and las- sies dress 'd out in fash -ions gay. Some are short and some are stout, oth -ers lean and tall, but the on -ly one who takes my eye is the girl with the wa-ter- fall.

DAN McGINTY

Sung by Irene McCrady, Bemidji, Minnesota, for Franz Rickaby.

On Sunday morning at nine, Dan McGinty dressed so fine
Stood looking at a very high stone wall,
When along came Pat McCann, says, "I'll bet you five dollars, Dan,
I can carry you to the top without a fall."
So on his shoulders he took Dan; to climb the ladder he began.
When McGinty, cute old rogue, to win the five he did let go,
Never thinking just how far he'd have to drop.
Chorus: Down went McGinty to the bottom of the wall,
      And although he'd won the five, he was more dead than alive.
      Sure his toes and nose and ribs was broke from getting such a fall.
      All dressed in his best suit of clothes.

From the hospital Dan came home when they'd fixed his broken bones
To find he was the father of a child.
So to celebrate it right, all his friends he did invite
And they soon were drinking whiskey fast and wild.
Dan waddled down the street in his Sunday suit so neat,
Holding up his head as proud as John the Great.
In the sidewalk was a hole to receive a ton of coal
Which McGinty never saw 'til just too late.
Chorus: Down went McGinty to the bottom of the hole.
      And the driver of the cart gave the load of coal a start.
      Sure it took us half an hour for to dig McGinty out,
      All dressed in his best suit of clothes.

Then McGinty raved and swore, about his suit he felt so sore,
And he swore that he would kick that man or die.
So he tightly grasped a stick and he hit him such a lick
That he raised a little shanty on his eye.
Two policemen saw the fuss, they soon joined in the muss,
And they ran McGinty in for being drunk.
Then the judge said with a smile, "We will keep you here a while
In jail to sleep upon a prison bunk."
Chorus: Down went McGinty to the bottom of the jail,
      Where his board it cost him nix and he stayed exactly six.
      There were six long months he stopped there, for no one went his bail,
      All dressed in his best suit of clothes.

But McGinty, thin and pale, one fine day got out of jail,
And with joy to see his boy he near ran wild.
And home he quickly ran to see his wife, Madalia Ann,
But she'd gone and taken away with her the child.
So he gave up in despair and he wildly tore his hair
As he stood that day before the river shore.
Knowing well he couldn't swim, he did foolishly jump in
Though cold water he had never took before.
Chorus: Down went McGinty to the bottom of the sea.
      And he must be very wet, for they haven't found him yet.
      But they say his ghost comes 'round the dock before the break of day
      All dressed in his best suit of clothes.

Dan McGinty

On Sun-day morn-ing at nine, Dan Mc-Gin-ty dressed so
fine Stood look-ing at a ve-ry high stone wall.
When a-long came Pat Mc-Cann, says "I'll
bet five dol-lars, Dan, I can car-ry you to the
top with-out a fall. Down went Mc-Gin-ty to the
bot-tom of the wall, and al-though he won the
five, He was more dead than a-live. Sure his
toes an' nose and ribs was broke from get-ting such a
fall all dressed in his best suit of clothes.

FINIS.

Jack Malone, vicinity of Emery, Price County.
Iconographic Collection, SHSW.

INDEX TO SONG TITLES

Poplar school band, Douglas County.
Iconographic Collection. SHSW.

5000-3L70026-77